→FOUR STAGES

OF

RENAISSANCE

STYLE

Transformations in
Art and Literature
1400–1700

WYLIE

SYPHER

Anchor Books Original

DOUBLEDAY & COMPANY, INC.
GARDEN CITY, NEW YORK

TO LUCY, G. WYLIE, AND GALE

WYLIE SYPHER, who was born in 1905 at Mt. Kisco, New York, graduated from Amherst College and received his doctorate at Harvard University. He has served on the faculties of Tufts College, the universities of Wisconsin and Minnesota, and is now at Simmons College, Boston, where he is Professor of English, Chairman of the Language, Literature and Arts Division, and Dean of the Graduate Division.

He is the author of GUINEA'S CAPTIVE KINGS (1942) and ENLIGHTENED ENGLAND (1947), and has written articles on art and literature for such magazines as *Partisan Review, The Nation, Gazette des Beaux-Arts,* and *Kenyon Review.*

FOUR STAGES OF RENAISSANCE STYLE: *Transformations in Art and Literature 1400–1700* is here published for the first time.

Library of Congress Catalog Card Number 55–6749

Cover Designed by Antonio Frasconi
Typography by Diana Klemin

FOREWORD

Surely my heaviest debt is to Andrew Chiappe of Columbia University and Jason Epstein of Doubleday, without whose wisdom, care, and good will this essay could hardly have been done. The book is, in a dozen ways, theirs.

In addition, the John Simon Guggenheim Foundation made it possible for me to study in Italy and France during 1950 and to see again some of the works of art I most needed to keep in mind. For many years, also, I have enjoyed the proverbial and unfailing kindness of the staff of the Fogg Museum Library at Harvard, who treat everybody's problem as if it were their own.

A few of these pages have appeared in somewhat different form in *The Magazine of Art*, the *Gazette des Beaux-Arts*, and *Partisan Review*, and I am obliged to these periodicals for allowing me to adapt this material.

For permission to quote from certain texts I wish to acknowledge the courtesy of publishers as follows: Appleton-Century-Crofts (*The Student's Milton*, edited by Frank Allen Patterson), Princeton University Press (renaissance critics of art in Elizabeth G. Holt's edition of *Literary Sources of Art History*), American Book Company (renaissance critics of literature in Allan H. Gilbert's edition of *Literary Criticism, Plato to Dryden*), Charles Scribner's Sons (Ralph M. Eaton's edition of *Descartes, Selections* and Richard McKeon's edition of *Selections from Mediaeval Philosophers*), and The Clarendon Press, Oxford (poems by John Donne and George Herbert in the *Oxford Book of Seventeenth Century Verse* edited by H. J. C. Grierson and G. Bullough).

W. S.

Auburndale, Massachusetts
August 15, 1954

CONTENTS

THE ANALOGY
OF
FORMS IN ART

I

*If art is enjoyment it is not the enjoyment of things, but
the enjoyment of forms—*

ERNST CASSIRER Essay on Man

*The historian cannot help dividing his material into "peri-
ods," nicely defined in the* Oxford Dictionary *as "distinguishable portions of history." To be distinguishable, each
of these portions has to have a certain unity; and if the
historian wishes to verify this unity instead of merely pre-
supposing it, he must needs try to discover intrinsic
analogies between such overtly disparate phenomena as
the arts, literature, philosophy, social and political currents,
religious movements—*

ERWIN PANOFSKY Gothic Architecture and Scholasticism

Either by nature or doctrine the puritan is one who intends to worship God in the spirit, tempering his affections and putting away the weakness of the flesh. It is
not surprising that John Milton should praise the
Reformation in England for casting off the sensual idol-
atries of those who bow down in "eye-service of the
body, as if they could make God earthly and fleshly
because they could not make themselves heavenly and
spiritual." But is it not strange that puritan England—
iconoclastic and nearly barren of drama and the

other arts—should have nourished the poetry of John
Milton, whose Eden has the fleshly abundance of Venetian painting:

Groves whose rich trees wept odorous gumms and balme,
Others whose fruit burnisht with golden rinde
Hung amiable . . .
Another side, umbrageous grots and caves
Of coole recess, o're which the mantling vine
Layes forth her purple grape, and gently creeps
Luxuriant . . .
Two of far nobler shape erect and tall,
Godlike erect, with native honour clad
In naked majestie seemd lords of all . . .
His fair large front and eye sublime declar'd
Absolute rule; and hyacinthin locks
Round from his parted forelock manly hung
Clustring, but not beneath his shoulders broad:
Shee as a vail down to the slender waste
Her unadorned golden tresses wore
Dissheveld, but in wanton ringlets wav'd . . .

Milton's own ethic was, we know, austere, disciplining
strictly that "visible and sensuous colleague, the body."
Yet this Paradise of his shows how imperative a style
can be, for it was created by the golden and copious
vision of Counter-Reformation art. And it is no stranger
than the vision of that other northern artist thriving
after the Flemish iconoclasts had wreaked their righteous destructions—Rubens, who, however unlike Milton in temperament and faith, painted about 1620, col-
laborating with Jan Breughel, a landscape with Adam
and Eve in the Garden that could serve to illustrate
the Miltonic scene we have just read. Here too are the
rich groves and burnished fruits, the cool recesses, the
mantling vines, and the majestic naked images of man
and woman. The canon of a baroque style was written
as clearly in Flanders or England as in Italy, and in
poetry as well as painting.

For Milton shares with Rubens a certain domain of
baroque imagination. The topography of the grand vis-

tas belonging, in spite of the iconoclasts, to the baroque poet and painter has never been more accurately sketched than by that historian of renaissance culture, Jacob Burckhardt, in his brief essay on Rubens: "what still existed to yield Rubens the matter of his art was an established stock of ideas, forming a single whole blended of the ideal world and a recognized sphere of the real world, and predominantly southern in character. The Bible, vision, legend, mythology, allegory, pastoral, history, and even a piece of the everyday world, figures as well as scenes, still formed a whole, and a mighty naturalist, inspired by his own fulness of life, undertook to maintain all these things at the right temperature." It was a glowing temperature. With his huge debt to Italy, his bravura and plentitude, his vast designs, his passion for antiquity, his strong movement, his shimmering color, Rubens is a witness to the heroic traditions of renaissance humanism—a humanism powerful enough to create its own myths simply by the splendor of its scenes. The art of Rubens and Milton— whenever Milton works on his epic and colossal scale —is different from the fragile decorative art of Botticelli and Spenser, and brings to the renaissance vision of life a refulgent and harmonious surplus.

The nineteenth-century critics fixed their attention almost continually upon the heights of renaissance art which they called the grand style. Recently we have been more curious about that phase of the renaissance which produced Donne and El Greco. Nevertheless we can hardly understand the significance of Donne and El Greco without looking backward to Spenser and Botticelli, and forward to Milton and Rubens, following the trajectory of renaissance styles over its entire course.

Though we no longer agree what the renaissance really "was"—or even what centuries it embraced—the era between the fourteenth and the eighteenth centuries has been the scene of nothing less than a modern revolution in criticism. Burckhardt provoked this revolution by interpreting the renaissance as an upsurge of individualism in history, an interpretation lately much revised. Presently Heinrich Woelfflin, with his *Classic Art* and his more influential *Principles of Art History,* raised the fruitful question whether the renaissance artist did not have an entirely different form of vision from the baroque artist. Then the Continental art historians gradually became aware that Woelfflin's contrast between renaissance and baroque forms failed to reckon with an intervening form of vision now widely known as mannerism, a term long used by European writers but only recently current in British and American criticism. In France, Émile Mâle studied the effects of the Council of Trent upon the arts of the later renaissance. In England, meanwhile, Sir Herbert Grierson had turned his attention to Donne, and his selection of *Metaphysical Lyrics* (1921) led T. S. Eliot to write his review suggesting that the poets and dramatists of the later sixteenth and earlier seventeenth centuries could accept and reconcile discordant impulses and could "feel their thought as immediately as the odour of a rose", but that during the seventeenth century came a "dissociation of sensibility"—a fissure between the mind and the feelings, the idea and the poetry. So Grierson's book became "a provocation of criticism," and Donne and Elizabethan or Jacobean playwrights like Webster, Tourneur, Middleton, and Ford were reappraised to find how this mechanism of sensibility operated. Thus literary critics insisted on widening the gulf between Milton's poetry of "magniloquence" (really baroque) and the earlier "metaphysical" poetry of tough "wit" (really mannerist). In America the "new" critics, indoctrinated by I. A. Richards as well as Eliot, promptly gave themselves to a close scrutiny of tensions in poetry, ambiguities, complexities of meaning, shifts in tone, and ravaging ironies in Donne and others. So, as Mario Praz well puts it, the revaluation of the "metaphysicals" shook the slopes of Parnassus like an earthquake, and reshaped the contours of its summit (from which Milton was forced to descend). Whether or not we choose to define them as being "the renaissance," the fifteenth, sixteenth, and seventeenth centuries have furnished the *mise en scène* for the drama of modern criticism.

They are also the scene of our present essay, which asks whether the changing "styles" of this period do not appear in literature as well as in the fine arts, and whether the techniques of "renaissance" architecture, painting, and sculpture do not correspond, by analogy, to the techniques used in certain poems, dramas, and epics. If the revolution in modern art criticism has been led by Continental scholars and has focused largely upon Italy, the revolution in literary criticism has been vigorously led by Anglo-American scholars and has focused largely upon English poetry of the sixteenth and seventeenth centuries. Yet both groups have been occupied with the same problems, the same era, and the same kinds of style. This situation will perhaps explain why I am concerned to apply chiefly to English poets and dramatists the definitions of style lately formulated for interpreting the fine arts of the Italian renaissance; this, and the fact that English literature seems to represent more fully or exactly than others the stages following each other in the Italian fine arts, which usually evolved more rapidly than the fine arts in northern Europe, and more decisively. During most of the renaissance England had a pre-eminence in literature equivalent to Italy's pre-eminence in painting, sculpture, and architecture. Neither geographic nor chronological distance blurs the correspondences in style.

Ever since Woelfflin contrasted renaissance with baroque forms, critics have tried, often unsuccessfully, to invoke the categories of art history in discussing literature. Admittedly a term like "baroque" has been used confusingly, if not absurdly. Perhaps literary critics have fallen short because they did not have adequately precise definitions of styles in the fine arts, or because they ignored that eccentric style now called mannerism and that reformulation of high-baroque into late-baroque. In any event a simple contrast between "renaissance" and "baroque" styles will not suffice, for there are several different orders of style competing during the period included within "the renaissance," from the opening of the fourteenth to the closing of the seventeenth centuries. One might, indeed, say that styles in renaissance painting, sculpture, and architecture run through a full cycle of change in which we can identify at least four stages: a provisional formulation, a disintegration, a reintegration, and a final academic codification—a cycle roughly equivalent to a succession of art styles or forms technically known as "renaissance" (a term, here, of limited meaning), mannerism, baroque, and late-baroque (having close affinities with academism and neoclassicism). In this larger circuit of changing styles, only the earliest tentative formula is, accurately speaking, to be called "renaissance."

The very term *style* is treacherous—as treacherous as the word *form*—and any attempt to recruit the definitions of art history for use in literary criticism is risky, particularly if one tries to press parallels to extremes. However, we cannot profit fully by our late critical revolution until we gain some *rapprochement* between our specialized, incisive art criticism and our specialized, incisive literary criticism. To venture this *rapprochement* I should prefer to abandon the notion of parallels and have recourse to that more amenable, if less exact, term "analogy."

This notion of analogy between styles has often appeared in critics who accept the premise that compositions in the same medium and in different media resemble each other, or differ from each other, in formal organization,[1] and that the internal changes always going on in society are inevitably reflected in the emergence of new styles in the arts, each with its own evolution, transformation, and eventual disappearance. A style is only an aspect of the course of a larger history, and the critic must try to relate the emergence of different styles with the emergence of the human attitudes which represent themselves, in one direction, by the arts. It seems safe to grant this relation between art and society without going on to propose any "organic" theory of either history or style. There are, in short, relations between styles themselves and relations between styles and history.

Investigating these relations usually leads into the no-man's land of criticism where there are few reliable maps, where one must always be guided by looking hard at the particular work at hand, guarding against wide generalizations, and above all not presuming that every work of art or literature reveals fully (or, perhaps, at all!) the style of the period to which it might be thought to belong. *Style is not an absolute*, and here we shall assume that a style seldom has total control over any poem, painting, sculpture, or building whatever. A style emerges only from the restless activity of many temperaments. A critic of the arts must invoke Proteus, not Procrustes.

We shall, of course, assume that the artist in any medium does not present us with objects themselves or experience itself, but instead with a *representation* or *portrayal* of objects and experience; that is, the object or experience appears in art only after it has been reduced or emancipated from actuality. The instrument of reduction or emancipation is the artist's style, the schema, composition, or "form" in which he makes his statement, the structure or organization he imposes upon the object or experience to which he refers. Art filters life. Between us and actuality the artist or writer places a special style or technique-of-representation. Surely this is what critics imply when they say that art subdues the world to a style.

Or, conversely, a style is not so much a "way of seeing the world" as it is a technique for representing what is already seen. The primitive arts, especially, suggest that the feeling for form is always limited, controlled, defined, by technical experience. Since nature offers the artist only the materials for a style, the formal patterns of art (as in the distinct fields of decoration in primitive designs) are modified by craft and medium. Then, in turn, whenever the representation is conventionalized into formal patterns by craft and medium, these patterns themselves acquire symbolic meanings and emotional values. Technique influences form, and form, by a kind of reflexive activity, influences the techniques of representation. So far as they are techniques, therefore, the styles of the various arts are separable and distinguishable, for each art has its own techniques to exploit its special medium, subject, or substance.

Yet again, if the "substances" of the various arts are not interchangeable, techniques sometimes are: for techniques may resemble each other even when the media differ. It is possible, on occasions, to treat stone *as if* it were wood, and the Doric column may be one consequence. So we come to the useful idea of "interferences,"[2] and can see how the techniques of different arts can be "exchanged" when, for example, the technique of sculpture penetrates Michaelangelo's painting, the technique of painting penetrates Rembrandt's etching, or the technique of water color penetrates oil painting in the British landscapists. Wherever techniques interpenetrate, they cause ambiguous "transformations" of style. Thus the medium of music is not the medium of painting or literature; but the tone poem in music uses techniques that are pictorial and narrative, generating at the intersection of three opposing techniques an equivocal order of art with inherently non-musical values of color and anecdote. The tone poem, like Rembrandt's etching, becomes a point of interference in the arts where there may be "correspondences" between perfumes, sounds, colors, as Baudelaire said, or where Rimbaud found the "colored" vowels of symbolist poetry—"*A* black, *E* white, *I* red . . ." Renaissance art and literature are filled with intersecting techniques, which is one reason for the mannerist "disintegration"—or transformation, if you will.

Under certain conditions styles seem to have a destiny which they must work out as if they obeyed a personal will. It is true that an artist evolves his own style by waging a conflict against the styles of preceding masters, rejecting or accommodating "the forms which others have imposed upon life." Doubtless there are cycles of styles, and recurrences also; for mannerism in European literature is a perennial overgrowth of ornate, clever, strained, abnormal phrasing that perverts the canon of classic rhetoric. There is mannerism in antiquity, in the Middle Ages, and in the seventeenth century.[3] A cycle of mannerism—baroque—rococo seems to repeat itself during the renaissance and the nineteenth century, since Ingres is mannerist, Delacroix baroque, and Constantin Guys rococo, corresponding to the earlier Bronzino, Rubens, and Watteau.

If, then, styles have a life of their own, there are analogies between types of formal organization in different arts, although the arts themselves differ in medium and content. The notion of this sort of analogy is clearer in biology than in the fine arts, and Kant in his *Critique of Judgment* employed it to suggest the strange correspondences between the structures or "forms" of widely different species of animals. It is praiseworthy, Kant remarks, to survey the orders of living beings to try to find some traces of a biological system expressing itself in similar structures:

. . . there gleams upon the mind a ray of hope, however faint, that the principle of the mechanism of nature, apart from which there can be no natural science at all, may yet enable us to arrive at some explanation of the course of organic life. This *analogy of forms*, which in all their differences seem to be produced in accordance with a common type, strengthens the suspicion that they have an actual kinship.

If we can find analogies of form within the various arts of the renaissance, we possibly can define for literature as well as for painting, sculpture, and architecture the mechanisms of a changing renaissance style that emerges, transforms itself, re-emerges, and at last plays itself out in a severe equation.

And "form" will mean the way in which the artist organizes his material or statement. As long as we are discussing painting, sculpture, or architecture, form does not seem to be a metaphorical term, since the form is actually the visible, tangible structure erected there in the art object before our eye, our hand. But in literature and music form has a metaphorical meaning, for the medium of literature is words, and words are complex symbols for sensuous impressions, for ideas, for feelings. However, literary form, like musical form, means simply the way in which these symbols or notations are arranged, the laws by which they are composed, the configuration or schema with which the writer creates in the imagination of the reader a scene or action (an "imitated" or "virtual" scene or action). In any work of art the primary medium is cast into a formal pattern, and there are analogies between patterns in unlike media, for spatial configurations can appear in literature as well as in painting or architecture. Tennyson, for instance, gains "distance" by presenting minute details in his descriptive foreground and leaving his backgrounds dim, vast, glimmering. So also, rhythm is one of the techniques of a style in either music, architecture, painting, poetry, or sculpture; a pattern of recurrence that is, by analogy, similar in a minuet, a rococo panel, a painting by Watteau, Pope's verse in *The Rape of the Lock,* and a sculpture by Falconet. The tempo in this style is kindred; and tempo is one device to mark structural accent. By contrast, the rhythm is very different in the style to which belong the polychoral sacred music by Giovanni Gabrieli, Saint Peter's in Rome, Rubens' painting, *Paradise Lost,* and Bernini's statue of Saint Teresa. Even in literary "form" there are changing laws of composition governing the sequence, development, and mode of statement or representation. A poem by Pope is not composed on the same formal principles as a poem by Swinburne.

This is because the artist—literary, plastic, or visual—begins with a conception, a configuration, a schema, to which his "subject" conforms. The novelist, who appears to be more subservient to actuality than the poet or painter, also employs a schema which is his "layout" —"the layout of those porches where a Balzac or a Dostoevski seems, as it were, to lie in wait for his characters." [4] In the first draft of Dostoevski's *Idiot* the murderer was Muishkin, not Rogojin; it is not the anecdote itself, but the *configuration* of the action that matters—more than the actors, who are often, in Henry James' perpetual phrase, "available" (*disponible*). James never forgot what Turgenev told him about "the fictive picture"—that the novelist's problem is "to find the right relations" for his persons, "those that would most bring them out." Just so, a painter needs a figure—"the image *en disponibilité*"—in a certain passage in his composition, a figure to "fit" the contours of his style, which, in other words, is a canon of form, of initial conception, or what Dante Gabriel Rossetti called "fundamental brainwork." Tintoretto evidently relied upon lay figures and a camera obscura to find the proper "layout" for his "composition."

Thus any comparison of the arts on the basis of their content or subject alone is deficient. The form of literature is not in the "story" it tells, for a drama or novel is controlled by its own kind of style, its own mode of vision or representation. Paradoxically, literature, so far as it uses a style, is non-literary, since the anecdote or situation is a vehicle only, an instrument to make "a complex of fine measurements," as James knew. There are other values than "subject" in poems, dramas, and novels so far as they aspire to formal composition. The same is true of painting and sculpture, where the subject or anecdote has imposed upon it a certain mode of presentation. It is not enough to say with Horace that poetry is like painting, if we merely imply that some pictures utilize the same subjects as poetry. Here we intend to examine analogous modes of treating the subject.

Nor can the arts be compared only by the range of emotional response they evoke; this is the sort of fallacy in criticism that damaged nineteenth-century aesthetes and moralists like Ruskin, who habitually confused technique (style or form) with the emotions roused by means of that technique. Ruskin admits in *Modern Painters:*

I am always led away, in spite of myself, from my proper subject here, invention formal, or the merely pleasant placing of lines and masses, into the emotional results of such arrangement. The chief reason for this is that the emotional power can be explained; but the perfection of the formative arrangement, as I said, cannot be explained, any more than that of melody in music.

Possibly formative arrangement cannot be "explained"

either; but it can be described, and in describing it we discover the technique of the painter, the poet, the composer. Homer and Vergil use the same kind of epic material, and evoke some of the same emotive responses; but the real difference between their arts is not so much between their legends or their moods as between their literary techniques, their angle of vision, their method of composition. In spite of the superficial resemblances between the Homeric and Vergilian poems, the analogy is not really between Vergil and Homer but rather between the style of the *Iliad* and the style of an early Dorian architecture, clarifying, as it does, each structural element; and between the rich style of the *Aeneid* and of imperial Roman architecture, where elegant "rhetorical" materials are used as facing (revetment) over plain, solid, monumental masonry.

Admittedly the subject of a work of art is involved to the extent that we can hardly imagine "a Dance of Death painted by Fragonard"; or, we may add, a *Rape of the Lock* written by Dostoevski or Kafka. The relation of an artist's subject to his style is "elastic." His style is his language, and if this language does not allow him to say everything, it allows him to say what he chooses to say.[5] To this degree style is both "vision and design." Technique is not merely a technical feat: if it is a way of representing what is seen or experienced, then it involves the whole cultural and social world that influences the artist to try to represent reality as he does. If style is a mode of representation, yet the artist is bound to represent the kind of world in which he lives, to which he belongs. Therefore not all kinds of style are available at any given time, since a style is modified by the artist's own vision, and his vision, in turn, by the world he inhabits. Vision has its own history. There are "period" styles, period techniques, period angles of approach, periods of history.

Who can deny that the egg-tempera technique in painting, which yields compartmentalized areas of color and abstract designs, was peculiarly suited to express a late-feudal view of the world, when social ranks had not yet disintegrated and when a formal scholastic logic had not yet dissolved into Bacon's half-scientific mode of thinking? Who can deny that the oil technique in painting, available for easel pictures, rendering full color and a naturalistic atmosphere, was an apt vehicle for representing the dreams of the sumptuous commercial world of the Venetian renaissance, given as it was to visions of mortal splendor? Who can deny that the minute and indiscriminate observations in a Balzac novel had some relation to the need for photography, the attentive vision of the nineteenth-century scientist seeking his "evidence," and to the loss of absolute values in the fat world of middle-class France?

Every art technique has a social context. As society changes, techniques change, along with the media of the arts and the modes of recording experience. So a style becomes an index to the structure of the contemporary consciousness and to the prevailing attitude toward experience in the contemporary world. It has, for example, been pointed out that Greek illusionism in painting has a certain pertinence to the growth of the philosophy of Heraclitus proving that all things are in flux, that nothing retains its form. Thus at the time of Zeuxis the Greek painters of still life used an almost impressionist technique—while the plague raged through Athens and while the Peloponnesian wars bred the doubts of the sophists. Similarly, it has been inferred that the rather prosaic and atomizing style of Lucretius, and his melancholy, accompany the concept of an unlimited space, without center or circumference, into which the Euclidean geometers needed to extend indefinitely their parallel lines. A more daring theory is that the techniques of an abstract art always appear whenever man feels himself alien from the natural world; on the contrary, when man is at home in nature, the artist uses a naturalistic technique, indicating that the mind submits to nature and does not need to impose its symbols upon the cosmos.

However skeptical we may be of such theories, it is apparent that any authentic style—or even a pastiche—is influenced by our outlook on the world. We can hardly suppose that the baroque artist could remain baroque in the world of Einstein or Freud, or that the renaissance artist living in a Copernican world could organize space exactly as did the medieval artisan living in a Ptolemaic world. Because the artist is unusually sensitive to the changing cultural temper, frequently he shifts his techniques before social changes become historically apparent; then some time later the already evolved style is rationalized by a substructure of aesthetic theory. The emergence of gothic architecture after 1140 from the system of vaulting at Saint Denis foretells the so-called secularizing of medieval culture bringing with it a proto-humanism, a victory for nominalism, and all the refinements of thirteenth-century scholastic logic, together with the growth of towns, bishoprics, and a new middle class. The proto-gothic mason was as truly an *avant-garde* artist as was Coleridge writing "Kubla Khan," that fantastic poem obeying the laws of free association of ideas, premonitory of the techniques and nightmare theories of surreal art and logic. Almost invariably a new style like gothic or mannerism or late-baroque is first practiced by a certain generation of artists before the critics endow the style with a rationale; indeed, it took the Italian theorists far more than a generation to catch up with Giotto's painting, and just about a generation for the French academicians to catch up with Poussin. There is among German art historians[6] a "generational theory" attempting to prove that styles arise in a kind of horizontal rhythm, each generation of artists finding it necessary to invent a style capable of expressing the consciousness they share (their *Gleichzeitigkeit*). Thus, it is argued, the "generation of 1430" (with Desiderio da Settignano, Mino da Fiesole, Rossellino, Pollaiuolo, Mantegna, and Memling) creates a style different from the "generation of 1450" (Perugino, Francia, Botticelli, Signorelli, Leonardo).

So the "spirit of the forms" alternates with the tides of history. Every style is a symptom. Howbeit, we are to be occupied not with the cultures surrounding renaissance styles but, instead, with styles as available indices to the cultures embracing them; that is, not with "culture history" but with "style history." A style is a vocabulary. It may well be the most sensitive and explicit vocabulary of any society.

If style is a vocabulary, it is also syntax; and syntax expresses the way in which a society feels, responds, thinks, communicates, dreams, escapes. By tracing changes in literary syntax we are able to interpret the varying modes of consciousness in different eras of European culture.[7] Doubtless the abrupt phrasing in *The Song of Roland* shows that the poet thinks and sees in sharply divided categories; the very parataxis indicates a rigidly feudal view of the world, when the concept of reality is limited, static, simplified, hierarchal, unarticulated. So too the syntax of Rabelais is adapted to the somewhat disorderly, disoriented, expanding world opening before the renaissance consciousness. Syntax is conditioned by the structure of the world in which we believe we live; and the whole organization of the artist's sensibility is a screen through which appears the world he represents. A prevailing style in the arts is the configuration (the *Gestalt*) of our experience of reality (for according to the Gestalt psychologists the organization of our mind and eye is itself a "given" structure for experience).

Consequently each style tends to reveal, and to create, a world of its own. Woelfflin said: "Styles crystallize the world in certain forms."

Our proposal is to outline the changing configurations of the worlds revealed, and created, by the changing styles of art from the fourteenth through the seventeenth centuries; and because a style serves as a syntax of consciousness, many of the definitions of style in the visual and plastic arts should have certain uses in analyzing the structure of literary experience erected by the word. It would, however, be foolish to suppose that all the artists in any period use the same syntax. The syntax of Spenser is not the syntax of Marlowe; the syntax of Montaigne is not the syntax of Tasso. None of these four writers inhabits the same world as the others. So, also, an artist can modify his syntax as he matures. In his youthful painting, dominated by the forms he inherited from mediocre artists like Lastman, Rembrandt had not yet found his own style; and when he does so, he evolves other styles from it, so that the tense phrasing of The Syndics of the Cloth Guild is very different from the earlier phrasing of The Supper at Emmaus. Michaelangelo, like Titian, runs through a gamut of styles ranging from the syntax of the high-renaissance and mannerism to baroque. And Milton's course is the most devious of all, emerging from the distinctively renaissance form of Comus, gathering violence in the mannerist techniques of Lycidas, realizing its full baroque power in Paradise Lost and Samson Agonistes, and then modulating itself in the late-baroque order of Paradise Regained. Almost outside this more or less consistent development fall those two gentle tone poems L'Allegro and Il Penseroso, which are preludes to the kind of style that in the eighteenth and nineteenth centuries finally identified itself as picturesque. Especially in any period as fertile as the renaissance two or more different styles can

be current at not only the same moment in different
artists but even in the same artist; for in certain phases
Caravaggio utilizes simultaneously mannerist and baroque techniques, and Shakespeare within the same
year (c. 1604–5) wrote both *Measure for Measure*
and *Othello*, the first mannerist, the second baroque, in
style. Shakespeare's course is so alternating, various,
and questing that any effort to contain his art within
the category of a single style is self-defeating; like Milton, he demonstrates the coexistence of unlike styles
and the intricacy of their relations.

In spite of—or perhaps because of—these interchanges, these divergences and complexities of direction, there is "a life of forms in art." Furthermore, we
may take for granted that every work of art must "be"
in a certain style, or possibly in more than one—some
works being syntactically pure in style, using the accepted idiom of that style, and some being transitions
between one style and another, as would be the case
with the great Titian Pietà, which derives from high-
renaissance style, accepts also the mannerist imbalance, and embodies some of the titanism of baroque.
Milton's *Samson Agonistes* is equally composite, deriv-
ing from the idealized "grand style" of the high-renaissance, but transformed by the laws of baroque structure and portending the academic system of
late-baroque neoclassicism; meantime its imagery and
verse bear the marks of mannerist distortion and torment.

II

Thus a style nearly always qualifies itself in any
particular poem, painting, sculpture, or building. Yet
we stand in need of definitions of various styles, since

many differing types of art structure exist in the realms of aesthetic space, matter, color, time, and language. Frequently art critics have used a vocabulary of polar terms to contrast the modes in which artists see, feel, and represent their world, crystallizing it in certain forms. In his *Principles of Art History* Woelfflin reduced the distinctions between renaissance and baroque styles to five opposing "forms of representation," and his vocabulary has been enlarged by recent critics. A few of these polarities are relevant in discussing the evolution of renaissance styles in the fine arts, and can be easily illustrated by well-known painters like Botticelli and Rembrandt, Leonardo and Michaelangelo, Rubens and Poussin, or by acknowledged architectural styles like gothic and baroque. Only by the loosest analogy can some of these contrasts be directly applied to literary form; yet all are helpful in defining the structure of various styles:[8]

Linear-Painterly: A linear style, whether in painting, sculpture, or architecture, emphasizes clarity of contour, sharp edges and boundaries, and each separate detail in an "isolating" way (sometimes known as the "decorative isolation" of details). By contrast, a painterly (*malerisch*) style, in Woelfflin's sense, blurs the limits, contours, and boundaries of visual or plastic forms, merging objects and images in a shifting semblance of illusory, impalpable appearances. If Botticelli's vision is linear, Rembrandt's is painterly, especially in a work like his Man with a Gold Helmet, or The Night Watch. If a Spenserian sonnet is "linear," Milton's vistas in *Il Penseroso* are "painterly." Sometimes this contrast resolves itself into one between an art of contour and an art of color.

Plane-Recessional: In general a linear style uses a sort of "horizontal perspective," arranging objects or designs upon the surface of a well-defined plane, or upon a succession of well-defined planes. This kind of style "holds the surface" as if space were essentially two-dimensional. The façades of early-renaissance palaces like the Rucellai in Florence seem "flat," all the architectural features being held in low relief. In recessional forms the plane is broken or may even disappear, and the representation is "in depth," with foreshortenings and spatial illusions of "distance" and, sometimes, shifting or oblique angles of vision. Again, Botticelli illustrates a planimetric art in contrast to the (mannerist) funnel or *coulisse* space in paintings by Tintoretto, or the strong forward-backward movement in the façades of baroque churches. And again, Spenser's sonnet seems to be an art of "surface" decoration in contrast to the "deep" plastic and spatial effects in Milton's *Paradise Lost*.

Closed-Open: As the name implies, a "closed" composition is a self-contained whole bounded by apparent limits; whereas an "open" composition looks limitless and "flowing" and seems to merge into space outside the design. In a closed composition a balance of vertical and horizontal usually dominates the structure. In an open composition this stability and balance are often wanting, as are also clearly stated geometric proportions. Woelfflin's contrast here is between "tectonic" and "atectonic" forms of art. The tectonic, closed, forms usually imply that the world is a cosmos; the atectonic, open, forms that there is no commensurable or stable order in the world. Leonardo's Last Supper suggests a closed, tectonic situation, and El Greco's Toledo one that is open and atectonic. A closed style employs, so to speak, an exact meter, in contrast to the free rhythm of an open style. Jonson's lyrics or Racine's plays are "closed" and tectonic; Milton's *Il Penseroso* or, in a different way, Marvell's "To His Coy Mistress" would be "open" and atectonic.

Multiplicity-Unity: In the multiple composition (as Woelfflin used the term) individual details maintain their identity and independence although they fit harmoniously and proportionately into the entire design. Ordinarily, but not always, multiple details appear in a closed composition. Woelfflin's "unity" is similar to the customary idea of "organic" art; that is, in a unified composition the details are submerged in a total rhythm or direction, with one "unconditioned dominant" force moving through the whole painting, sculpture, or building. In a distinctively "renaissance" painting like Botticelli's Primavera the many details are set down with fussy precision, each one sharply visible; but there is an organic "unification" of details in baroque painting like the Rubens' Garden of Love, dominated by broad rhythms surging through all parts of the design. Sometimes art critics use the phrase "fractional seeing" (fragmented vision) instead of multiplicity. Woelfflin's idea of "unity" must be treated cautiously because a composition need not be "organic" to be unified. For example, Poussin's painting—though not "organic"—is unified rather than "fractional" because it is tectonic, symmetrical, self-contained, and classic in repose and proportions; these proportions, harmoniously conceived, strongly integrate the whole design and emphasize the coherence of the vision. In any event, it is clear that Spenser's Faerie Queene does not have either the broad "organic" unity of Milton's Paradise Lost or the calm classic unity of Racine's plays.

Absolute Clarity-Relative Clarity: This contrast (clearness-unclearness) borders upon the contrast between linear and painterly; but in "absolutely clear" composition the design, color, and light serve to define the structure of individual forms, whereas in "relatively clear" composition color and light have their own value and are not used simply to define contours or objects. In relatively clear styles there may be "conflict between form and lighting," or between color and line, and the accents of color and light may distort and disguise objects until they become flickering subjective symbols for things. The already mentioned contrast between Botticelli's and Rembrandt's painting illustrates Woelfflin's distinction, as would also the contrast between Spenser's "Prothalamion" and Milton's *Il Penseroso,* with its fugitive definitions of objects.

Rest-Motion: Although the contrast between Hardouin-Mansart's Chapel at Versailles and the architecture of the gothic system is not a mutually exclusive distinction between a static and a dynamic art, the Versailles Chapel is a relatively stable form of architecture as compared with the relatively mobile form of the Beauvais cathedral. So also the composition in Poussin's classic painting is relatively static as compared with the restlessness in Tintoretto or El Greco. Similarly Jonson's lyric "Drink to Me Only with Thine Eyes" has a stability lacking in Marvell's "To His Coy Mistress."

Cyclic-Broken (Cyclothym-Schizothym): Attempting to explore the "psychology" behind the "disorganized" painting of certain periods, some critics have suggested that when an artist is in conflict with the world in which he lives, his art represents forms that do not "hold together." Then painting becomes "schizoid" as it does in modern expressionists like Picasso (or, we can add, El Greco and the mannerists). When the artist is in harmony with his world, he conveys his sense of adjustment to society and nature by untroubled "cyclothym" designs, which resemble, perhaps, Woelfflin's "closed" compositions. Raphael's art in The School of Athens is cyclothym; El Greco's Toledo schizothym. Ordinarily a "cyclic" form of art is symmetrical, and a "broken" form asymmetrical. Here we might contrast Milton's *Comus* with his troubled *Lycidas.*

Exact-Abstract (Representational - Nonrepresentational): This kind of contrast is implicit in a distinction between "abstract" and "empathic" art; that is, whenever man senses that the world is hostile or beyond his power to control, the artist employs abstract, anti-naturalistic forms, into which he reads the violence of his own emotions. In contrast, during eras when man has "the unproblematic sense of being at home in the world," he reads into nature his own self-assurance, submitting to the natural order and representing it with pleasure and confidence. Abstract art is transcendental, crystalline, and often geometric, or at least distorted. According to this distinction the artist of the early renaissance is at home in the world, whereas the mannerist artist, uneasy, doubtful, alienated, arbitrarily distorts space, light, color, and contour, and uses naturalistic details in a forced, unnatural way. Thus, Giotto would be more at home in the world than El Greco. Byzantine mosaic is "abstract."

Visual-Haptic: The two latter contrasts are related to a current but overworked distinction between an art that builds a world from optical impressions and one that projects its "visceral" and tactile sensations into the world. The blind person is entirely haptic, and Sir Herbert Read notes: "As the importance of the sense of sight diminishes, so that of the sense of touch, as the intermediary between sensations and the concept, increases." The distinction is important for us only because Milton, the blind poet, charges his baroque art with visceral and tactile effects—as does the "sculptural" Michaelangelo. By contrast, mannerist art, like Impressionism, often seems "visual" and disembodied, as in the "optical" and illusory Tintoretto. The oppressive languor of Michaelangelo's Adam, roused by God's finger, has a strongly visceral effect; so, also, does baroque sculpture or a baroque façade.

Nearseeing-Farseeing: We owe to Ortega y Gasset this ingenious distinction between "distant vision" and "proximate vision," which is really the difference between the kind of vision in early-renaissance "carto-

graphic landscapes" painted by Sassetta, the Lorenzet-
tis, or Benozzo Gozzoli, and the vision in El Greco or
Cézanne. In Ortega's "distant" vision the eye leaps afar
over a wide horizon or scene, but does not focus upon
one point; instead, by a kind of "optical democracy,"
it embraces the whole field of distant objects, each of
which seems to exist separately in hollow space. Paradoxically, the farther away the object, the clearer it
becomes; but it also loses its bulk, solidity, and "plenitude." When, however, we bring the object closer and
closer to the eye, the bulk, the plenitude, reappears,
and the field of vision shrinks into a peculiar "bent"
structure as the eyes converge upon the object immediately before them, observing only vaguely, in an in-
definite zone of indirect and inattentive vision, the confused color and "atmosphere" surrounding the object
upon which we are focusing. In fact, the peculiar structure of mannerist vision, especially in painting by Tintoretto or El Greco, seems to have the distortion of
"nearseeing," when the object in close focus is vaguely
surrounded by zones of impressions that diffuse or blur.
This is true of El Greco's Toledo, or his Crucifixions,
where the space about the fringes of the composition
seems to "curve away" from the central focus. Ortega
observes that the history of western painting is the
gradual retraction from the object to the subject, from
the distant to the proximate, and finally to the interior
or wholly subjective focus. If the *Faerie Queene* uses
a "distant vision," Milton's *Lycidas* has moments of
curiously "proximate" focus.

Geometric-Free: This polarity has some bearing
upon Ortega's. Although it is a distinction chiefly relevant to modern painting, architecture, and sculpture
(for instance, the difference between the lucid geometric statement by Mondrian and the flowing statement by Miró), the half-geometric space of renaissance "perspective" painters like Mantegna must be

contrasted with the "free," vaporous, non-perspective vision of El Greco; so, also, the precise relations in a play like *Romeo and Juliet* disappear in a mannerist play like *Hamlet*.

Intensified Seeing-Relaxed Seeing: Not exactly equivalent to Woelfflin's contrast between multiple and unified vision, or absolute and relative clarity, this polarity is useful to discriminate between the extreme tension of Botticelli's wire-drawn vision and the sweeping, abandoned, saturated vision of baroque painters like Rubens; or, perhaps, between the nervous contours of Verrocchio's sculpture and the exuberant volumes of Bernini's. Spenser "sees" more sharply in the "Prothalamion" than Milton does in *Il Penseroso*.

Dark-Light: There is a technique of "dark" vision, as the art of Rembrandt suggests. A different kind of vision ignores shadow and presents forms in a kind of monotone, with uniform illumination. Botticelli is not given to shadows, and uses, like most painters of multiple or fractional vision, contour instead of chiaroscuro; and Caravaggio is a "tenebrist" as somber as Milton is in depicting Hell.

Horizontal-Vertical-Oblique-Spiraling: In painting, sculpture, and even architecture the prevailing "direction" (or spatial dynamics) of the composition can be suggested by some such terms as these. During the early renaissance arts in general there is a degree of equilibrium between horizontal and vertical energies of the composition, and the point of view in painting is so managed that there ordinarily is a bilateral symmetry and a central focus or axis. During the mannerist period oblique and spiraling motions developed, as in Tintoretto's painting or Cellini's figures, which often twist in serpentine "flamelike" curves. In this same period both architectural and pictorial composition tends to shrink within a narrowed, if not unstable, design, and heightened, oblique, or eccentric angles of vision are manipulated to gain atectonic effects. The baroque and late-baroque arts return to principles of symmetry, balance, and tectonic form. The clear equilibriums in the structure of *Romeo and Juliet* are surrendered in the devious, oblique, and seemingly improvised structure of *Hamlet*.

Points-Lines-Planes-Volumes: These terms suggest very different orders of artistic vision and technique. The renaissance painter at first was inclined, like the architect and sculptor, to arrange his clear linear contours upon a plane, or within a succession of receding planes. He was nevertheless also tempted to paint in high relief or to break the wall of the façade and use sculpture and columns in their full rotundity and volume; and in general, as the renaissance fine arts mastered the third dimension, the tendency was to create "in depth," in cubical space, in sculptural volume, or to shatter, perforate, and complicate the plane. In fact this indecision between accepting the plane and realizing the full sculptural mass of objects in deep space was a major cause of the instability of renaissance painting, sculpture, and architecture, and eventually led to a mannerist "disintegration" of style. The mannerist painter, dissolving planes and twisting or scattering space, sometimes discharged the energies of his composition at illogical, unexpected points—thus willfully diverting the eye from what ought to be important and focusing off center. The irregular stress at these points of discharge gives mannerist art a wavering accent, and the intervals between structural elements seem more expressive than the structural elements themselves. In mannerist painting the space about bodies, or the interval between bodies, is illogical but dramatic. The baroque arts reintegrate the world by accepting symmetrical and regular space, the wall in all its density, the full sculptural and volumetric bulk of the image, as a basis for composition.

Other less exact contrasts are also employed by art historians to distinguish between styles. Among the devices of mannerist painting, for instance, is strong foreground framing—a boundary that seems more arbitrary than the foreground framing of the renaissance painter, who does not like to crowd his figures into an unnaturally confined space. There can be relatively strong or weak foreground framing of even sculptured figures, either by a niche or an ideal boundary. Or again, we shall need to distinguish between "color" and "tonal value" in painting, since there is a difference between the brilliance of the hues of pigments and the "tonal relation" between pigments, which establishes light-and-dark values. Tonal value can arise from modulating a single color or hue, or hues of similar intensity. In Rembrandt's painting the hues are not bright, but the play of light and shadow absorbs everything into an atmosphere the German critics call *Hell und Dunkel*. Rembrandt's etchings have maximum values of light-and-dark—in contrast to Rubens, who prefers to triumph in baroque color.

Finally, there are many different kinds of perspective operating at once in renaissance styles, in painting, sculpture, and even architecture. Ordinarily we think of perspective as optical or "vanishing-point" perspective, an arrangement of objects within cubical space so that each object is clearly "located" in relation to the enclosing space and to other objects by a system of co-ordinated lines ("orthogonals") converging in a "visual pyramid" toward an exact focal point situated upon an implied or defined horizon. This sort of mathematical perspective—as artificial as any system of vision ever invented—became an orthodox mode of representing space in renaissance painting. But throughout the renaissance, painters, consciously or not, were actually using quite other codes of perspective, relating figures to scene in quite other ways. Inevitably a "surface" perspective, in breadth—a horizontal or shallow perspective—was always tending to counteract "deep" perspective, thus creating a tension between seeing in planes and seeing in funnel-like recession. Then too, a conceptual or hierarchical perspective, essentially medieval, persists curiously in Botticelli and mannerist painters like Parmigianino—a method of scaling figures according to their psychological, social, or ritual importance, much used in romanesque sculpture. Atmospheric perspective, in the evolution of which Leonardo played so large a role, locates figures in space by immersing the more distant ones in a "blue" vagueness. Leonardo used a "twilight" vision, and everywhere in renaissance painting the Vale of the Arno serves as a "distant" blue atmosphere opening behind the portrait figure in the immediate foreground. Perspective need not be single; it may be "double" whenever the painted scene is a place of intersection for two or more systems of perspective. In this event there may be no precise vanishing point but, instead, as in late-medieval painting, a vanishing area or vanishing axis in relation to which the figures may be loosely and approximately located. Botticelli's Birth of Venus uses a complex and inconsistent perspective. There is also color perspective, which results from using cold or warm, receding or advancing, colors side by side; or there may be, as in Velázquez, a reflexive or "mirrored" perspective, implied by reflected images; or inverted perspective, as in Rembrandt's Syndics of the Cloth Guild, where the vanishing point is outside the picture somewhere in the space from which we ourselves look at the painted group. This vanishing point is "introspective" because it shifts with *us* as the attention of the painted people follows us in our space. Above all, a system of perspective has a close relation to the kind of space in which it operates; for in painting, sculpture, and architecture space can be treated in very different ways according to whether it is conceived in "blocks" (as it was in a romanesque nave), whether it is perforated (like gothic or mannerist space, making "shadow-holes" in a façade or funnels in Tintoretto's painting), or whether it is modeled (like baroque space, which seems to well up from within walls and statues).

The space existing about a statue has been thought to obey a "law of the receding plane" apparent in three phases of the development of sculpture. In the archaic statue the contour of the figure is sharp, and the statue must be seen from the front, as if the marble had been "cut" by a plane running through the facing surface of the image touching it at every point. The archaic figure is rigid, frontal, and defined by this planimetric outline. In the classic statue this ideal plane no longer touches the front of the figure but moves inward from the facing surface and passes medially through the torso and head, giving the image a mature naturalistic "freedom" and rotundity. In the "baroque" phase sculpture loses its ideal plane of reference entirely and stands, as it were, unoriented in space, expanding outward in all directions with an explosive force. This law has been rephrased to show how the renaissance statue requires us to take a "profile" or "contour" view from the front, or from either side; whereas the mannerist statue requires us to take a circulating or revolving view of it because it twists with a flamelike, serpentine motion as though it were made to stand on a swivel; the baroque statue again accepts the one-view principle because our approach to it is from a restricted angle—an angle which, however, allows the volumes of the figure to spread out into the "flattened" space around its energetic contours. Donatello, Cellini, and Bernini illustrate, respectively, this theory about renaissance, mannerist, and baroque figures, which have a certain correspondence to Romeo, Hamlet, and, perhaps, Othello.

In any event, these theories involve a basic difference in sculptural techniques—carving and modeling. In carving, the figure is released from the enclosing marble by a process of chipping off the stone until the contours of the image appear. In modeling, the figure emerges or swells from within by a process of expanding volumes growing about an armature. If Donatello's sculpture gives a carved effect, Bernini's is, rather, modeled. The paradox of Michaelangelo's statuary is that the vigorous carving creates, strangely, an effect of modeled volumes. Generally, however, we may think of early renaissance sculpture as being carved and of baroque sculpture as being modeled. This distinction between carving and modeling forms is also relevant to painting since Botticelli's figures are "delineated" by a technique analogous to carving, whereas Rubens' images seem to emerge into pictorial space by a technique of expanding pigment and color analogous to modeling.

All these contrasts, we repeat, are directly pertinent only to spatial and visual arts, not to literature. Yet a style—and particularly a major style—being a symbol of contemporary consciousness, will usually express itself in several media; it *is* a mode of vision as well as a technique. Consequently if we are dealing with an authentic style and not a mere pastiche or imitation, a structure in the fine arts will normally find its analogy in literature. We can hardly hope, or wish, to define the structure of a poem in spatial or visual categories; the problem, instead, is to use these categories to help define the style or syntax in question, which is a far more embracing structure than appears in any one medium.

In tracing the cycle of renaissance styles we must not ignore the "law of technical primacy in the arts," according to which all the arts in certain periods fall under the domination of the technique of one of the arts.[9] To take an instance: in the romanesque era the controlling art was architecture, and thus sculpture and painting (as well as a *chanson* like *The Song of Roland*) were dominated by the techniques of romanesque architecture with its monumental, inexorable "law of the frame"—the tyrannical system of the wall divided into compartments. The rigid, mosaic-like decorative patterns of romanesque sculpture and literature, monotonously repeating images in a highly stylized series of units, are therefore due to the demands of an architectural logic governed by the sharply defined areas of the romanesque wall. During the gothic period the dominance passed from architecture through sculpture (which was the prevailing gothic art) to painting. During the early renaissance the technical primacy in the arts remained vested in painting largely because the painter inherited certain problems of architectural and sculptural space left unsolved by gothic craftsmen. By the end of the seventeenth century architecture had recovered from painting a certain supremacy; though eventually, during the nineteenth century, the technical primacy passed to music, the romantics and symbolists accepting the principle that all the arts tend "to approach the condition of music"; even architecture was thought of as a frozen melody—and not only by the Wagnerians.

We enter upon the renaissance cycle of art at that moment when the painter realized that he was facing the task of assimilating architectural space and sculptural volume to the flat surface of the wall or canvas. This is the moment of shift in technical primacy, and Leonardo da Vinci speaks like a true renaissance man when he insists that the painter is superior to the poet, the musician, the sculptor—he is the paragon among artists.

This shift marks an interval in the cycles that seem to

run through western art, with phases of integration, disintegration, and reintegration of styles. The largest of these cycles appears to sweep, in vague sequence, through the many changes from archaic to classic to baroque-romantic-naturalist art, which is followed by a reintegration of style in a new kind of abstract art. This gigantic cycle is perhaps discernible in the developments from Helladic to Hellenic art, then to Greco-Roman and finally Byzantine-Romanesque art. The same huge cycle seems to repeat itself in the era between the dark ages and the twentieth century: the first phase would be Byzantine-Romanesque, which was followed by a Gothic-Renaissance style, then a Romantic-Naturalist style, which yielded, about the time of Cézanne, to a neo-archaic abstract Cubism. Such giant cycles, if they exist, are too inclusive to be of much critical value.

Quite outside any such monstrous circuit is the limited sequence of styles during the period from the fourteenth through the seventeenth centuries, with certain analogies between the shifts in technique in both the fine arts and literature. Here again we must hardly presume that the stages in this sequence—"renaissance," mannerist, baroque, late-baroque—everywhere follow in exact chronological order. For example, the renaissance in England happened belatedly and very swiftly, with overlappings in history, so that, inconveniently enough, different phases can at moments be seen running concurrently in Jacobean or Caroline literature, when Donne follows hard on Spenser, Milton hard on Donne, and Beaumont and Fletcher almost contemporary with the others. As early as 1611 traces of a late-baroque style are perceptible in Beaumont and Fletcher, before Milton has written his mannerist poem *Lycidas,* and long before he wrote his baroque *Paradise Lost.* A living style often violates the logic of geography and history. Yet after all we shall be less concerned with historical sequence or geographic latitude than with defining the alternations in style occurring everywhere in the renaissance arts—just as, today, they occur in Picasso's paintings—in an aesthetic, not a chronological, pattern. Like the burning phoenix, a style can resurrect and transform itself in a miraculous way. It has its own fate, but not always the fatality of the history that is written in time.

Our cycle does not properly open until the style known as gothic had played itself out—or "decayed" or transformed itself—into a naturalism that usually betokens the dissolution of a formal technique. The reintegration of style could be said to begin in Italy, at least, by the first of the fourteenth century, and centers in the attempt of the fifteenth- and sixteenth-century arts—painting, architecture, sculpture, and literature—to achieve a new and formal principle of composition to give "unity" to the world of the artist. This principle of unity was found in the renaissance notion of harmonious proportion, ideal ratios, and the coherent "realization" of a scene or action from a fixed point of view. The renaissance artist, critic, and scientist believed he could integrate the world by obeying the Golden Measure and Probability, which was the foundation of "the grand style," an affirmation of Logos and Proportion in each of the arts as well as in physics, astronomy, and philosophy.

But the renaissance harmony was based upon an artificial and enforced unity, which often raised more problems than it solved. Thus between 1520 and 1620 came a phase of further experiment, or disintegration, in style accompanying a crisis in faith and conscience leading to the Council of Trent (1545–63) in Romanism and the severities of Protestantism, and marked by disproportion, disturbed balance, ambiguity, and clashing impulses in painting, architecture, and sculpture as well as in "metaphysical" poetry, Jacobean drama, and all the witticisms of Cultism, Marinism, Gongorism, and emblematic verse. This is the era of mannerism.

The unresolved tensions in mannerist art are presently resolved in the grandiose affirmations of a new style—sumptuous, pompous, invigorating, fleshly, authoritarian—the baroque, which appears as early as 1600 and swells to *fortissimo* shortly after mid-century. It returns to the idealism of the renaissance grand style for some of its formal laws, but exercises these laws with an exultant, if somewhat thoughtless, spirit and a satisfaction in the textures of the material world. This splendid resolution might be said also to derive from the Council of Trent, convened during a phase of dissolution but inaugurating a phase of reintegration in the arts. If Rome is the scene of baroque triumph in the fine arts, *Paradise Lost* is the flood tide of baroque poetry.

The full glory of baroque style does not extend much beyond 1660–70 in any country in Europe. Yet the vigor of baroque art has its last, and loudly rhetorical, expression in the heroic style of late-baroque, which is common to France and England after 1640. This strident form of baroque, with exaggerated contrasts, presently is sobered and purified under academic jurisdiction, and late-baroque finally achieves intense moral and psychological force in the controlled, naked style of Racine and Milton's *Paradise Regained,* a style marked by dramatic conflict and a spiritual testing of baroque energies. The cycle of renaissance styles is closed.

NOTES

1. *My remarks on interchanges between media and analogies between types of formal organization derive largely from Theodore Meyer Greene's systematic discussion in* The Arts and the Art of Criticism. *I adopt Greene's premises, also, about the relations between a style and the*

social history in which it matures, although I have felt free to utilize the more dramatic language with which Malraux treats style in The Voices of Silence.

2. *The term and the idea come from Henri Focillon's* Life of Forms in Art, *where there is subtle comment upon "exchanges" and "transformations."*

3. *A full and learned account of mannerism as a "constant" is in Ernst Robert Curtius:* European Literature and the Latin Middle Ages. *The following reference to the mannerist—baroque—rococo cycle is based upon Karl Scheffler:* Verwandlungen des Barocks in der Kunst des Neunzehnten Jahrhunderts (1947).

4. *Malraux:* Voices of Silence, *p. 335.*

5. *So Malraux puts it in* Voices of Silence *(p. 447), where there are many striking remarks on the relation of subject to style. Woelfflin* (Principles of Art History) *earlier said that subject, style, and "vision" are a reflex of history.*

6. *Notably Wilhelm Pinder, who in 1926 published* Das Problem der Generation in der Kunstgeschichte Europas. *The "cultural lag" between the practicing artist and the theorist who follows in the next generation is illustrated by Joan Evans in* Pattern.

7. *Erich Auerbach in* Mimesis *analyzes a succession of passages in writers from Homer to Virginia Woolf, treating each as a mirror of consciousness.—Dante, Rabelais, etc.*

8. *The following synopsis of contrasts opens with the widely known polarities on which Woelfflin based his* Principles of Art History. *But I have also drawn the Cyclic-Broken polarity from Walter Winkler* (Psychologie der Modernen Kunst), *the Exact-Abstract polarity from Wilhelm Worringer* (Abstraction and Empathy), *the Visual-Haptic polarity from Sir Herbert Read* (Education Through Art), *the Near-and-Far-Seeing polarity from Ortega y Gasset's essay "On Point of View in the Arts"* (Partisan Review, *August, 1949) and his other comments on art. Most of the other polarities come from Laszlo Moholy-Nagy's* Vision in Motion. *The paragraphs on the "law of the receding plane" in sculpture, and on the distinction between the form of renaissance, mannerist, and baroque sculpture, summarize the views of Adolf Hildebrand, Heinrich Woelfflin, and Erwin Panofsky.*

9. *The "law" is so named by Henri Focillon* (Life of Forms in Art). *Focillon adapted the idea from Louis Bréhier.*

RENAISSANCE

I

THE GOTHIC SYSTEM: PROBLEMS   In spite of recent attempts to deny that there was any such event as "the renaissance," we must grant that Brunelleschi's Pazzi Chapel in Florence (1429) is not really like the cathedral at Amiens, and that Shakespeare's dramas are not really like mystery plays. Something decisive seems to have occurred in Italy during the fifteenth century, then all over Europe during the sixteenth.[1] There are many ways of describing what took place during this era; but however we identify it, there was a renaissance. This particular renaissance, which is well called "Italianate," is inherently different from the Carolingian and Ottonian revivals during the ninth and tenth centuries and also from the "proto-renaissance" of the high Middle Ages. Often these medieval renewals adapted to their own art and science the "classical" broken images of the Romans, or Aristotle's methodology; yet the Italianate renaissance used antiquity in a quite different spirit—one of nostalgia—and for quite different purposes—to affirm the dignity of man living amid the "wondrous setting out" of a universe shaped, as it seemed to Cardinal Bembo in Castiglione's _Courtier_, with "beauty and comeliness": the very celestial bodies "among themselves have such force by the knitting together of an order so necessarily framed, that with altering them any one jot, they should be all loosed, and the world would decay."

Such restored confidence in the comely order of the

world is, in effect, a reaction against the instability of
gothic art and thought, which had striven to reconcile
many contradictions of flesh and spirit by an Aristotelian logic of *sic et non*, yes and no. In the closing pages
of *Mont-Saint-Michel and Chartres* Henry Adams
suggested why gothic was a treacherously complicated system, fraught with risks and double meanings,
inspiring faith and doubt. He perceived that the spring-
ing vault, the earthward plunge of the flying buttress,
was a visible effort to throw off visible strain by seeking
an equilibrium delicate, as at Beauvais, beyond the
line of safety, with danger lurking in every stone:

The peril of the heavy tower, of the restless vault, of the
vagrant buttress; the uncertainty of logic, the inequalities
of the syllogism, the irregularities of the mental mirror—all
these haunting nightmares of the Church are expressed as
strongly by the Gothic cathedral as though it had been the
cry of human suffering, and as no emotion had ever been
expressed before or is likely to find expression again. The
delight of its aspirations is flung up to the sky. The pathos
of its self-distrust and anguish of doubt is buried in the
earth as its last secret.

All the subtleties of scholastic method, with its cun-
ning techniques of *yes and no*, could not reduce the
inherent strain of living in the double world of gothic
art and thought: the world of the abstract system, and
the actual, immediate world of human experience,
which needed to be contained within the system. This
strain is severe in the art of Dante, who in the second
circle of Hell, where the air is heavy with grief, meets
the souls of Paolo and Francesca, borne along on the
dim infernal wind because they loved too hotly in the
flesh. Francesca, the girl of Rimini, remembers in her
misery the happy hours of her earthly lust and speaks
so compassionately of her adultery with Paolo that
Dante must pause, bowing his face with pity, to hear
how the two came to their eternal sorrow. Francesca
says that one day while she was reading to Paolo, for

delight, of the love of Lancelot, their passion took the
color from their faces; then Paolo kissed her mouth
all trembling: "That day we read no farther." Dante
does not question the judgment of God upon these
lovers; but he falls swooning for sympathy. Gothic art is
indeed a humanization, filled with modulations of feeling, with a grave personal intimacy. Dante's poem has
the quality of "figural realism"; his eternal system—
both Heaven and Hell—is a framework for concrete
human experience, and his timeless order is dense
with anecdotes of Italian history. Every steep ledge of
Purgatory is a theater for human beings striving to master their human passions with human effort, to bring
their will to peace. Especially here on these dim ledges
the image of man almost eclipses the image of God.[2]
Thus the *Comedy* has two poles, like all gothic art and
thought: the ideal order of a universe expressing
God's unchanging will, and the changing existence of
each human being who feels desire and pain and the
sting of memory.

In this sense the Middle Ages had a double vision of
reality, presenting both the concrete fact and the conceptual form. At the very center of gothic art—whether
sculpture, painting, or poetry—stands the figure of
man. This humanizing of art suggests that some sort
of proto-renaissance was already occurring at the heart
of the thirteenth century, the age of abstract systems
erected outside space and time. Of course the humanism and naturalism of the Middle Ages were not those
of the renaissance, because medieval art used classic
forms without classic intents; yet gothic art and science
alike cause us to suspect that the "revelation of nature"
during the renaissance was, from another point of view,
only a survival and transformation of the strong medieval sense of what is local, personal, and actual.

The allegorical method is itself a means of representing the double range of gothic experience, personal

and abstract, historic and timeless, local and transcendent. Art historians have long been conscious of the high "tension between the specific and the universal" that sustains the finest gothic sculpture and architecture—and also Dante's poem. They have pointed out that gothic art does not ignore the material world but sees it in a new way—the way the romanesque artist never saw it—as "a relationship of plastic forms in a local area of universal space." These intensely felt local relationships and anecdotes, seen from the perspective of eternity, give a figural realism to gothic literature, stained glass, and sculpture.

The gothic philosopher met this double range of experience in the guise of the nominalist controversy, for within the confines of scholastic thought the so-called nominalists were always inquiring whether truth is not in "things" as well as in "universals" (or abstractions). Aquinas himself had presumed that knowledge rises from a kind of double experience, beginning in the senses and perfected in the understanding. But in the mid-thirteenth century the nominalist Roger Bacon (c. 1214–94) used the term "double experience" as if he were already writing about a modern "dissociation of sensibility":

. . . experience is double: one is by means of the exterior senses; . . . but this experience does not suffice man; . . . it touches on nothing at all of spiritual things. Therefore it is necessary that the understanding of man be aided otherwise, and therefore the holy patriarchs and prophets, who first gave the sciences to the world, received interior illuminations and were not dependent only on sense. . . .

Earlier in the century Grosseteste (c. 1168–1253) had conceded that "there is another truth than the supreme truth," an order of reality to be found in corruptible and contingent things. "Truth is double," he explains, since there is a truth of particular things, an accidental as well as a substantial truth. This "principle of individuation" necessarily leads one to believe that the concrete object is as real as the abstract essence; or as Grosseteste says:

We think . . . that the truth of things is multiplex; . . . if one descend to single things, a diversified principle will be found for each truth. . . . Wherefore the intention of truth, as the intention of being, is ambiguous; from one part it is one in all truth, and, nevertheless, by appropriation it is diversified in particulars.

The modern experimental method arose in the thirteenth century with Grosseteste, who tried to relate theory to observation, especially in his experiments with light. Thus Roger Bacon, Duns Scotus, and William of Occam simply extended Grosseteste's curiously duplex inductive-deductive method. Bacon sought a knowledge of the Creator through a study of created things and developed nominalism into a mode of experimental science, "because without experience nothing can be known sufficiently":

There are, in fact, two ways of knowing, namely by argumentation and experience. Argumentation concludes and makes us grant the conclusion, but does not make certain nor remove doubt that the mind may be quiet in the contemplation of truth, unless it finds truth by way of experience. . . . For if a man who has never seen fire should prove by sufficient argument that fire burns and that it injures things and destroys them, the mind of one hearing it would never be satisfied by that nor would a hearer avoid fire until he had put a hand or a combustible object into the fire that he might prove by experience what argument had taught. But once he has had the experience of combustion, his mind is made sure and rests in the brightness of truth. Therefore argumentation does not suffice, but experience does.

In gothic art and science, then, there is a strong current of empiricism. Just as Roger Bacon sought to understand combustion by putting his hand into the flame, the gothic sculptor often turned his eye toward the living model nearby instead of merely relying upon "type" figures. The renaissance came when the Italian artist and scientist tried to impose mathematical and aesthetic theories upon this loose medieval empiricism. Late-gothic architecture is less systematic than high-gothic; for there entered into late-medieval culture an aesthetic and religious subjectivism, a reliance upon private judgment and experience (*intuitus*) expressed in Eckhart's mysticism and in the new "subjective" space being created by optical perspective in Giotto and Duccio, who try to see the world from a certain individual standpoint. In any case, Grosseteste opens the way for Francis Bacon and his *Novum Organum* and his aphorisms that man "can do and understand so much and so much only as he has observed in fact," that "our only hope lies in a true induction," that "we must lead men to the particulars themselves" until they "lay their notions by and begin to familiarize themselves with facts."

Dante's extreme attentiveness, his inquiring—almost experimental—attitude toward the events of the *Comedy*, is a sign of the capacity of the gothic artist and thinker to undergo a double experience. Leonardo da Vinci, with his talent for observing every local thing, might have entered in his notebooks the episode in Canto V of the *Purgatory* when one of the shades, staring at Dante's body, exclaims that he casts a shadow *on the left*. At once Dante pauses to look, and Vergil must warn him that the pilgrim's mind should not be diverted by any such curiosity. The intensity of Dante's psychology is partly due, no doubt, to his having looked so directly into his heart and so eagerly into the streets of Florence. The *Comedy* is a poem of exciting recognitions made from personal experience. This is the genuine humanizing of gothic art, deeper than the mere cult of the Virgin or the intimacy of troubadour verse. Dante enters Paradise bearing the scars of his Florentine love. He is greeted, "I am indeed, I am, indeed, Beatrice." From the *New Life* through *Paradise* Dante

burns away the ritual of feudal codes until we can behold, naked and self-conscious, his own passion told
with a new intelligence of love, the wonderful tremor
beginning in his breast on the left side and running
through his flesh when he feels the presence of Beatrice
in a house by the Arno, or below the spheres of Heaven.
So Proust in our own day feels the power of Albertine;
so Swann feels the presence of Odette. The *Inferno* is
peopled with small gentry from Pisa, from Donoratico,
from Perugia, from Siena. In Paradise the Tuscan
nobles keep their local temperaments, Heaven itself
becoming Italianate. In eternal places Dante encounters the fullness of human experience. His struggle is to
discipline his human will, to find peace, like his relative
Piccarda, by obeying God. Beatrice tells him that the
universe is filled with individual forms created by God
—a plenitude of local beings; that man must learn to
curb his impulses, which means that the gothic drama
is played in man's own soul, where he suffers and assumes the heavy burden of his self.

So we see why medieval proto-humanism is the root
of renaissance humanism, why the double experience
in gothic art and thought is essentially modern; for
gothic does not belong to a very old order of art, as
does romanesque. The proto-humanism of gothic poetry
and sculpture is a sign that culture was becoming secularized. Gothic art, developing as it did in the region
about Paris between 1140 and 1270, is a result of semi-
modern conditions, a creation of town-dwelling pro-
fessional scholars and craftsmen. The so-called
"revolution of the twelfth century" brought the rise of
international business, the growth of lay power, the
building of cathedrals by wealthy guilds and wealthy
master architect-masons whose names we know in considerable numbers. The romanesque age of crusade and
monastery was done; Chaucer's Canterbury Pilgrims do
not belong to the same realm as Roland, Oliver, and

Raymond IV, Count of Toulouse. The abbot had yielded
to the bishop; the bishops meant cathedrals; the cathedrals meant towns; and towns meant the trader, the
worker, and, at last, the secularizing of both religion
and art, a "laicization" bringing with it Van Eyck's
Arnolfini and His Wife (1434), a world full of the
poetry of ordinary objects, where the painter is at
home in a new pictorial domain—for on the wall behind
Arnolfini and his bride is the clear legend "Johannes de
Eyck fuit hic": the painter "was there" himself to see
and record this little episode from middle-class life, to
make his layman's remarks. This Arnolfini world is sufficient to itself in its "creatural" realism; it no longer
needs support from the structure of a system of faith
which had given Dante's realism fourfold meanings.

This new pictorially convincing art appeared partly
because details were congenial to the late-medieval
mind, along with nominalism, and partly because
gothic art had failed. When in 1144 the builders of the
choir at Saint Denis used their ogives, they created an
intricate realm of space that gothic art could neither
control nor organize. Essentially the ogive, the rib, the
pointed vault, were counter-structures against the inert,
solid, blocklike romanesque architecture, which accepted, in its full imperious density, the masonry wall.
By a process of opening up the wall and "aerating" the
interior, the gothic ogive led to a highly intellectualized   7
design of buttressing and ribbing that emptied the system and finally, in its flamboyant phase, reached a negation of architecture, if by architecture we mean an
enclosure of space. Gothic architecture, gradually
making a great refusal, reasoned away the architectural
problem by penetrating space instead of defining and
encompassing it; thus the cathedral became a projection of lines through voids, converting architecture into
a framework for the non-architectural elements of sculpture and glass. When architecture ceased to master

spatial experience, the sculptor, and then the renaissance painter, whether he willed or no, necessarily
dealt with the problem of organizing three-dimensional
space. And by rights this is not the painter's problem
at all. Thus when the renaissance painter sought to
represent cubical space by inventing vanishing-point
perspective, he damaged the integrity of both architectural and painted space. One might, indeed, define
renaissance art as an attempt to resolve the spatial problems gothic architecture evaded.

One instance will suggest how the renaissance
needed to recover architectural space from the fluid
and intricate environment created by the rib-vault and
buttress. In the Chapter House at Lincoln the primary
walls disappear, and the whole structure becomes, like
the choir at Beauvais, a scheme *for* architecture, not an
enclosing fabric but a skeleton; meanwhile the wall has
reappeared *outside* as a complex *exo*skeleton of flying
buttresses thrown against the primary wall, which has
been treated like an illusion. The humanism of the renaissance builder consisted in finding again, by returning to antique principles, the proper function of the
wall as an envelope and boundary. The Lincoln Chapter House proves that the gothic "visual logic" is not
necessarily architecture but a system of armatures
transforming itself, as we walk within and about it, into
a painterly illusion—which is at the same instant an
illusion of logic. Thus the renaissance painter shared
with the renaissance architect the task of re-establishing, controlling, and rationalizing the third dimension.

Once gothic relaxed its architectural control, space
became "environment," and during the Middle Ages
technical primacy in the arts shifted from architecture
through sculpture to painting. When the rib-vault dissolved the mural plane, the sculptured figure and the
painterly images of stained glass found a freedom to
exist independently of the architectural system to

which they once belonged. The essential problems of romanesque architecture can be solved by a geometry of plane and cube, but the problems of gothic architecture cannot. In the complex and delicate logic of Beauvais, where dimensions are merely outlined and not solidly possessed, architecture opens and enriches itself with new values of direction, vista, and extension. Whereas romanesque space is determinate and impenetrable, the interior space of early gothic is "indeterminate and penetrable." As soon as it appears, the ogive behaves equivocally; it is still disputed whether the ribbing of gothic vaults is a structural necessity or simply a pattern of linear decoration upon a roof. If the ribs fall, many vaults seem unimpaired. At Bourges, where architecture is an abstract logic of buttressing, space becomes a shifting appearance of voids in the mass, and can be defined only by a complex diagram drawn in stone about the exterior of the building. Within, all is a bewildering vision through arcades and aisles, rib running into rib, bay into bay, with extremely refined transitions, a sinewy plausible logic as intricate as the "questions" pursued through every phase of *sic et non* by scholastic philosophers, who practiced a tactic of "sufficient interrelation" and "sufficient articulation." The same elastic transitions sustain the movement of Dante's *terza rima*, a form of verse allowing the poem to develop continually in many directions through an involved and subtle syntax. Every nuance of inflection, pace, and meter—every inversion, elision, echo, overflow, and pause—is heard in the shifting tempo of the *aba, bcb, cdc* terzains which carry the narrative ceaselessly through canto after canto with a fluid restrained progress. There operates in Dante's *terza rima* and gothic architecture a principle of "progressive divisibility" analogous to the co-ordinations, the delicate articulations, of syllogism in a scholastic thesis, ramifying incessantly into parts of parts until it comes to its conclusion after traversing its argument encyclopedically. Scholasticism discriminates finely.

In this new fluid space, pierced or traversed rather than enclosed, the gothic architect could hardly avoid optical illusions. As the late-gothic system becomes more fragile, more intellectualist (like the scholasticism of Roger Bacon, who found certainty in mathematical systems alone) architecture is transcribed into an ever-changing pictorial geometry: capitals are suppressed; thin pilasters cluster about piers; liernes and tiercerons spring into dainty webs over the surface of vaults; gables, mullions, and moldings everywhere leap into flamboyant curves; and we glance through thin stone armatures diagonally, vertically, horizontally. This painterly, linear decorated gothic liquidates boundaries, penetrates planes, opens volumes, and leaves to the renaissance architect and painter the obligation to reintegrate this disproportional space by re-establishing the wall and constructing a new perspective from a fixed point of view. Gothic architecture employed three diverging kinds of logic at the same time: of the eye, of the structure, and of the pure intellect. To enhance the illusion of length, some naves were intentionally built on a bent, or "deviated," axis.

In this dynamic environment the sculptured figure, emancipating itself from the control of the wall, gained, along with its freedom in space, a more convincing humanity. Gothic art is the revenge of the person upon the inhumanity of the romanesque ikon.[3] Certainly this art attains its classic phase in the graven image of man, who now bears the marks of suffering and that private sensibility by which Dante, in his sweet new style, humanizes and "spiritualizes" the artifices of courtly love. When the statue-colonnette no longer performs a solely architectural function, it assumes another "morphology" and takes on the frail contours of the living flesh; the stone people set about cathedral porches tend to group themselves, as at Chartres, into dramatic ensembles, responding to the impulses now moving them strongly from within. The gothic statue ventures to take its role with "gentle animation" in the vivid local anecdotes of figural realism. The logic of the architectural scheme no longer has power to deny individuality to the images it contains. In the second ring of the ninth circle of Hell Dante finds Count Ugolino della Gherardesca, of Donoratico, gnawing upon the skull of Archbishop Ruggieri degli Ubaldini, the Ghibelline who cast the Guelf count treacherously into an oubliette and there left him and his sons to starve. Looking up from the ice, Ugolino tells Dante how he was turned to stone within as he watched his sons die; for two days after they had perished he called them by name, groping over their bodies in blind hunger: "Then fasting was more powerful than woe." The episode has the immediacy of Italian hatred and human pain, and we exclaim, with Dante, as Ugolino wipes his bloody mouth upon Ruggieri's hair, "Ah! Pisa!" Similarly in the gothic cathedral the statues have, like the local foliage on capitals, the authenticity of secular and provincial life, as sculpture emerges in the round from the thin and emptied architectural framework. In his *Dictionary* Viollet le Duc says of such gothic statues that each "possesses its personal character which remains graven on the memory like the recollection of a living being whom one has known." At the portals of any gothic cathedral we feel the ambience of human beings, the pathos and dignity of those philosophers Dante met in Limbo, antique people "with slow and grave eyes, of great authority in their looks; they spoke seldom, and with soft voices." There in the dim silence are Socrates and Brutus and Plato, and Caesar in armor with his gerfalcon eyes. These people of Dante's always live and move in a certain quality of light, whether the dusk of Limbo, the tempests of Hell, the sapphire dawn of Purgatory, or the flaming glory of Paradise; for Dante's art is also pictorial. In the *Comedy*, as in the porches of Amiens, the tensions are complex between an abstract system, a plastic humanity, and a painterly vision.

Throughout the "environmental" space created by the pointed arch occurred many "interferences" among the techniques of architecture, sculpture, and painting, because as gothic space became fluid and mobile the light within it was broken up and modulated until both architecture and sculpture were used pictorially. In the high-gothic cathedral,

Light is form, since it is admitted to the nave only after it has been patterned by the colored network of the stained glass windows. To what realm, to what region in space do these structures, situated between heaven and earth, and pierced through and through by light, belong? The flat, but limitless expanse of the windows, their images, shifting, transparent, disembodied, and yet firmly held in place by bands of lead, the illusory mobility of volumes which, despite the stubborn rigidity of architecture, expand with the depth of shadows, the interplay of columns, the overhang of many-storied, diminishing naves —all these are like symbols of the eternal transfiguration forever at work upon the forms of life and forever extracting from it different forms for another life.[4]

When the Beau Dieu and other carven people at Amiens stirred within the architectonic frame encompassing them, they entered a world of space we call sculptural, and they began to lead a double existence: as an architectural element and as a volume plastically felt almost with a sense of touch passing around the contour of the figure. Already the statue-colonnettes on the west porches at Chartres are adjusting themselves to the realm of sculptural space; and presently the Vierge dorée in the portal of the south transept at Amiens (c. 1280) stands forth graciously under her

own canopy, occupying her own private situation. As
the light passes over such images, they seem to live a
voluntary existence, independent of the design of the
portal. Meanwhile the architectural system was itself
generating painterly space, for the late-gothic portals
are so deep as to be porches within which the play of
shadow and light transforms the structure to a pictorial
scene. The light falling over and within Amiens is fugitive, colorful; the façade needs dawns, twilights, the
gray mists of northern storms. By the close of the thirteenth century the sculptural figures at Reims entered
a third relation with space; now they are felt not alone
with the touch but with the eye; they seem no longer
to be stone but to belong to some painterly composition where they exist as forms of light and shade. The
façade of Rouen beguiled the Impressionists like
Monet into seeing this architecture as a shimmer of
pure color. Was Grosseteste led to his experiments with
light by dwelling in this luminous gothic atmosphere
where all structures transform themselves? Does the
gothic statue belong to the realm of architecture, sculpture, or painting?

The gothic window was also a point of interference
between the techniques of architecture, sculpture, and
painting. The early windows at Le Mans treat glass in
a mural—almost romanesque—form: the figures are
controlled by the architectural design and function of
the window; the areas of color are large and make an
abstract pattern defined heavily by coarse leading
(*cernes*). Then in general the trend was away from
large, severe architectural patterns toward pictorial
and descriptive fluency. At Chartres the half-architec-
tural, half-sculptural figures of La Belle Verrière and
the west lancets were followed by windows of the thirteenth century which break up the design of the medallions into complicated details, with a succession of
anecdotal scenes where the figures enter a half-realis-

tic narrative of great variety. Though Henry Adams
has denied that the windows of Chartres have "perspective," the figures often seem "raised" into bas-relief by accents in the leading, by fine etchings of the
background color, by "mounting" red and yellow details against a blue field. In some windows this "mounting" achieves a color-perspective decisive as Matisse's,
the small yellow figures, especially, appearing to
"move" against the blue ground of the medallion. So
again at the height of a gothic technique we find interferences: are these windows architectural, sculptural, or painterly? Like the image in sculpture, the
image in glass lost architectural immobility and entered new relations with space. In late-gothic windows,
of course, the diapered pattern of the ground was gradually replaced by more "naturalistic" motifs, and the
value of the glass became so pictorial that stained glass
was transformed to painted glass.

Gothic light is tenderly modulated by that neutral
glass known as "grisaille," of which English builders
were fond. The restrained glow admitted into interiors by this sensitive medieval glass has all the intimacy of Dante's gray scenes in the *Comedy*—as when
in the seventh circle of Hell some souls come through
the thick air, each of them staring at Dante "as a man
is wont to look at another at evening under a new
moon." This scene is penetrated by the ambiguous twilight atmosphere that excited Leonardo da Vinci. The
sweet color of oriental sapphire falls over the easter
shore of Purgatory, and in the Valley of the Princes
(*Purg.* VIII) figures like Leonardo's gray people
move quietly, mysteriously. So the shadows fall, waveringly, within the porches at Amiens. In the third
round of the seventh circle of Hell Dante uses his light
with the nuance—the chiaroscuro—of sophisticated renaissance painting:

. . . . Over all the sand, with a slow falling, were raining

down large flakes of fire, as of snow on alps without a
wind . . . ; so was descending the eternal heat whereby
the sand was kindled, like tinder beneath the steel.

Or there is the vision of Dis, lurid city, or the bleak
foggy atmosphere of the nether ice, or the slopes of
Purgatory where night comes softly.

Thus gothic art holds, perilously, for a moment an
equilibrium between an architectural framework, a lib-
erated sculpture, and a pictorial illumination. This
doubtful gothic world is crowded with intensely human anecdotes and closely recorded details from nature; all these images from actuality being presented
in a simple linear succession, like the story unfolded
in the medallions of stained glass or in the statues
arranged side by side within a cathedral porch or along
a façade. The gothic "style" has the movement of trac-
ery or the foliation wreathing about the borders of
an illuminated page. Gothic literature, too, accepts this
simple linear arrangement of episodes, as in the mystery play, presented on pageant wagons—wagon following wagon past the same spot until the cycle of
playlets is complete. This one-dimensional form of theatric movement has been called "processional" because
the episodes, dramatic as each may be, are not compressed within a "unified" plot or scene. Gothic space
furnishes a dramatic environment but lacks a dramatic
focus, a point of crisis to which all characters and acts
inevitably draw, converging toward a climax.

Dante's *Comedy* uses this gothic dramatic environment and is organized, almost like a mystery play or
gothic window, into pictorial episodes arranged in linear progression, causing the curious medieval tension
between space and time. Gothic space is different from
renaissance space, and each sort of space requires its
own kind of time.[5] The renaissance painter accepted
the laws of optical perspective, constructing his scene
about a vanishing-point so that his composition had a

three-dimensional space conceived from a fixed point of view. Within this "closed" vanishing-point perspective the figures were situated in a coherent, limited "deep" space enabling us to see them together "simultaneously" in their relation to each other and to the cubical boundaries of the scene they occupy. This sort of pictorial space (really architectural in its conception) uses instantaneous time; thus the renaissance optical perspective in painting fuses time with space by reducing time to a moment when the painted figures are associated in a unified action like that of the "regular" renaissance drama.

In contrast to this renaissance unified time-space perspective, the medieval time-space perspective seems linear and non-Euclidean, having a one-dimensional extension, unrolling like the episodes on a film. The gothic nave is a continuous passage from bay to bay, a motion in a single direction or in several linear directions; amid the bays of Amiens we feel the gothic principle of "transparency," a delight in "flowing transitions." So the episodes in romances by Chrétien de Troyes follow each other lineally through many engaging incidents that are not co-ordinated toward a climax from many directions at once. In Chrétien's genteel and finicking narratives there is every gothic diversity, affectation, and grace, but no focus for the action, no proportional movement of force and counter-force.

Dante's poem is a *passage,* a linear traversing of space, scene after scene; and Dante's time is a linear extension taking the course of a journey. The pilgrim reaches the eternal through time. The term needed to characterize Dante's space-time vision is used to describe the "spread" perspective in Sienese painting in contrast to early-renaissance Florentine painting—"cartographic." The Sienese narrative painters depicted "landscapes that display the world from the top to the bottom of the picture, not in depth, but in a bird's eye view." The eye runs in a linear course over the episodes of a scene in "flattened" space, in "transparency":

The need to grasp the totality of space is here satisfied by a wholly arbitrary and yet fertile structure—a structure which is neither the schematic abbreviation of a ground-plan, nor a normal perspective. . . . In an eye-level horizon objects are hidden one behind the other, and distance, by progressively diminishing their size, also tends to efface them. But beneath a raised horizon, space unfolds like a carpet, and the shape of the earth is like the slope of a mountain. (*Life in Forms of Art*)

This form of "horizontal" vision is apparent when Dante ascends to the Crystalline sphere and, looking down through the heavens, sees the earth spread out in a cartographic space-time dimension not unlike that of the frescoes along the walls of the Campo Santo in Pisa, a perspective which allows for distance, passage, and environment, but without focus; and it operates episodically in linear time, displaying the world from "top to bottom":

I saw that, since the hour when I had first looked, I had moved through the whole arc which the first climate makes from its middle to its end; so that beyond Cadiz I saw the mad track of Ulysses, and on the other side almost the shore on which Europa became a sweet burden. And more of the site of this little threshing-floor would have been discovered to me, but the sun was proceeding beneath my feet, a sign and more removed. (*Par.* XXVII)

Dante's "Sienese" vision of the Mediterranean is like the medieval map drawn before the renaissance Mercator projection was invented to enable us to see things simultaneously and in proportion. Although the *Comedy* attains the realm of the timeless and eternal, its art form is controlled by a technique of passage, transition, and transparency. The movement through the topography of Dante's universe, a spiral and ascent, is so fluid that in Paradise it becomes almost an illusion and can be indicated only by modulation of light—almost as we feel our passage along the nave of a gothic cathedral as a transition through an ever-changing atmosphere, deprived of architectural substance, but filled with human meaning and crowded with human images.

And in truth gothic art gave us dramatic episodes with very human actors, but could not furnish the proper stage, the proper space, for an entirely humanist drama. The proto-humanism of the gothic imagination is expressed in that supreme and final achievement of medieval painting, the Villeneuve-Avignon Pietà (*c.* 1465), where the anguished stiff body of Christ is bent at an angle full of pathos over the lap of a weeping and mannered Mary, beside whom piously bow two gracious figures, and before whom kneels, with prayerful hands, some layman so literally portrayed that he is doubtless the donor. In the background, at the left, and very small, are the walls and towers of Jerusalem. The sky is vacant bronze. The humanity of these figures is as authentic as anything in renaissance painting; here are the gothic *dramatis personae.* But there is wanting a stage; or rather, the stage is not yet arranged for a completely human drama, a secular drama. The gothic figures are secular, but their world is not. They do not *fit into* a humanized perspective. The space in which they exist is very expressive, of course, but not proportional: the eye runs from the donor to the kneeling Magdalen and from the dead Christ to the other figures, arranged cartographically in powerful linear design. There is implied space, and we cannot say it is unorganized; it is simply not organized convincingly in depth. We see man as he is in the flesh, gothic man whose pain is redemption; but he belongs only vaguely to the world; or else this bronze world, with Jerusalem, does not belong to him. The focus is double, suiting the double gothic experience of reality—worldly and other-worldly; and the proportions of the scene are alien to the men who inhabit it.

The space is incommensurate: we cannot measure the interval between the kneeling donor in front and the group "behind" him, or possibly a little "beside" him; and it is harder to say how far the Magdalen is "behind" Mary. The intensely realized gothic figure of man with all his personal authenticity needs to be seen in a new perspective, a new world-order, a new space— a space with a single, not a double, focus. The arts of the renaissance provided this space, this focus, this perspective.

II

RENAISSANCE COMPOSITION   The renaissance humanists brought their world into a single focus, though it is hard to say whether the focus was scientific, platonic, or Christian. Marsilio Ficino exclaims: "Certainly the universal motion of the cosmos itself cannot be lacking in perfect order . . . In this common order of the whole, all things, no matter how diverse, are brought back to unity according to a single determined harmony and rational plan. Therefore we conclude that all things are led by one certain Orderer who is most full of reason." Sometimes it is hard to relate Machiavelli's politics to Pico della Mirandola's platonism, or Brunelleschi's gothistic dome soaring above Florence to the frigid "classical" arcades screening the Certosa of Pavia; and we wonder whether the renaissance was not hopelessly at a loss for any sure direction—a condition we may call either "chaos" or "experiment." Yet flexible, inconstant, diverse as were the many forces working in humanism, the renaissance, especially during the fourteenth and fifteenth centuries, was able to sustain an optimism that could come only with a sense that one lived in a closed, intelligible universe.

This felt order is perhaps more apparent in renaissance art than in renaissance thought, for the architect, sculptor, and painter resolutely set about attacking the "problem of the third dimension" which, being solved, furnished an adequate theater for the image of man created by gothic artisans. Inevitably this new rendering of space brought man into new psychological, as well as physical, relations with reality. As we know, there were two diverging strains in medieval art and thought, idealism and naturalism (philosophical "realism" and "nominalism")—the "double experience" of gothic existence. When the tension became too great between these diverging strains, there emerged between them the world of renaissance experience: the world of beauty, an aesthetic world, an order of reality unknown to the Middle Ages. The forms existing within the renaissance world of art, which owes so much to science, are "significant" because they have an aesthetic rather than a moral, religious, or naturalistic value. The order of reality represented in Leonardo's painting is ambiguously related to human life as medieval art, with its grace of tears, seldom is; but Leonardo's world has a new kind of enchantment and gives to illusions a new kind of power frightening to those neo-Thomists who have accused the renaissance of letting loose the great beast Beauty to prey on man and art. The renaissance painter did, indeed, give "a higher coefficient of reality to the object," [6] the coefficient of aesthetic representation. The old medieval order of God's ideal system could hardly hold together this secular aesthetic world, where images needed to be related to each other by some formal law of beauty, a canon of proportion unnecessary in the linear style of gothic art. The architectural discipline of renaissance space—the "window frame" view in painting—

brings the spectator into psychological adjustment with this aesthetic representation and safeguards this formal order of reality from disintegrating.

In his theory of Being, Aquinas had no idea of proportion, since God is infinite and incommensurable, and one cannot easily adjust the infinite to the finite in any closed ratio—another reason why the symbolic landscape in the Villeneuve-Avignon Pietà does not seem to belong to the persons who inhabit it. Instead of the double experience of gothic art—the tension between realistic anecdote and the symbolic system that contained it—renaissance art achieves a single vision, for the world of renaissance art and science was founded upon a theory of correct proportions. Writing on architecture in 1452, Alberti assumes that "a certain and regular order," which he calls congruity, is the law of art and nature:

The business and office of congruity is to put together members differing from each other in their natures in such a manner that they may conspire to form a beautiful Whole . . . ; nor does this Congruity arise so much from the body in which it is found, or any of its members, as from itself and from Nature, so that its true seat is in the mind and in reason; and accordingly it has a very large field to exercise itself and flourish in, and runs through every part and action of man's life, and every production of Nature herself, which are all directed by the law of congruity. . . .

Thus the painter and architect and sculptor were able to erect their realm of aesthetic experience upon pure mathematical ratios like the "golden measure." The Middle Ages did not believe that the artist could create; only God could create. The renaissance painter and poet created a formal domain of Beauty regulated by algebraic equations and platonic notions of harmony. This is the renaissance "composition."

Bernard Berenson once said that the Italian renaissance painter was usually a man with a native gift for science who took to painting for purposes of research;

consequently "the humanist in him was always killing the artist." Here is one difference between the Middle Ages and the renaissance: in the earlier period theories of art grew out of practice; in the renaissance the practice of the arts grew out of theory, and the renaissance artist, unlike the medieval artisan-builder-sculptor-craftsman, was often a doctrinaire scientist, attempting to impose upon his aesthetic world a unity, a closed system of ratios. That is why medieval science developed outside a context of scientific thought, and also why so much renaissance science rose within the context of art. If the Florentine painters reached their notions of Beauty through science, sometimes they did not succeed in reconciling their science with their painting. Nor did Sir Philip Sidney succeed in reconciling his notion of regularity in drama with the practices of the English stage—even the academic stage. If Giotto practiced a classic technique in painting, his near successors did not follow him but turned instead to mathematicians who were busy inventing coherent visions of space, so that it took better than a generation before a mature renaissance style grew from the art of Giotto and Masaccio. The renaissance devoted itself to erecting critical theories with an energy almost unequaled in western culture; fortunately for the arts the theories were sometimes more honored in the breach than the observance, as Shakespeare's theater suggests.

Implicit in the theory itself is a kind of intellectualism Ruskin once called "rigid, cold, inhuman." In fact, the renaissance, commonly presumed to be an era when art was "humanized," is far less human, less filled with pathos, with a sense of suffering, than gothic art, which was deep in the human condition. Uccello, for example, who gave his life and his art to exploring perspective, is one of those humanists who used his painting for research. Berenson complains that Uccello merely illustrates scientific problems, that his zeal for converging lines causes him to forget local color; so he presents us with green and pink horses. Uccello's Deluge, Berenson adds, looks as if a milldam had burst; in the Sacrifice of Noah, Uccello studies the figure of God "with nothing but the scientific intention to find out how a man swooping down head-foremost would have looked if at a given instant of his fall he had been suddenly congealed and suspended in space." However, in the next century did not Galileo watch a lamp swinging in the cathedral at Pisa? Today we admire Uccello and the "intellectual" painters—Piero della Francesca, for instance—because we too have given our arts to solving technical problems of time and space. We detect in Uccello's Rout of San Romano the same sort of experiment with objects we find going on in Braque when he "disintegrates" a bottle into planes. There is no reason to deny that a great deal of renaissance art is bloodless and inhumane in a cold rational way, especially since the nineteenth century mistakenly supposed the renaissance to be a reaction against the "otherworldliness" of the Middle Ages. The Elizabethan critic Samuel Daniel could have been referring to modern painting when he said, "It is ever the misfortune of Learning to be wounded by her own hand."

Sometimes the renaissance was so intellectual that it did not see, or even try to see, the world as it "is." In "Fra Lippo Lippi" Browning takes the nineteenth-century view of renaissance man, who was presumed to have rediscovered "the value and significance of flesh." Explaining how he wants to record "the look of things," Browning's painter Lippo says, "Zooks, sir, flesh and blood, that's all I'm made of." Today, by contrast, we recognize that the ability to observe "the look of things" is rather an inheritance from gothic man than an original renaissance talent. As we know, Burckhardt is chiefly responsible for the assumption that ren-

aissance man was for the first time flesh and blood,
an individual being—*uomo singolare, uomo unico*. The
shapes of things, the color, the lights and shades—why
not paint them just as they are, asks Browning's Lippo.
The only reply is that Jan Van Eyck tried to, and often
did, along with half-medieval painters of the North
and South, who saw the commonplace object for what
it is. If the nineteenth century overstated the importance of renaissance sensuousness, we now are struck
by the severity of renaissance critical theory. The renaissance did not discover man in the flesh or in his
human condition—the medieval sculptor and poet already had done so; but he *situated* the image of man,
confidently, within a new world-order, within a new
coherent space and perspective. The mastery of the
third dimension, in painting especially, required a kind
of realism that was at the same instant plastically convincing but technically an illusion; so the renaissance
set about forcing a synthesis in the face of this contradiction. Leon Battista Alberti, Piero della Francesca, Sebastiano Serlio—these austere scientists
devoted to proportion and perspective—seem increasingly to be the "representative men" of renaissance art.
As we now see it, the final problem of all renaissance
artists is not to represent objects naturalistically but
instead to *dispose* objects within a rationalized composition, to reconstruct about the figure of man a cosmos whose proportions are determined from a fixed
point of view.

Therefore the humanist concept of "nature" is really
an assertion of a will to reconstruct man's environment
from a certain angle of vision, which is, in effect, not
only a technique—a style—but also a perception of how
things "happen" and "appear." By means of his principles of "composition," the renaissance artist treats the
world as a "realized" area for man's action. This understood, it is not difficult to interpret "the enthusiasm

of the Early Renaissance for simple mathematical relations in space." The fifteenth-century "space enthusiasm," the effort to integrate the design of buildings, paintings, and sculpture, is comparable only with our own attempts to master space from contemporary points of view. In this sense the renaissance artistic "form" means, in the last analysis, the imposition of a theory of proportion, whether that proportion expresses itself in the "regularity" of drama and epic, the "unified" stage of the Teatro Olimpico, the painter's "visual pyramid," the ideal ratios of sculpture, or the "golden measure" of the architect. The renaissance artist-and-scientist has an abiding faith that space is strictly measurable and can be formally arranged within a cosmos, that all the constructions of art have a law of unity, harmony, and coherence. Consequently the disposing of elements proportionately in architecture, sculpture, and painting corresponds, by analogy, to the literary attempt to organize episodes and characters according to a principle of propriety, decorum, or "probability." The renaissance evolved its aesthetic world from an almost Pythagorean belief that all is number; it tried to obey in both art and science a theory of quantitative relations. And Leonardo, renaissance scientist and artist, relied upon "the supreme certainty" of mathematics: "No human investigation can be called true science without passing through mathematical tests." Speaking as a painter, Leonardo continues: "the painter in his harmonious proportions makes the component parts react simultaneously so that they can be seen at one and the same time both together and separately; together, by viewing the design of the composition as a whole; and separately by viewing the design of its component parts."

The first premise of the renaissance artist is the sanctity of the mathematical ratio, which reveals itself both philosophically and scientifically in neoplatonism.

The most famous renaissance definition of Beauty is in
Alberti's treatise *On Architecture* (1452): "I shall define Beauty to be a harmony of all the parts, in whatsoever subject it appears, fitted together with such proportion and connection, that nothing could be added,
diminished, or altered. . . ." Beauty, he thinks, arises
from the number, figure, and collocation of the several
members, which must be united into a whole with "an
orderly and sure coherence and agreement of all those
parts." For Alberti, the law of nature in the arts is "a
consent and agreement of the parts of a whole as to
Number, Finishing, and Collocation." Woelfflin defined
the renaissance art-structure as being a harmonious
adjustment of clearly bounded units, with absolute
clarity of statement. Writing about prose style, Ben
Jonson said that "The congruent and harmonious fit-
ting of parts in a sentence hath almost the fastening
and force of knitting and connection as in stones well
squared, which will rise strong a great way without
mortar." This symmetrical structure in language is the
prose of Alberti's Rucellai Palace in Florence (1446–
51), where each unit of the façade is neatly defined
and exists as a harmonious feature on a plane surface.

The renaissance builder rationalized his system by
basing it upon the ratios of the circle and musical harmony. Far from being licentious, renaissance architecture is constructed upon measures at once platonic
and scientific, so that the round church is the most
adequate symbol of a humanism having two facets,
mathematical and aesthetic, as in the writings of Pico
della Mirandola. Since the circle is the perfect figure,
the sign of divine order, the change from the long-
naved medieval church to the renaissance circular
churches (sometimes called "temples") is token of a
confidence in a harmony between microcosm and macrocosm, between man and his universe. Furthermore
the proportions of the human figure with arms and

legs spread, like an extended compass, is the archetype for the "cyclothym" renaissance sculpture, painting, and architecture. Following Vitruvius' measurements of the human body, Leonardo notes that "if you open your legs so much as to decrease your height by 1/14 and spread and raise your arms so that your middle fingers are on a level with the top of your head, you must know that the navel will be the center of a circle of which the outspread limbs touch the circumference; and the space between the legs will form an equilateral triangle."

The centralized church, whether it be a circular temple or the church in form of a Greek cross or the church like Santo Spirito, Florence, with transepts and apse in identical proportions, is a reaction against the incommensurate space of the gothic nave. Within this church we are not induced, as we were in the gothic nave, to move; when we stand at the proper focal point, we discover that man is the measure, that the nave of Santo Spirito is in a golden ratio, twice as high as it is wide, with bays half as wide as they are high, with ground story and clerestory of equal height.[7] Giuliano da Sangallo in 1485 also designed Santa Maria delle Carceri, Prato, as an ideal Greek-cross structure in simple ratios, the depth of the arms being half their length, and the four walls perfect squares where planes meet. In these churches so luminously planned Christ is no longer the suffering medieval man who is crucified but a Pythagorean creative principle, Christ Pantocrator, a Logos-God whose divinity is expressed by symmetries. Bramante and Michaelangelo designed Saint Peter's to be a centralized structure with the great dome rising above it like a diapason. Alberti speaks as a platonist in writing "Nor does this congruity arise so much from the body in which it is found . . . ; its true seat is in the mind and in reason."

Trissino, author of the heroic poem *L'Italia Liberata*

dai Goti (1547–48), was patron of the architect Palladio, and himself obeyed Vitruvius' law of *symmetria* in laying out the Villa Cricoli. Palladio agreed that to preserve decorum churches must be round because the circle has neither beginning nor end, all its parts being alike: "the extreme in every part being equally distant from the center, it is therefore the most proper figure to show the Unity, infinite Essence, the Uniformity, and Justice of God." So the critic Minturno set the ideal ratios for the composition of a poem:

. . . for truth is one, and that which is once true must of necessity be true always and in every age, nor can the differences between various ages change what is true, though they may be able to change customs and life, yet in all their mutations the truth still remains stable; . . . it is according to reason that in every poem there should be treated one sole and single action which should be perfect and of suitable length.

In those amazing "Fowre Hymns" to Love, Beauty, Heavenly Love, and Heavenly Beauty, Spenser sang of this formal humanist system, the mystic order to which Ficino devoted his *Theologica Platonica* (1463) and Pico his *De Ente et Uno* (1494):

What time this worlds great workmaister did cast
To make al things, such as we now behold,
It seemes that he before his eyes had plast
A goodly Paterne, to whose perfect mould
He fashiond them as comely as he could;
That now so faire and seemely they appeare,
As nought may be amended any wheare.

That wondrous Paterne wheresoere it bee,
Whether in earth layd vp in secret store,
Or else in heauen, that no man may it see
With sinfull eyes, for feare it to deflore,
Is perfect Beautie, which all men adore,
Whose face and feature doth so much excell
Al mortal sence, that none the same may tell.

To Spenser, love is a celestial Harmony, and the frame of the wide universe is an idea of Pure Intelligence.

Thus the single vision of the renaissance humanized the world; for as Leonardo asks: "Do you not know that our soul is composed of harmony and that harmony is only produced when proportions of things are seen or heard simultaneously?" Leonardo, man of the renaissance, finds proportion "not only in numbers and measurements, but also in sounds, weights, times, spaces, and in whatsoever power there may be."

If the form of the gothic cathedral was most clearly defined by its exterior, where the buttressing showed the tensions of a linear system, the renaissance arts gave to space a new internal coherence and amplitude. This interior dimension makes the world a "realized" area for human action; it is the humanist space generated within Copernicus' revised world-order, where "all the spheres revolve about the sun as their midpoint, and therefore the sun is the center of the universe." By setting the sun at the focal point of his cosmology, Copernicus endowed universal space with the renaissance three-dimensional increment already created in painting, architecture—and literature as well. His book *De Revolutionibus Orbium Coelestium* (c. 1530) reorganizes the Ptolemaic system he found in Dante and medieval science by looking at it from inside, as if it were a self-contained realm. The old "cartographic" perspective takes on three-dimensional plenitude, and the medieval feeling for space as linear extension now is consolidated "in depth." Magnificently enclosed by the sphere of the fixed stars, the Copernican universe is enriched and unified by an internal coefficient we ordinarily associate with "space":

First and above all lies the sphere of the fixed stars, containing itself and all things, for that very reason immovable; in truth, the frame of the universe, to which the motion and position of all other stars are referred. . . . Of the moving bodies, first comes Saturn, who completes his circuit in xxx years. After him, Jupiter, moving in a twelve-year revolution. Then Mars, who revolves biennially.

Fourth . . . is contained the Earth. . . . Venus. . . . Mercury. . . . In the middle of all dwells the Sun. . . . And thus rightly in as much as the Sun, sitting on a royal throne, governs the circumambient family of stars . . . We find, therefore, under this orderly arrangement, a wonderful symmetry in the universe, and a definite relation of harmony in the motion and magnitude of the orbs . . .

We have this sense of harmonious enclosure inside the cubical system of Brunelleschi's Pazzi Chapel (1420–29), where the simple equations are constantly restated by the pilasters, the dome, the frieze, the blind arcades. The proportions are so clearly written that the building seems to be a theorem inscribed in black lines upon white planes. Every interval, every boundary, every member, reaffirms the coherence, the "wonderful symmetry," of this three-dimensional space, firmly and logically defined in luminous, intelligible measure. If we look too intently, the delicate structure seems to vibrate: the domes, for instance, do not quite touch the moldings on which they rest and thus have a power to "float" above the white walls; and the black medallions seem "suspended," or the pilasters, moldings, and frieze seem to "advance" and "recede." But Brunelleschi never exploits such opportunities for illusion; instead he disclaims them by setting every element of his architecture in known relation to every other element. There are no oblique approaches, no overlapping or concealed surfaces, no doubtful functions. Within this building we are always confident of the scale; we are continually reminded of our position. This is space to be entered by man, adjusted to the scope of his mind.

Renaissance aesthetic space is not simply extension or projection: it is composition within three dimensions proportionately arranged from a fixed point of view. Essentially it is architectural space bringing us a sense of security and giving coherence, limit, and probability to medieval "environment." By creating

the illusion of such an architectural space, the painter,
Berenson says, can have a "potent" effect upon us:

This art comes into existence only when we get a sense
of space not as a void, as something merely negative, such
as we customarily have, but, on the contrary, as something
very positive and definite, *able to confirm our consciousness of being*, to heighten our feeling of vitality. *Space-
composition is the art which humanizes the void, making
of it an enclosed Eden.*

This heightened "realization" of being comes whenever the technique of perspective and proportion
makes us fully aware of our situation within a cosmos.
When we exist, confidently, in this renaissance increment of space, we attain the humanist conquest of
reality, a supremacy in a secular, aesthetic Eden invented for us by the scientist-painter. Composition in
depth, with measurable intervals and dimensions
adapted to the image of man, places us, as it were,
within the confines of a stage where human action
takes on a dramatic meaning. The medieval artist did
not have such a stage at his disposal, for he saw with
a double perspective; he drew man toward the center
of his vision, but he lacked a secular theater in which
man could act, since the cosmos still belonged to God,
not to man. Gothic art humanized the anecdote. The
renaissance scientist-artist, having a single and humanist vision, built a new scene, in depth, about man, who
could now appear in tragic focus.

The evolution of "deep" space—that heroic dimension—in medieval painting, the enclosing of the scene
from within, its internal co-ordination in a rationalized
perspective, began in the thirteenth century among the
gothic figures grouped in "implied" space "behind" the
ornamental architectural screen in triptychs. Presently
these figures lost their immobility and, like the statues
in a cathedral porch, appeared to intercommunicate,
to fall into clusters by a law of psychological and anecdotal gravity. Though they still were actors in a linear

narrative spread out across the foreground plane, they
became more closely and intricately associated
"within" the shallow stage of the architectural system.
As the area behind these figures deepened into a
"scene," this space was at first rationalized by means
of a "vanishing area" or "vanishing axis," not by a precise vanishing point. In some such way Jan Van Eyck
adjusted his persons inside a "deep" enclosure, the action being seen simultaneously within the confines of
a stage that "belongs" to human beings. Since the
logic of this early perspective is not entirely consistent,
the figures fit somewhat loosely—"bifocally"—into three-
dimensional space that "slides" into double or even
triple adjustments. When during the fifteenth century
the Italian painters used a "boxed" or "window-frame"
area to encompass their figures, this "deep" space was
more rigorously closed in a vanishing-point perspective.
Thus the Italian painting came to resemble the picture
or *coulisse* stage like that built later by the architects
Serlio and Palladio for the Teatro Olimpico in Vicenza.

During the evolution of this dramatic perspective
we can see the difference between medieval and renaissance realism; for though medieval art placed man
at the center, its structure did not have a convincing
humanistic focus. The intricate romances of Chrétien
de Troyes, for example, have many realistic anecdotes,
and the characters have a sensitive psychological
mechanism resembling the "delicate nerves and fine
perceptions" of Henry James' persons. Yet Chrétien's
responsive creatures inhabit a "romantic" or magical
landscape, which allows the marvelous to happen, but
not the "probable," so that the anecdotes cannot take
on their full human meaning. The probable does not
occur until characters live in a coherently organized
world where events are more responsibly managed
and converge, inevitably, toward a climax—or a "vanishing point" of plot. Chrétien's is a lively and pleasant

and genteel world, but an undependable one, lacking resemblance to any theater where there can be a "recognition" of the human situation in a "closed" reliable perspective.

Chaucer's *Troilus and Criseyde* gains a degree of probability partly because the characters coexist within a more convincingly realized world. However diffused the narrative may be, as if Chaucer were writing a novel, the co-ordinations between characters and society and between each other are becoming dramatic with involved psychological interplay, a responsible logic of events, which are no longer arranged in a mere anecdotal succession. We can *enter* the secular and recognizable world of Troy as we cannot possibly enter Chrétien's world except by fancy. Similarly we can enter the box-settings of Italian fifteenth-century painters as we cannot enter a medieval cartographic landscape; and we are encouraged to do so. However, the situation in Chaucer's poem, like the situation in a painting by Van Eyck, is not completely rationalized or unified, and the figures fit a little loosely into their milieu, as if the scene were organized about a vanishing area or axis, rather than a vanishing point. There is an exciting effect of approximation, as if the point of view wavered. Perhaps some of the mystery of Cressida's behavior is due to this doubtful perspective allowing Chaucer to shift slightly, or relax, his view of his heroine. Somehow we understand Cressida's conduct better than we can explain; though she is "slyding of corage" we do not wholly condemn her. She is certainly human enough even if we cannot precisely define her adjustment to her world or even to Troilus, Pandarus, and Diomedes. The world of Troy remains here and there out of focus; some relationships are uncertain. Chaucer's irony, his sympathy for everyone, and Troilus' half-cynical, half-pathetic surrender of the world as his soul mounts to heaven are evidence of this

somewhat equivocal point of view, which allows the
poet to readjust his angle of vision at some expense of
logic. The probabilities here are answerable but re-
markably free, as they are in Giotto's half-medieval
scenes not yet entirely rationalized in space.

Then Masaccio's Holy Trinity, painted about 1427
for Santa Maria Novella, Florence, closes the perspective with great skill and dignity; this half-gothic motive
of Christ on the cross, with the Dove and the Father
immediately above, is contained within a strictly defined stage where, as Woelfflin says, there is a "strong
feeling for the relation between man and architecture,
for the resonance of a beautiful space." Masaccio
places Christ crucified in architectonic space created
by painted columns supporting a huge coffered vault
narrowing logically from a fixed point of view toward
the background plane of the wall. The symmetry is
nearly perfect, the body of Christ forming the major
axis, the center of the foreground plane being his navel,
the two figures on each side kneeling in such a way as
to form the legs of an equilateral triangle with its apex
at the head of the Father, who is set beneath the axis
of the vault. The walls of the enclosing painted
"chapel" recede with mathematical precision toward
a vanishing point indicated by the feet of Christ in the
foreground plane. The architectural values of this
space are also human values, and though the angle of
vision is raised, the painted scene extends the amplitude of our own space convincingly inward, heightening our consciousness of every dimension. Thus Masaccio lays the groundwork for those later majestic
constructions of a classic painting—"weighty masses
bound together by strict rule" in a style which "has its
being in the wide echoing spaces of the churches of
the High Renaissance."

This reintegration of space is probably the most important aesthetic achievement of renaissance human-

ism. Technically it expresses itself as a rationalizing of sight, which imposes upon our experience of reality a certain kind of unity gained through an "artificial perspective." The "optics of antiquity" used a "natural" perspective, which is nothing more than a subjective impression caused by the eye itself as it "bends" space and line toward the point upon which the eye is focused.[8] When one uses this "natural" or subjective perspective, the size and position of objects depend upon the visual angle. Sometimes the medieval painter tried to rationalize his subjective impression by means of a "synthetic" perspective, using "bifocal" constructions like the vanishing area or vanishing axis. Consequently the perspective of painters like Fouquet is "empirical," having great optical freedom within an inconsistent space and keeping man in a somewhat subjective relation to the outside world. Then by a new technique of vision Brunelleschi and Donatello attempted to impose upon aesthetic space a rational structure enabling the artist to represent reality in a mode convincing to the mind as well as to the eye, consistently to relate solid objects to each other and to the area about them, and to unify the composition. Thus was erected the coherent perspective of the renaissance, defining space by means of orthogonal lines converging toward a vanishing point. By this technique the painter was enabled to represent three dimensions upon a plane surface, creating an illusion of a "deep" self-contained consistent space where all lines can be conjugated with respect to each other. In effect mathematical perspective transformed a system of rectangular co-ordinates to aesthetic dimensions. At least three incompatible purposes were inherent in the very conception of aesthetic-mathematical space perspective: to organize the composition formally, to create pictorial space, and to harmonize this new "real" space with the surface upon which it was represented.

Certainly it was an artificial system, and often over-rationalized. In the fifteenth century some painters set about demonstrating spatial relations with a desire for precision that is almost naive: their perspective is so forced as to seem arbitrary; the recession is not so much convincing as astonishing; the foreshortening has the overconfidence of many *tours de force* in renaissance logic. This learned command of space is no more artificial, however, than the "unities" finally imposed upon epic and drama, as when Castelvetro dogmatically—and scientifically—explains, following, he presumes, Aristotle, that there is reason for "limited time and limited place" in tragedy and for the canon of "twelve hours." In his *Art of Poetry* Minturno asks with the doctrinaire tone of the renaissance scholar, "Who ever agrees to what he does not understand? How can that be luminous which is hidden?"

Painters were compliant to the law of unity imposed domineeringly by Alberti, who in 1435 in his treatise *On Painting* formulated a mathematical system to "close" the world in a coherent perspective. Accepting the vanishing point as the focus of his aesthetic space, Alberti takes a fixed point of view from which any painting becomes a "visual pyramid." With the pride of system Ruskin so hated, Alberti calmly explains: "Painting is nothing other than a cross section of a visual pyramid upon a certain surface, artificially represented with lines and colors at a given distance, with a central point of view established, and lights arranged." He says that he "borrows from mathematicians" to make his theory of painting clear, for beneath the sensuous appearances of things one must discern those mathematical forms that are primary and stable. (One already detects in Alberti the Cartesian spirit, the ambition to construct a world from geometric ideas.) Even color has proportion. By his mechanism of angles and visual cones Alberti determines the exact

point of view from which the mind can represent
reality. This system was "too difficult and abstract" for
his predecessors. The necessities of painting are, he
thinks, the "circumscription" of objects as defined by
the visual pyramid, the composition of relations between parts, and the harmony of features arranged in
mathematical ratios; also the harmonious distribution
of light. In brief, Alberti insists again, "the painter's
task consists in defining and recording by line and
color each body presenting itself on any surface, at a
specific distance and situated by means of a central
axis, with the effect that all will be represented as a
relief imitating closely the object seen." This is the
strange renaissance synthesis of seeming naturalism
with a highly theoretical closed system. It is vision and
design at once.

During the cinquecento, critics overintellectualized
this renaissance unity into an abstract system that bears
the mark of "mannerist" academism. For example, Sebastiano Serlio's treatise on perspective (1545) congeals
Alberti's theory into pedantic rules:

Perspective consisteth principally in three lines: the first
line is the base below, from whence all things have their
beginning. The second line is that which goeth or reacheth
to the point which some call . . . the horizon. . . . The
third line is the line of the distances, which ought always
to stand as high as the horizon is far or near, according to
the situation.

By means of some such mathematical theorems the
renaissance painter had hoped to recover the values
of antique art. The most gravely "classic" of renaissance
artists, Piero della Francesca, wrote (1480–90) a treatise on perspective to prove that the painter must situ-
ate objects in planes falling away proportionately toward a vanishing point; for painting is the science of
knowing every dimension, by which "many ancient
painters gained eternal fame." Piero accepts optical
perspective as a structure for interpreting human ex-

perience. He tried to measure accurately the proportions of his own scenes by blocking out foreshortened squares on a pavement, a mechanical device known as the *costruzione legittima*, "since painting is nothing else than representations of foreshortened or enlarged surfaces and objects placed on an established picture plane."

When we see Piero trying to reconstruct his art by these "antique" formulas, we recall Panofsky's opinion that during the "Italian, or main, renaissance the classical past was looked upon from a fixed, unalterable distance, quite comparable to the distance between the eye and the object in that most characteristic invention of the same renaissance, focused perspective." The humanists were aware of the distances of history as the Middle Ages were not, and they looked backward to antiquity across a dark abysm of time with a sense of interval and direction; they have an angle on the past. Shakespeare's history plays, too, have a sense of the direction and continuity in political tradition. However imprecise these history plays were, the Elizabethan theater had its own form of "perspective consciousness," [9] which gives Henry IV, 1 and 2, and Henry V a deep focus. To be sure, Shakespeare was unacademic; yet the "rules" served most renaissance literature as a kind of *costruzione legittima*, a formula for reintegrating human experience in a supposedly antique perspective. This is the reason for the controversy about the Aristotelian unities in epic and drama.

Again the cinquecento critics—"mannerist" or academic—overintellectualized the literary rules. Minturno, writing in 1564, insists that the poet must, like Vergil, design his epic in such proportions as to "make up a unified and perfect action":

He will compose correctly the plot of an epic poem who imitates and describes excellently a subject that is entire

and perfect, made up of actions that are illustrious and
serious, and having suitable size, because, as has been said,
the plot is the imitation of an action which is one and
complete and of proper length. . . . But though the epic
has this prerogative of being carried to great length, the
plot should not be made up of more than one unit of material, nor composed of actions that came about in a longer
time than a single year, for the epic narrative is not a history. . . . But the poet, as we have shown (since in one
poem he comprehends those things which tend to one
end) does not treat everything that happened to one man
at the same time and in the same group of events, if they
are varied and not of one sort.

The same rigorous unity, with proportional episodes
and restricted time and space, controlled the perspective in tragedy. Castelvetro was able by 1571 to summarize the law of classic style: the plot of a tragedy
or comedy "should of necessity contain one action of
one person, or of two that are mutually dependent, and
the plot of an epic should contain one action by one
person." Willingly and willfully epic and drama accepted the "foreshortening" of Aristotelian fable, time,
and place. Palladio used Vitruvius very much as Trissino used Aristotle's *Poetics*—to gain the antique unity
and perspective.

The renaissance intention to achieve unity in painting, epic, and drama accounts for a perspective technique that coherently organized the action of the figures into consistent relations with each other and with
the limited scene they occupy. For the techniques of
composition in renaissance painting and renaissance
fable are cognate, the painter using a system of orthogonals that can be conjugated with respect to each
other, the poet a decorum that "should be considered
not merely in actions but also in the speeches and answers of men among themselves," as Cinthio put it in
1549, writing of romances; and he says about "The
Composition of Comedies and Tragedies" (1543):

It appears to me also that reason is able to present the

same truth to us with sufficient probability, because the
power of moving tragic feelings depends only on imitation
which does not depart from probability. . . . Therefore
it seems to me that it is in the power of the poet to move
at his wish the tragic feelings by means of a tragedy of
which he feigns the plot, if that plot is in conformity with
natural habits not remote from what can happen and often
does happen.

(The various characters and episodes must be designed
according to some literary *costruzione legittima,* adjusted to one another by a law of probability, since,
Cinthio insists, the success of a plot depends upon an
"arrangement . . . with which one part is joined and
combined with another just as the parts of the human
body are bound together."

(The tyranny of this law of probability at last reduced
the structure of renaissance "regular" drama to an imitation of life seen from a designated point of view—
the artificial perspective of a pseudo-Aristotelian
canon confining the action to twelve hours, special
motives, and "noble" characters) Cinthio thinks that romance itself must be scaled as proportionately as architecture, and in 1549 furnishes the poet with still
another *costruzione legittima:*

The writer should use great diligence that the parts of his
work fit together like the parts of the body. . . . And in
putting together the bony frame he will seek to fill in the
spaces and make the members equal in size, and this can
be done by inserting at suitable and requisite places loves,
hates, lamentations, laughter, sports, serious things, beauties, descriptions of places, temples, and persons. . . . For
there is nothing above the heavens or below, nor in the
very gulf of the abyss, which is not ready to the hand and
choice of the judicious poet, and which cannot with varied
ornaments adorn the whole body of his composition . . .
for such things give to all the parts their due measure and
fit ornament in such proportion that there emerges a body
well regulated and composed.

He speaks the language of the renaissance scientist-
painter. The law of decorum, warns Cinthio, will show

"what fits times, places, and persons . . . ; for the composition and arrangement of the parts will avail little if the parts are ineptly placed." Minturno expects the actions in the epic to have a "suitable size"; Scaliger would have the episodes neatly proportioned to each other; Vida urges that the drama and epic be kept within strict limits.

Thus as the imitation of reality became more "regular" in poetry and painting, the angle of vision narrowed, and the artist surrendered the freedom of an earlier subjective approach. In the cinquecento, when Raphael is able to locate things exactly, he sacrifices Uccello's inventive incongruity in perspective; when Trissino writes his *Sofonisba* (1515) he boasts that he first laid out the action and speeches "generally" and then "inserted the episodes." Bramante's scholarly Tempietto (1502) at San Pietro in Montorio is a rather chill and bloodless monument. It is one of the ironies of renaissance art that as soon as the system was completely and successfully rationalized and the science of perspective, proportion, and unity had been perfected, thus creating a convincingly realized scene for human action, there fell upon the artist the mortal rigor of academic rules—and we almost prefer the curiously empirical and human ambiguity of Chaucer's *Troilus and Criseyde*. We admire without much warmth Averlino's discourse (1451-64) proposing to regularize civic life itself by using a classic plan for a city: "The principal streets will lead to the Piazza from all the eight gates in the obtuse angles of the city walls and from the eight round towers in the right angles of the city walls." At the eastern end of the piazza will be the principal church; to the west will be the princely palace; on the south the market; on the north the merchants.

For the Italian theater Serlio, perhaps inspired by scenes for masques and pageants or various settings for "garden dramas," designed about 1545 a "fixed" and "closed" perspective stage—a piazza bounded, on three sides, by houses and arcades receding like the *costruzione legittima* in *coulisse* foreshortening. In the "antique" unity of this setting the "regular" drama like *Sofonisba* at last found its logical *mise-en-scène,* giving to the action optical, as well as psychological, probability. The most celebrated perspective stage was built by Serlio and Palladio for the Teatro Olimpico, Vicenza, between 1580 and 1585, although here the "deep space" took the mannerist form of "vistas" opening into the backstage wall. Belatedly Scamozzi erected at Sabionetta in 1588–90 a *coulisse* stage on which the characters acted inside the confines of genuine "deep" space, the foreshortened vista having become the actual stage. In Italy, therefore, there is some parallel between the development of artificial perspective in painting and the "picture" stage.

The Elizabethan playhouse did not so exactly fix the point of view as this "classical" Italian theater; but the richness of dimension on the London stage was even more convincing, for there the character existed powerfully within a dramatic scene none the less probable though it lacked the optical logic of Serlio's piazzas. We need not review the evidence that we have overstressed the influence of the innyard upon the London stage and that we should, instead, look to the *tableaux vivants* presented in the Low Countries to understand how the players on Shakespeare's "unworthy scaffold" were clustered into sculptural, pictorial, and architectural groups.[10] Shakespeare's stage had multiple dimensions, and provided ample depth to enclose its action. In early-renaissance painting one of the devices to represent deep space was to group figures within a baldachino—a room with the walls taken away, leaving columns to support a roof. Sometimes Italian paintings of the Nativity used the baldachino to create an "interior" perspective. The columns and "shadow" (roof) of the London stage offered the same sort of interior-exterior dimensions for grouping figures in an action that could range freely from outer to inner stage and evolve, through adventurous movements in space, every sort of composition.

Being no scientist ~~or~~ academician, Shakespeare could hardly have gone about writing his plays by theories of unity, proportion, and decorum; but he was able to construct, psychologically and scenically, about his characters the fabric of a world so convincing that the dramatic perspective is "deeper" than in other renaissance theaters. Shakespeare's plays preserve, as a residuum from the medieval drama, perhaps, the half-subjective empirical perspective that generates imaginative dimensions rather than literal boundaries for tragic action. As with all great renaissance artists—that is, those who were not primarily scientists—Shakespeare's profoundly human representations do not focus by any mechanical perspective but, instead, upon some implied poetic vanishing point, making "things seem small and undistinguishable, like far-off mountains turned into clouds." Under the spell of this perspective we find, with Hermia, that we "see these things with parted eye, when every thing seems double." The authentic renaissance perspective attained by major painters and poets is not an artificial and exacted unity, but a heightened consciousness of being in the world, a dramatically foreshortened view of man's fate. As a result of this strong perspective-consciousness each of Shakespeare's plays has its own climate and landscape, its own dominating and recurring symbols, making a dramatic firmament from whose arc every stroke of fate seems to fall with its own meaning. Even the domain of the supernatural is seen within the confines of this dramatic perspective, so that "both the worlds suffer" when Macbeth steeps himself and Scot-

land in blood. Shakespeare enveloped his action in an
imaginative fabric as solid and rich as the Othello-
world or the Titian-like sensuality of Cleopatra's
Egypt, a scene broad and deep enough to accommodate the imperial course of history and the secret house
of death. Because of this imagined perspective Shakespeare's stage is thoroughly humanized.

In the early performances like *Romeo and Juliet*
Shakespeare uses a mechanical foreshortening in a
very limited scene, with proportions exactly stated.
The action in this "tragedy," confined as it is by the
walls of Verona, its orchards, squares, and rooms, is
measured in the careful ratios of those Italian paintings whose composition was subjected to simple geometric solutions. The contrasting movements of the
plot are arranged like the conjugation of lines in orthogonal space, and the dramatic illusion is won in
an almost naive way by forcing the perspective—which
has the effect of destroying the "middle ground." The
mechanics are too clear: Romeo is scaled against
Paris and Mercutio; Juliet is scaled against Rosaline,
the Nurse, and Lady Capulet; Tybalt against Benvolio;
Romeo's love, and his pseudo-heroic stature, against
the affectations of Paris; the fury of his passion is scaled
against the common sense of Friar Laurence and the
callow exertions of a courtly lover. Even the values of
this play fall into symmetrical patterns like love and
hate, courtly and romantic love, rashness and caution,
tolerance and intolerance, wit and grief, purity and
sensuality, day and night, sleep and death, Montagu
and Capulet. Romeo's exile to Mantua opens a false
"distance." Tragic time is compressed to forty-two
hours. The foreshortening of events in Verona is too
contrived to permit a mature enchantment; the stagecraft, though it requires lyrical gestures, is too obviously
invented to create those mysterious dimensions that
envelop the action in *Macbeth*, which is quite as regu-

lar but not limited by its precisions, its clarity of structure.)

(The maximum tragic shock occurs when the movement and situation cannot be rationalized by any intellectual or moral design, any formula of proportion, unity, probability, or justice. When Shakespeare is at the top of his tragic power he troubles us with final ambiguities and imprecisions; then the instruments of darkness tell us truths; then arise black vesper's pageants, and imagination bodies forth things unknown. Shakespeare's farthest vision, like Leonardo's, entertains conjecture; and Hamlet's bourne from which no traveler returns is like the "perspective of disappearance" in The Virgin and Child with Saint Anne. At this range of vision Leonardo and Shakespeare face problems that cannot be entirely resolved by that "supreme certainty of mathematics" in which the renaissance humanist set store. Thus arises the deepest contradiction in humanism: the techniques of renaissance art assumed that space is strictly measurable and proportional, that action obeys a law of probability, unity, and decorum; but actually the renaissance imitation of life is most humanistic whenever it touches an order of reality beyond the confines and precisions of this artificial perspective. Humanism was indeed wounded by its own learning. The renaissance artist often tried too hard to close his system, to make probability a reasoned certainty.)

III

INTERFERENCES AND TRANSFORMATIONS

In fact the humanist philosophers sought to reintegrate experience by methods as fictitious as the optical perspective that enabled the painter to make his conquest of space. To be sure, the arts have in common a *theory* for a "renaissance style"; but the mathematical-platonic ideas of harmony, proportion, and unity concealed thoroughgoing inconsistencies in technical practice that finally caused the style based upon these very ideas to disintegrate.

The divergence between theory and practice is illustrated in the painter who used artificial perspective to integrate his composition. Theoretically the *costruzione legittima* made it possible for the painter to unify his scene in depth; actually there remained an unresolved, and perhaps unresolvable, conflict between the flat pictorial surface of wall or canvas and the deep architectural space he represented, by illusion, upon this surface. Thus occur many enigmatic relations between cubical space and surface space, with dissonance between two different and incompatible sorts of perspective—horizontal and recessional. In many renaissance paintings we feel a dramatic disharmony between the surface tension of the foreground plane and the orthogonal space suggesting a third dimension. Therefore the painter was usually driven by a double intention: to use both flat space and volumetric, cubical space—a dilemma that meant a choice between a decorative surface and three-dimensional realism. Sometimes he resorted to that other kind of perspective known as aerial, which in turn qualifies his "linear" perspective. The conflict, in brief, was between representation on the surface and representation in depth, distance, and volume.

These indecisions are everywhere apparent in Italian painting between Giotto and Raphael, whose style is the triumph of high-renaissance art. Theoretically the new perspective should have kept a "careful counterpoise of depth and surface"; yet there was always a contradiction between the design on the surface and the orthogonal design in depth. Even the theory of receding planes did not entirely compromise the opposition between "shallow seeing" and "deep seeing." Theoretically, also, the new perspective required a fixed point of view; actually the point of view does not govern the perspective of many renaissance paintings, Botticelli's, for example, where the perspective is not very deep and is shifted slightly from a central foreground axis to a diagonal view of the background, a symptom of Botticelli's "distrust of depth." And Fra Angelico's figures seem to have volume but not weight, perhaps because, as with Botticelli, the space about them is not fully realized.

The same problem takes other forms in architecture and sculpture. When the renaissance architect re-established the wall, he thought of mural space as a plane divided harmoniously into symmetrical units by moldings, pilasters, friezes, or other elements clearly indicating the boundaries of each unit. In the façades of Alberti's Rucellai Palace in Florence, or of the Cancelleria in Rome, the moldings, pilasters, and frames of windows and doorways tend to be held flush with the mural plane. But there always arose before the renaissance architect, inspired as he was by the classical theories of Vitruvius and by the antique Roman triumphal arch, the difficulty of handling the column against the wall—how, in short, to treat this volume set against the inviolable surface.[11] This technical difficulty has many implications and a very long history, dating from the Romans. The Greeks ordinarily treated the column as the basic architectural unit, for, as in the Parthenon, it is disengaged from the wall of the cella to stand free as a support for the roof, entablature, and pediment. The Romans on the contrary thought of the wall as the essential element, and the column in the basilica, amphitheater, and triumphal arch was handled inconsistently as both a unit in the wall and also as an "engaged" feature, bulging sculpturally from the primary mural surface. Since the renaissance architect followed Vitruvius' practice, not the Greeks', he met this dilemma as soon as he tried to enrich his façade by columns. Alberti desperately struggled to reach a solution when he remodeled San Francesco at Rimini (1450), where he imposed the rather heavy columns of a triumphal arch upon the plane surface of the west front, treating the wall as a basic structure, then engaging columns and arches as classic ornament. The trouble remained, however, for the engaged columns and arches break the plane, falsify the logic of the façade, and make the front sculptural rather than architectural; the plastic features obscure and coarsen the fine mathematical harmony of the proportions. Thus the Roman triumphal arch becomes a sculptural "screen" for the essential architectonic surface. At Sant' Andrea, Mantua (c. 1470), Alberti tried a different solution by using "giant" orders, that is, running huge pilasters up the whole height of the façade. Later, in Venice at the Redentore (1576) Palladio used these giant orders, the effect of which inevitably was to transform the purity of renaissance architectural surfaces into a heavy—almost a baroque—display of sculptural mass. And sometimes where there are interlocking orders, with interplay of engaged columns and pilasters, the architecture looks "mannered." In any event the ambiguity of using the column or pilaster as either fragment-of-plane-wall or as sculptural volume was not resolved.

The same ambiguity in style causes a crisis in another medium—sculpture. In the early renaissance Brunelleschi as architect and Donatello as sculptor alike were troubled by the painter's problem of using relief-perspective. It is possible to read the history of renaissance sculpture as a prolonged conflict between two opposing techniques, carving stone and modeling stone; and when modeling eventually wins, the integrity of renaissance sculptural space is destroyed. According to this interpretation the purest renaissance style in sculpture is reached at Rimini, where Agostino di Duccio's reliefs are so low that they have surface tension instead of mass, and the carving of the stone is felt actively as the technique of the art. The sharpness of contour makes the stone come to life. Moreover, the style of sculpture seems to be authentically renaissance only so long as it keeps its clarity of profile, the figure never looking bulging or "stuck on." Again, the "horizontal perspective" or "flattening" is due to a technique that holds the image close to the surface of the block from which it is carved. When the image begins to emerge in higher relief, then the surface vitality is lost, and renaissance sculpture takes on a baroque sensuousness and volume. The low relief of fifteenth-century Italian sculpture does, indeed, resemble a profile on which the naturalistic details make a decorative pattern.

This interpretation is worked out more completely in a theory suggesting that even free-standing renaissance sculpture is created and looked at as a "two-dimensional pattern," a relief rather than a round object; it is made to be seen from one side or another, front or back, left or right.[12] The renaissance figure is easy to "read" because it is a melodious "contour" standing clear on a central axis, without foreshortenings or overlappings. The structure of a typical renaissance statue like Donatello's David or Gattamelata is controlled by a simple plane running through it medially. It reveals its maximum aesthetic "form" only in profile. Strongly in agreement with this theory are the renaissance artists themselves, who prefer—before mannerism and baroque set in—to think of both sculpture and painting as a "circumscription" of objects which are "realized" by defining their "edges." Alberti, like Piero della Francesca, emphasizes that painting is constructed upon drawing; and drawing, Piero explains, means "profiles and outlines which contain the objects." Alberti says outright that no composition is good unless there is clear "outline" and "circumscription"— that is, "the going around of the edge." Even Leonardo, sensitive as he was to nuances of color, bathing his figures in twilight shadow, thinks of painting as a low relief, saying, "The first thing in painting is that the objects it represents should appear in relief." Leonardo's Madonna of the Rocks, as well as the work of Mantegna, Piero, Botticelli, and the Bellinis, proves that some of the gravest, noblest renaissance composition is founded in drawing, with profiles that seem inscribed. The decision in Botticelli's line gives his forms an almost unearthly transparency, a surface tension and horizontal perspective.

Earlier we were saying that renaissance style humanized the world in three dimensions. Now we see that there was a dramatic tension between shallow seeing and deep seeing, between decorative surface realism and three-dimensional realism, between horizontal and recessional vision. The early-renaissance architect held the plane surface of the wall; then the Strozzi Palace and Alberti's giant orders utilized strongly plastic features in "depth"—rusticated stonework and massive columns or pilasters. Baldovinetti's painting of the Madonna Enthroned kept the simple architectural planes of the Pazzi Chapel or the Rucellai Palace, ranking its figures in a shallow foreground before a curtain. But Signorelli's great blond Crucifixion, with its bulky sculptural bodies of Christ and Magdalen and its grave empty landscape, shows how the thin patterns of Italian painting were gradually remolded in deep space —a space which tends to "confirm our consciousness of being" and to make the world dense and volumetric. In sculpture the profile figures of Donatello yielded to the massive creatures of Michaelangelo.

The renaissance has a two-dimensional as well as a three-dimensional style. The integrity of the wall surface, the profile contour, the delicate circumscription, the low-relief view of things—all these suggest that renaissance style is marked by the plane, the clear line, the "multiplicity" of single units; they also explain why quattrocento painting uses fussy details and "petty flourishes," giving to it an air of "breathless complexity." In spite of the humanist's architectural feeling for reality, enabling him to imagine a world in spacious deep perspective, it is undeniable that early renaissance art, in particular, is marked by a high degree of "decorative isolation" and "fractional seeing" in a flat pattern with sharp naturalistic details. Here is a point of interference in techniques. Further, one might say that the naturalistic technique of renaissance art— which is inherited from the linear and cartographic techniques of the Middle Ages—best represents itself in shallow seeing, whereas the more intellectualist and theoretical technique of renaissance art appears in the effort to enclose the world in proportional cubic space.

In the renaissance style of decorative isolation or "fractional seeing" Botticelli and Spenser are unequaled. So fastidiously do both perceive single flowers, leaves, hairs, wavelets, and fluttering of garments that their art tends to be illustrative; their ornamental and sometimes agitated passages read like elegant excerpts from a cartographic scene. And indeed the perspective in Spenser and Botticelli seems anachronistic, as if some medieval artist had been born out of his time into the humanism of a later age. Thus the two are very self-conscious and treat allegory with a sophistication that is, at times, almost preciosity. Spenser is as "romantic"—and as neoplatonic—as Botticelli. Berenson writes sympathetically of Botticelli's fragile, almost disembodied, vision, his "linear decoration" and "linear symphony"—"and to this symphony, everything is

made to yield." Botticelli discovered a way to translate
values of the flesh into values of movement, excitable,
undulatory, naive, sedulous. Thus he was able to ren-
der tactile values transparently, without having to ren-
der the volume of the body itself. Among renaissance
poets Spenser has an equivalent transparency and un-
dulation; although his art is less wiry and nervous than
Botticelli's, it has the same capacity to transcribe sensuous and tactile values into values of movement, into
linear symphony, working itself out through illustrative flourishes. Spenser and Botticelli have the same
virginal and studied grace, the same cursive energy.
The *Prothalamion* is almost a libretto for the singing
contours of Botticelli's Primavera:

> There, in a Meadow, by the riuers side,
> A Flocke of *Nymphes* I chaunced to espy,
> All louely Daughters of the Flood thereby,
> With goodly greenish locks all loose vntyde,
> As each had bene a Bryde,
> And each one had a little wicker basket,
> Made of fine twigs entrayled curiously,
> In which they gathered flowers to fill their flasket:
> And with fine Fingers, cropt full featously
> The tender stalkes on hye.
> Of euery sort, which in that Meadow grew,
> They gathered some; the Violet pallid blew,
> The little Dazie, that at euening closes,
> The virgin Lillie, and the Primrose trew,
> With store of vermeil Roses,
> To decke their Bridegromes posies,
> Against the Brydale day, which was not long:
> Sweete *Themmes* runne softly, till I end my Song.

Perhaps the only comparable poet is Poliziano, whose
Giostra also shows this sophisticate and decorative naturalism. *The Faerie Queene* retains the medieval processional movement, and in spite of Spenser's effort to
impose upon this allegoric romance the discipline of
some regularity and "unity," its proportions remain capricious and its narrative ornate, anecdotal, unfocused.
Spenser is so little attentive to probability that the

Redcrosse Knight slays a dragon "three furlongs" from head to tail.

The mobile and clear vision of Botticelli and Spenser belongs to the art of the earlier renaissance, before the "grand style" of the cinquecento attained a classic dignity by simplifying the composition of painting and poetry. Many years ago Woelfflin pointed out that "the whole conception of form possessed by the fifteenth century is two-dimensional," bound as it was by "the spell of the flat plane, placing its figures side by side across the breadth of the picture and composing in strata." Then, after Fra Bartolommeo and Andrea del Sarto, the painter used "a grander kind of co-ordination" and gained "the capacity to see parts collectively and simultaneously, the power of grasping the variety of things in the field of vision as a single unit." Elevated by this ideal of a calm and spacious beauty, the artist "conceived everything *sub specie architecturae*" and figures were assigned a fixed position in architectonic space, framed, enclosed, and sculptured: "Weighty masses bound together by strict rule, grandiose contrasts of direction and a mighty rhythm in the movement of the whole." This mature composition in generous space was the triumph of renaissance humanism and the antecedent of baroque style.

Vasari's *Lives of the Painters* notes the difference between these two phases in the development of renaissance technique. After Masaccio, he says, the masters tried "to impose rules of perspective, and to carry the foreshortenings precisely to the point which gives an exact imitation of the relief apparent in nature and the real form." Uccello "reduced all to strict rules, by the convergence of intersecting lines, which he diminished towards the center after having fixed the point of view higher or lower as seemed good to him." In contrast Vasari mentions the illustrative technique of

Alesso Baldovinetti, whose sensitive talent was for fluent calligraphic detail:

He drew exceedingly well, and in our book there is a mule depicted from nature by his hand, wherein every turn of each hair all over the animal is represented with much patience and considerable grace of manner. Alesso was extremely careful and exact in his works, and of all the minutiae which mother nature is capable of presenting, he took pains to be the close imitator . . . ; thus we find in his pictures rivers, bridges, rocks, herbs, fruits, paths, fields, cities, castles, sands, and objects innumerable of the same kind; . . . he represented the Nativity of Christ, painted with such minuteness of care that each separate straw in the roof of a cabin figured therein, may be counted; and every knot in these straws distinguished. . . .

Because of this graceful draughtsmanship Baldovinetti's painting is almost rococo in its charming optical notations.

And indeed there is something rococo in the decorative conceited language of Elizabethan prose and verse, accepting as it does Alberti's principle that ornament is an "auxiliary brightness" on the surface of Beauty, which consists in proportion. The renaissance literary critics were always talking about the need for "decoration" and "variety" in diction. Du Bellay and Ronsard wanted to "illuminate" the French language by elegant phrases chosen from Greek and Latin poets, "which make the verse glitter like precious stones." Whatever were the objections to using "inkhorn" terms, the Euphuists everywhere "decorated" their prose with fantastic conceits, like the petty flourishes in quattrocento Italian painting, to give it an "auxiliary brightness" and high surface tension. The Euphuistic style —for example, in Greene's *Carde of Fancie*—has the breathless complexity, restlessness, and fractional accent we find in Baldovinetti; in this preclassic phase of renaissance art the separate units, however neatly proportioned, always keep their clear identity within the composition:

. . . . for as I have one childe which delights me with her vertue, so I have another that despights me with his vanitie, as the one by dutie brings me joye, so the other by disobedience breeds my annoy: yea, as the one is a comfort to my minde, so the other is a fretting corasive to my heart; for what griefe is there more griping, what paine more pinching, what crosse more cumbersome, what plague more pernitious, yea, what trouble can torment me worse, than to see my sonne, mine heire, the inheritour of my dukedom, which should be the piller of my parentage, to consume his time in roysting and ryot, in spending and spoiling, in swearing and swashing, and in following wilfullye the furie of his owne francticke fancie.

Almost any passage of conceited prose has this illustrative visibility, this dainty extravagance which is distracting in its multiplicity. We could say of Greene what is said of Pisanello's fussy paintings: all the many details are held in the same plane of interest. There is vivid naturalism, but the total effect is dilettante. In fact, like much early-renaissance painting, the conceited style elaborates its naturalistic details within a decorative surface pattern: the ornamental and learned design of the Euphuist sentence (with isocolon, parison, paromoion) accommodates every fantastic precision and could be taken as an early phase of mannerist art if its verbal sophistication involved any psychological sophistication.

The renaissance liking for the "gallant invention," the ornamental surface, is best expressed in the witty form of the emblem, the "device" that appears in literature and the graphic arts. The emblem is an ornamental figure inscribed upon any surface and is defined by Geoffrey Whitney in 1586: "The word [emblem] is as much to say in English as *To set in,* or *To put in:* properly meant by such figures or works as are wrought in plate, or in stones in the pavements, or on the walls, or such like, for the adorning of the place." The emblem has a maximum surface vitality, and is, almost literally, the *inscription* of a decorative pattern worked out in naturalistic flourishes. Consider, for a moment, the witty Elizabethan sonnet as an overwrought inscription in low, taut relief; especially one of Spenser's *Amoretti:*

Sweet is the Rose, but growes upon a brere;
Sweet is the Iunipere, but sharpe his bough;
Sweet is the Eglantine, but pricketh nere;
Sweet is the firbloome, but his braunches rough.
Sweet is the Cypresse, but his rynd is tough,
Sweet is the nut, but bitter is his pill;
Sweet is the broome-flowre, but yet sowre enough;
And sweet is Moly, but his root is ill.
So euery sweet with soure is tempred still,
That maketh it be coueted the more:
For easie things that may be got at will,
Most sorts of men doe set but little store.
Why then should I accoumpt of little paine,
That endlesse pleasure shall vnto me gaine. (XXVI)

The logic and design have a symmetry alien to mannerist art; but the images are fractional and the wit, with its busy illustration, is like the shallow ornament in the emblem. Frequently the design of the Italian painter conformed of necessity to the surface available inside some conventional framework like the triptych, the equilateral triangle, the semicircle, the rondo —frames analogous to patterns of the sonnet, the eclogue, the madrigal, and other forms.

Inherent, then, in renaissance style there is a dramatic disharmony between the foreground surface and unified deep space—the noble spaciousness that seems to be the calm signature of the classic human self. In tracing the changing styles of Shakespeare's drama, we might say that Richard II is a transparent profile, sensitively outlined, like Botticelli's figures with nervously drawn edges, and having a decorative grace. Everyone regards the melancholy figure of Richard as predecessor to Hamlet; but Hamlet exists over an abyss of malaise that has not yet opened beneath this frail king, who is seen in a sequence, almost processional, of

clearly held poses, a thin helpless character wearing
the haunted and decadent features of the luminous beings floating in a Botticelli scene. Richard has the
charm of external appearance we see in Botticelli,
whose beauty has in it "something afflicted," so that
even when he smiles, it seems, as Woelfflin says, "only
a transitory lighting up." Amid the pageant of English
history Richard is arrested in lyrical attitudes, merely
a contour of royalty, who studies his worn image in the
mirror he holds before him, telling, in his solemn trem-
olo, sad stories of the death of kings, playing the wanton with his woes, descending lithely to his little,
little grave.

The foreground of other early plays is as brilliant as
that in *Richard II*, notably in *Love's Labour's Lost*,
where the action has all the artificial contours of events
in the courtly Academe in Navarre, still and contem-
plative with art. And since the very fabric of this play
is verbal—those dainties bred in a book, the odoriferous
fancies invented by those who have drunk ink—there is
over almost all five acts the glassy surface tension of
the conceited sonnet. But suddenly—almost shockingly
—this shallow design of pose and language opens into
another dimension when the King of France dies and
the scene begins to cloud. Then Berowne, alone, re-
cedes into another dramatic world—remote—where he
must bring wild laughter in the throat of death and try
to master his wit by special grace. At this moment
Shakespeare is adjusting his deeper insight to the glit-
tering bas-relief of his dramatic form. Berowne takes
a long perspective upon the human condition, a perspective that the screenlike structure of this play
hardly allows. Similarly Mercutio suddenly retires behind the screen of superficial and artificial conflicts
that does for a tragic action in *Romeo and Juliet;* and
he too must be imagined in another dramatic context;
he does not fit the structure of events at Verona and

dies outside their pattern, saying, "A plague o' both your houses!" Berowne and Mercutio need the distances of a mature theater. Eventually, like the Italian painters of the cinquecento, Shakespeare creates a more architectural space to accommodate his action, and by a deeper perspective is able to gain a higher coefficient of reality, a scene resonant with the full consciousness of being in all its complex relations. The nocturnal world of *Macbeth* has, in Berenson's phrase, "that feeling for reality which made the great painters look upon a picture as the representation of a cubic content of atmosphere enveloping all the objects depicted." Macbeth realizes that he is moving in fathomless reaches beyond the bank and shoal of time, where man is smothered in surmise, and nothing is but what is not.

Shakespeare uses no one dramatic form. On the contrary: in plays like *Hamlet* he revises all the dimensions of dramatic art, and in *The Tempest* revises them again. Such transformations occur whenever the techniques of renaissance art were pressed beyond the solutions they were devised to reach; then the experiment causes techniques to interpenetrate each other, as they often do in Leonardo's painting. Uccello's perspective, intended to be a syntax for defining position, became also a syntax for expressing motion. From these interferences in renaissance techniques evolve the structures of mannerist and baroque art. Already the affectations of mannerism are in the fantastic grace and conscious elegance of Botticelli and Spenser. The academic paralysis is already inherent in Alberti's theory of beauty, and in Piero della Francesca, in Mantegna, in Trissino, in Sir Philip Sidney's high-minded defense of poetry. The Pazzi Chapel has the clear proportions of renaissance style; but any heightening of the illusion, any shift in accent, any inequality in design, will transform the structure and become manneristic. The balance is too delicate. Or any more formal unity will seem academic. Over Andrea del Sarto's poised madonnas and saints already falls the morbid uneasy shadow of mannerist painting; and their figures have, already, the mannerist pliability. The saints and Marys painted by Perugino are somewhat too suave, chill, self-aware; there is too much mechanical mourning and posing about the foot of the cross. Pollaiuolo's engraving already has the tortured energy of the mannerist line. Any further expansion of Raphael's grand style will produce the spectacular, the pompous. In the theater, *The Merchant of Venice* already uses the double valencies of mannerist tragi-comedy; and Marlowe's *Tamburlaine* approaches baroque overstatement. Any experiment with renaissance harmony, unity, perspective, or contour will generate a manner; any intellectuality more assertive will lead to unconditional academic dogma, or else eclecticism.

A panoramic view of Italian renaissance painting discloses where the interferences, the transformations, occurred among the three modes of vision between 1275 and 1575 [13]: the earliest mode—of the Sienese painters—was to define contour; then after Giotto there was a mode of plastic volume, of substance and flesh arranged sculpturally and architecturally in receding planes; finally there was a "pictorial" mode, created when Giovanni Bellini and the Venetians tried to see the world as color. As soon as the world is represented by hue instead of by volume and contour, color tends to acquire the values of both contour and volume, and forms become illusions shimmering away into "tonality." The world does indeed shimmer away in some paintings by Titian, and in most paintings by Tintoretto and Rembrandt. It becomes musical, perhaps, instead of being architecture or contour or mass; then space takes on meanings that elude mathematical ratios. Space is melodic when Leonardo's renaissance sci-

ence dares dissolve line ("which," says Leonardo, "is
of invisible thickness") and wherever his light is a
penetrating ambience, a "blue" perspective, a plastic
dimension. Thus when Leonardo's techniques intersect, his interpretation of space is not alone mathematical; it is also a feeling for atmospheric tone—a
Stimmung. A cubical quantity is transformed to a
painterly quality. Another sort of transformation happens in Raphael's School of Athens (1509–11), where
the three grand coffered vaults, the mightiest composition of renaissance painting, do not, in a sense, define
architectural space in firm ratios but give it an acous-
tical quality, a momentum that seems to vibrate off
into free energy. Here space becomes echo and motion.
Even before Copernicus has imposed his mathematical
symmetry upon the universe, Raphael's classic spaces
are already resounding with incalculable forces. This
resonance mounts to full volume in the mysterious
color of Titian's painting, where all transformations
occur, where all known values are changed to other
values. Giorgione's pastoral landscapes are filled with
transformations: the contours of hills, the intervals of
space, the accents of local color, are fused into a poetic
sonority. One of the most illusive structures of renaissance painting—in which techniques intersect to revise
all aesthetic values—is Giovanni Bellini's Allegory of
Purgatory (c. 1490). Bellini firmly grounds his composition in all the techniques of renaissance style, for the
space is geometrically enclosed, the masses are sculpturally realized, the contours are tightly drawn, the
color is stabilized by cool greens, browns, and pale
blues; yet there is a constant transforming of reality—
color becomes contour, contour becomes space, space
becomes mass, mass becomes color. These interferences
and transformations appear at the groundwork of renaissance style in Ghiberti's bronze doors for the Flor-

entine Baptistry, which are, at the same time, architecture, sculpture, and painting.

In poetry, too, there are interferences and transformations, for Spenser's Bower of Bliss is contour, color, relief, and music; it has both surface tension and sculptural mass, both horizontal and deep perspective, both optical texture and audible melody or "movement." All its values can be transvalued, as the repetition of the verb "seemed" indicates:

> And in the midst of all, a fountaine stood,
> Of richest substaunce that on earth might bee,
> So pure and shiny, that the silver flood
> Through every channell running one might see;
> Most goodly it with curious imageree
> Was over-wrought, and shapes of naked boyes,
> Of which some seemd with lively jollitee,
> To fly about, playing their wanton toyes,
> Whilst others did themselves embay in liquid joyes.

> And over all, of purest gold was spred,
> A trayl of yvie in his native hew:
> For the rich mettall was so coloured,
> That wight, who did not well avis'd it vew,
> Would surely deeme it to be yvie trew:
> Low his lascivious armes adown did creepe,
> That themselves dipping in the silver dew,
> Their fleecy flowres they tenderly did steepe,
> Which drops of christall seemd for wantones to weepe.

Lessing's theory that poetry is not painting, that each utilizes only its own technique, does not reckon with these interferences, these renaissance interchanges and correspondences between painting, relief, architecture, poetry, and music. Alberti must have had some intimation of these revisions in renaissance art when he wrote that in a clever painting, which defines all its contours, the faces will "seem to issue out from the panel like sculpture." The languid, saturated art of Tasso—which is inherently different from the more disembodied but nevertheless elegant art of Spenser— brings to the renaissance a poetic substance generated,

so to speak, from the painterly and sculptural techniques; Armida's Garden, with its luxuriant color and
texture, has the ambiguous values of Correggio's painting. It was Leonardo who wrote in the *Paragone* that
"Painting is poetry which is seen and not heard, and
poetry is a painting which is heard but not seen. These
two arts (you may call them both either poetry or
painting) have here interchanged the senses by which
they penetrate to the intellect."

The logic of renaissance techniques caused these
transformations, through which there was always an
escape from the algebra of the *costruzione legittima*.
Sometimes the perspective opens upon a pastoral landscape, Arcadia, or on the Vale of the Arno; then space
is a suffusion, not a measurement; the distance is a blue
silence. These interferences bring us to the threshold
of mannerism and the art of Tintoretto, and Shakespeare at Elsinore, where the russet dawn cannot dispel Hamlet's bad dreams.

NOTES

*1. This is the uncomplicated but deeply reasonable view
held by Erwin Panofsky in an article called "Renaissance
and Renascences"* (Kenyon Review, Spring, 1944). *No one
has contributed more wisely and learnedly to understanding the structure of gothic and renaissance styles than Panofsky, and throughout this chapter I have been heavily
dependent on his description of gothic principles in such
books as* Early Netherlandish Painting *and* Gothic Architecture and Scholasticism.

2. So argues Erich Auerbach in Mimesis. *Auerbach's analysis of "figural" and "creatural" realism in this book is
only one of the sources I have used in my discussion of
gothic literature and art, which in general follows Joan
Evans' many studies of romanesque and gothic art (and
also her more inclusive study,* Pattern), *Charles Rufus
Morey's* Mediaeval Art, *and Max Dvořák's ingenious*
Kunstgeschichte als Geistesgeschichte. *Readers of Nikolaus Pevsner's* Outline of European Architecture *and Henri
Focillon's* Art d'occident *will recognize that my phraseol-*

ogy often derives from these art historians. I have also accepted Charles Singleton's opinions of Dante's Comedy.

3. Focillon's Art d'occident, *where this claim is made, is a sequel to the discussion of the hieratic romanesque imagery in Jurgis Baltrušaitis's* La stylistique ornementale dans la sculpture romane.

4. Focillon: Life of Forms in Art, *1948, p. 22.*

5. This distinction between gothic and renaissance spacetime is based on Dagobert Frey's Gotik und Renaissance *and Panofsky's* Gothic Architecture and Scholasticism.

6. See Berenson: Italian Painters of the Renaissance.

7. These descriptions are drawn from Pevsner: Outline, *pp. 110–15, and Rudolf Wittkower:* Architectural Principles in the Age of Humanism.

8. The stages in the evolution of optical perspective are indicated in John White's article "Developments in Renaissance Perspective" (Journal of the Warburg and Courtauld Institute, XII, 1949, and XIV, 1951). The present paragraph, and those which follow upon the nature of optical perspective in renaissance art, utilize this article as well as Panofsky's classic account, "Die Perspektive als Symbolische Form" (Vortraege der Bibliothek Warburg, 1924–25). In addition I have used Miriam Schild Bunim's Space in Mediaeval Painting *to describe the genesis of renaissance space, the vanishing axis, etc.*

9. See Auerbach's discussion of Shakespeare's "perspective consciousness" in Mimesis.

10. George R. Kernodle's From Art to Theatre *considers fully the "form" of renaissance theater in England and Italy.*

11. This matter is discussed in Rudolf Wittkower's Architectural Principles in the Age of Humanism, *from which I drew my remarks on proportion in renaissance art here derive my paragraphs on the complicated problems of treating the column against the wall.*

12. The low-relief theory was the theme of Adrian Stokes' unsystematic remarks in Stones of Rimini. *The definitive statement of this theory, distinguishing between the form of renaissance, mannerist, and baroque sculpture, is in Erwin Panofsky's* Studies in Iconology. *Panofsky, of course, adapts the theories of Adolf Hildebrand, not Stokes.*

13. These modes of vision are identified by Berenson in the closing pages of Italian Painters of the Renaissance.

MANNERISM

I

THE MISSING TERM   As the renaissance wore on
during the sixteenth and seventeenth centuries, all
western Europe was inwardly shaken by some tremor
of malaise and distrust. The evidences are everywhere:
in the growth of the Reformation, the blood baths of
Saint Bartholomew and the Thirty Years' War, the disciplines enforced by the Council of Trent, and the
equivocal policies of the Jesuit order; also in philosophy, literature, and the arts—in Montaigne's easy skepticism, Bacon's "very diligent dissection and anatomy
of the world," Shakespeare's "dark" plays, the troubled
Jacobean dramas, Michaelangelo's freakish architecture in the Medici Chapel, Cellini's overfacile sculpture, the restlessness in Tintoretto's painting, the twin-
ing hollow forms in Parmigianino, the phosphorescent
world of El Greco. At the height of the renaissance order Copernicus thought that "the remarkable symmetry and interconnection of the motions and spheres are
not unworthy of God's workmanship and not suited
to these divine bodies." But to Hamlet this goodly
frame, the earth, the brave firmament fretted with
golden fire, seem a sterile promontory, a foul congrega-
tion of vapors; and presently Gloucester, who has a
monstrous son like Lear's monstrous daughters, fears
that "These late eclipses in the sun and moon portend
no good to us." Love has cooled, the bond has cracked
between son and father: "We have seen the best of
our time," Gloucester thinks, and "all ruinous disorders

follow us disquietly to our graves." In writing his "First Anniversary," John Donne, that profane and pious poet, serves as prologue to the tempest in *Lear:*

> And new Philosophy calls all in doubt,
> The Element of fire is quite put out;
> The Sun is lost, and th'earth, and no mans wit
> Can well direct him where to looke for it. . . .
> 'Tis all in peeces, *all cohaerence gone;*
> All just supply, and all Relation . . .
> . . . nor can the Sunne
> Parfit a Circle, or maintaine his way
> One inch direct; but where he rose to-day
> He comes no more, but with a couzening line,
> Steales by that point, and so is Serpentine . . .
> . . . but yet confesse, in this
> *The worlds proportion disfigured is;*
> That those two legges whereon it doth rely,
> Reward and punishment, are bent awry.
> And, Oh, it can no more be questioned,
> That beauties best, *proportion, is dead.*

About the same time Shakespeare's character Ulysses was explaining in *Troilus and Cressida* that when degree is shak'd, the planets wander in disorder; then discord follows until everything meets in mere oppugnancy, and power degenerates into will, will into appetite, which at last eats up itself. There is something rotten in Hamlet's world. This sweet prince is of heavy disposition; his mind is tainted; he confesses to Ophelia that he is only indifferent honest, and has more offenses at his beck than he has "thoughts to put them in" or imagination to give them shape. His oversensitivity tells him that he suffers from some "vicious mole of nature," the o'ergrowth of some strange complexion breaking down the pales and forts of reason. He speculates, in the graveyard, how my lady, though she paint an inch thick, comes, like the great Alexander, to dust, and could serve to stop a bunghole. Hamlet is somehow sick. He is obsessed with an almost late-medieval sense of death. And in the painting of

Tintoretto and El Greco there appear those strange
skeletal forms that seem to move through a *Totentanz.*
Both Hamlet and Angelo, that prenzie sinner in *Measure for Measure,* go "that way to temptation where
prayers cross." In their unsettled world, "quite athwart
goes all decorum."

Perhaps these manifestations are some shadowed
aspect of the renaissance itself. Nevertheless there is
in the arts, the religion, the politics, the science, and
the very conscience of this era some disturbance interesting to us because we also have been living
through a crisis of history and consciousness. Until recently we have lacked any name to denote this period
when the renaissance optimism is shaken, when proportion breaks down and experiment takes the form of
morbid ingenuity or scalding wit; art and thought
curve away unpredictably along private tangents; approximation, equivocation, and accommodation are accepted as working principles; the sensibility of writers
and painters seems overexercised; all directions are
confused and obscure when we enter that "waste of
shame" where the Jacobean drama is played. Apparently we have now found a name for this disturbance:
mannerism, a term adopted from art history. Even if
mannerism be a phase of the renaissance itself, it represents a "formal dissolution of a style"—the style of
renaissance art founded upon the concepts of proportion and harmony and unity. In literature, this disturbance, which in various ways has been associated with
cultism, Gongorism, conceit, wit, Marinism, and preciosity, is widely known through T. S. Eliot's description
of the English poetry of the seventeenth century as
showing a "dissociation of sensibility." Unfortunately
Eliot used the term ambiguously. When reviewing
Grierson's selection of "metaphysical poets" he spoke of
Donne as having "a mechanism of sensibility which
could devour any kind of experience," whether from

the heart, the nervous system, the cerebral cortex, or the digestive tract. The implication was that Donne could bring poetic unity into a "heterogeneity of material," a talent lost to later poets. Then when writing in *A Garland for John Donne*, Eliot mentioned Donne as a poet who shows "a manifest fissure between thought and sensibility."

Whatever Eliot may have implied by "dissociation," he was evidently referring to Grierson's idea that Donne and the truly "metaphysical" poets of the seventeenth century are "more aware of disintegration than of comprehensive harmony." Their verses are filled with "clashes" of attitudes and language; or, as Basil Willey puts it, the "metaphysical" mind has a capacity to "live in divided and distinguished worlds," and to pass freely between them without "being *finally committed* to any one world." The art historians' analysis of mannerism—an analysis constantly being revised—offers to literary critics a chance to look again at the "dissociations" in metaphysical poetry and Jacobean drama, the uneasy license in Donne's wit, the dubious motives in Ford's plays, and the sordid but dazzling world of Bosola in Webster's *Duchess of Malfi*, or the perilous world of Middleton and Rowley's *The Changeling*, where De Flores feeds strangely upon the impure virginity of Beatrice-Joanna. The madmen in Webster's plays inhabit a dissolving world; and Shakespeare and Tourneur have an uncanny insight into mental disorder such as Marlowe did not have even in *Tamburlaine*. In a character like Bosola the intrigues of Machiavelli's renaissance man are changed into the malcontent desperate irresponsibility of man caught in a region without sunlight: "We are merely the stars' tennis balls struck and bandied which way please them." Hamlet and Bosola exist in the unhealthful mannerist climate, and Shakespeare himself confesses

that he has gone here and there to play the fool and
to "gore" his own thoughts:

> Most true it is that I have look'd on truth
> Askance and strangely . . . (Sonnet 110)

.The mannerist temperament is inclined to gore its
thoughts, or, with Hamlet, to quarter them; even the
mediocre Polonius hopes he can "by indirections find
directions out." However much our "New" critics insist
that any sort of poetic statement is ambiguous and
ironic, the ambiguities and ironies in Donne are extraordinary. Shakespeare's lilies that fester smell far
worse than weeds; and in the troubled Shakespeare
there is much festering—in *Troilus and Cressida*, in
Measure for Measure, in *Timon.* T. S. Eliot takes Webster as an "example of a very great literary and dramatic genius directed toward chaos." His characters
are injured by the sort of "strange eruption" that shook
Elsinore and Hamlet's conscience; for Hamlet's inky
cloak and shows of grief are, he says, only tokens of
"that within which passeth show," and his very world
"is thought-sick" and corrupt. The intent scrutiny of
filth and purity in *Measure for Measure* is carried on
in a fetid atmosphere and in the spirit of Donne's quest
for Truth, who, Donne remarks, may be a little elder
than Falsehood but is not easily found on her craggy
hill; one must, to see her, go "about and about." This
circling examination occurred in a world thrown off
center, wanting repose and safety. Cellini's Perseus
stands cruelly and gracefully under "the troubled sky
of the later sixteenth century."

When we try to date this phase of instability in the
arts, we find that mannerism appears hard upon the
high-renaissance as a sign of irresolution, a movement
deprived of the sense of security, equilibrium, unity,
and proportion expressed in renaissance style; it comes
during an interim period while the energies of Counter-Reformation faith are being rallied at the Council

of Trent (1545–63), presently to burst into full baroque splendor. Shall we say that in Italy the mannerist period falls between 1520 and 1620, and later in the North, where the dissonances are still audible in Milton's *Lycidas* and Marvell's "To His Coy Mistress"? In England during the 1590's came some deep shift in sensibility dividing the *Arcadia* and *The Faerie Queene* from Shakespeare's "dark" sonnets and plays, and from Donne. Discords already play over the walls of the Medici Chapel, which Michaelangelo left unfinished in 1534, and the techniques of mannerist style are still discernible in Velázquez and Rembrandt until the 1660's.

One of the difficulties in describing mannerism is that the "Jesuit style" has been called baroque; yet the triumphant glories of baroque appeared long after the constrained Jesuit art. The Order was sanctioned in 1540 and baroque was not seen in its high pomp until seventy or eighty years later. The uncomfortable austerity of the Gesù façade in Rome (*c.* 1569) has little in common with the abandoned, full-blooded magnificence of baroque architecture and painting as seen in the façade of Sant' Agnese in Agone (1653 ff.), Pozzo's grandiloquent operatic roof in Sant' Ignazio (*c.* 1685), or even the roof of the Gesù (*c.* 1668–83). The compulsive severities in Jesuit style seem to reflect the policies of the Council of Trent, the organ by which the Roman Church tightened its authority over dogma and ritual. And the Tridentine Council antedates by many years a mature baroque architecture and sculpture. The truth is that the Council, summoned during the years of doubt, bad conscience, and skepticism characteristic of the mannerist temperament, did prescribe a discipline that suited the spirit of the Jesuit style; but it also firmly laid the foundations for a baroque philosophy, ritual, and art that came to fulfillment in the following era, during the seventeenth

century. Actually the Council presided over two
phases in Counter-Reformation styles: a phase of formal disintegration (mannerism) and a phase of formal
reintegration (baroque).

Literary critics have tried to see the relation between
the agitated "wit" in Donne's verses and the "magniloquence" of Milton's organ voice in *Paradise Lost*. Here
again the troubled and heightened piety of the seventeenth century appeared in two different phases of
English poetry, a Donne phase and a Milton phase.
Or in Milton alone the changing styles, ranging from
the mannerism of the hymn "On the Morning of Christ's
Nativity" and *Lycidas* to the baroque rhetoric of *Paradise Lost*, have a sequence we might, after examining
the course of the fine arts, expect: the "wit" belonging
to one phase, the "magniloquence" to another. In any
event the idea of a mannerist technique intervening
between renaissance and baroque helps bring logical
order into the criticism of art and literature in the
period, and enables us to appraise Donne and the metaphysical poets and playwrights against prevailing
styles of architecture, painting, and sculpture.

But first we must have some notion what mannerism
as a style involves. It becomes more and more evident
to both art historians and critics of literature that mannerism is a "constant" principle in the arts of western
Europe, since it is a reaction against the norms of "Classicism" in whatever period, ancient, medieval, or
modern. What at first glance seems to be overstrained
wit is one indication of a revolution or readjustment in
the arts; when a classical style is revised there are apt
to be feverish symptoms in poetry and painting alike.
That is, mannerism in style accompanies mannerism
in thought and feeling. Mannerist art is "troubled" and
"obscure," if not "illogical." It treats its themes from
unexpected points of view and eccentric angles, sometimes hidden. The mannerist uses thin or sour color,

nervous line, twisted or oblique space, and asymmetrical designs. His images and metaphors seem perverse and equivocal. His statements are intense and highly "expressive." Certain so-called baroque traits are in part, at least, mannerist—especially those Woelfflin referred to as painterly, open, atectonic, recessional, or "mobile." Mannerist forms are only "relatively clear."

Formerly art historians themselves presumed that the "mannered" figures used by Pontormo, Niccolo dell' Abbate, Parmigianino, and the first and second Schools of Fontainebleau—elongated, mincing, distorted—were a sign of degeneracy among minor renaissance painters. Yet we now think that mannerism is something quite different from merely painting with a certain affectation or "manner." We accept mannerism, like baroque, as an authentic style, not simply a mark of artificiality in conception or execution. It has long been noted that the eccentricities in some renaissance painters like Uccello, Botticelli, and Filippino Lippi resemble mannerism in Primaticcio, Tintoretto, and El Greco. However, a genuinely mannerist style, in contrast to a trivial or superficial "manner" or a strongly personal technique, originates with—or from—a "dissociation" of vision or sensibility in artists working between the height of a renaissance style and the triumph of a baroque style. Thus also, the "conceited" style of Elizabethan prose and verse is not authentically mannerist because the techniques of renaissance wit are only a kind of verbal affectation or complexity, not a mark of malaise, double vision, and tormented sensibility. Grierson makes this clear when he mentions "the finer psychology" of metaphysical conceit, and "above all the peculiar blend of passion and thought, feeling and ratiocination." Spenser's bright conceits are not Donne's subtle wit, or even the wit of the Cavalier poets. There is a difference between the clever and sensitive first generation of Elizabethan writers and the new generation of the later 1590's that is scourged by some personal disenchantment. Hamlet is no mere Euphuist; and the involutions in this stagecraft derive from a nameless psychological intricacy and unrest that, in turn, seem to arise from these techniques. Botticelli, Andrea del Castagno, and Piero di Cosimo use a "mannered" syntax; but Tintoretto and El Greco invent a new psychological vocabulary.

Many of the affectations in renaissance style were clichés; and sometimes the mannerist painters used clichés, too, in a very studied way, just as the metaphysical poets used clichés—to gain new effects. The erroneous idea of mannerism as being solely an ornamental, modish, sophisticated use of clichés derives chiefly from Vasari, who in his eclectic way admired painters adept in practicing a "truly good manner" by copying "the most beautiful objects, and afterwards combining the most perfect, whether the hand, head, torso, or leg, and joining them together to make one figure, invested with every beauty in its highest perfection." Mannerism is nothing if not intellectual, and Vasari's is the "fine manner" of the platonizing clever artists who are complicated, learned, dry, and abstract. There is, says Vasari, a variety of manners: those of Leonardo, Raphael, Correggio, Parmigianino, and Michaelangelo. Pollaiuolo's "manner" was "anatomical," treating the action of the muscles, and Parmigianino was said to have "sweetness" and a singular "grace of attitude." Often in mannerist portraits the cliché becomes a mask. Bronzino portrayed his sitters in a "diplomatic style," giving an "armored look" to the features (*panzerhaft*). Sometimes this cold intellectualizing manner is so sophisticated that it looks "mondain." With their long necks, their precious gestures, their sleek bodies, Parmigianino's Madonnas have something of the svelte quality of Cranach's nudes, so knowingly posed, or the exquisite breeding of Perugino's renaissance saints and Marys and Magdalens. The elegance of these figures, controlled and detached, suggests that neither Parmigianino nor Bronzino was capable of sympathy. The same chilly worldliness benumbs the transparent, sere nudes of the Fontainebleau painters.

So mannerism came to mean a kind of facile learning, an abused ingenuity, a witty affectation, a knowing pose, a distorting through preciosity, or a play with conventional proportions, images, and attitudes. In one sense mannerism has its roots in renaissance conceits and flourishes. Sonneteers like Drayton seemed interested only in contorting further Petrarch's already-involved cleverness:

> As other men, so I my self do muse
> *Why in this sort I wrest invention so,*
> And why these giddy metaphors I use,
> Leaving the path the greater part do go.
> I will resolve you: I am lunatic.
> *Idea*, ix

The bloodless devices in fashionable poetry at last caused George Herbert to ask, "Who sayes that fictions onely and false hair/Become a verse?" and "Is all good structure in a winding stair?" Henceforth in his religious verse he will "plainly say, My God, My King."

Given as the Elizabethan sonneteers were to "jerks of invention," their wit was at times salacious, turning platonism upside down:

> Would I were changed but to my mistress' gloves . . .
> Or else that chain of pearl (her neck's vain pride)
> Made proud with her neck's veins, that I might fold
> About that lovely neck, and her paps tickle!
> Or her to compass, like a belt of gold!
> Or that sweet wine, which down her throat doth trickle,
> To kiss her lips and lie next at her heart,
> Run through her veins, and pass by pleasure's part!
> B. BARNES, *Parthenophil*

Only superficially, however, does this renaissance ingenuity resemble the libertine wit of Cavalier poets, who practiced the same kind of "court mannerism" as the French mannerist painters, both being attuned to the exquisite neurotic society for which Thomas Carew wrote his "Rapture," that impudent trifle.

The renaissance used nudity without much self-consciousness—witness Giorgione's Venuses or Shakespeare's early erotic *Venus and Adonis*. But mannerism discovered the more insidious pleasures of nakedness —which is self-conscious nudity; and it used nakedness insolently, provokingly, with intent to shock or to mock. Donne's "Elegie XIX" is as knowing as Hamlet's unbridled pornographic mirth, although it was doubtless written in higher spirits than Hamlet's:

> License my roaving hands, and let them go
> Before, behind, between, above, below. . . .
> Full nakedness! All joyes are due to thee,
> As souls unbodied, bodies uncloth'd must be,
> To taste whole joyes.

The artificiality and salaciousness of authentic mannerism conceal introspective values we recognize at once in the work of Parmigianino, that highly characteristic and enigmatic painter who is only now beginning to be understood.[1] Though Parmigianino's strange art is a logical outgrowth of the techniques of renaissance painting, it is inspired and controlled by a mannerist psychology. Parmigianino "operates from within," seeming to turn his attention upon an interior image, a *disegno interno*, rather than outer reality. Because Parmigianino's relation to the world is subjective, his figures are lengthened by nervous, elegant serpentine lines or into ovals or slim rectangles. In these delicate, rather morbid-looking figures normal proportions break down. The strange verticality of design and movement suggests a "spontaneous re-emergence" of gothic. The contradictions in Parmigianino are sensational: he sets three-dimensional bodies in a shallow, flat, two-dimensional space, and makes the volumes of his figures meaningless by his supple, elastic, decorative drawing, which turns everything sinuous. The action of his people is far from convincing; there is no sustained or adequate energy behind their motion; their anatomy is not organic and muscular. In the Prado Holy Family, Parmigianino arranges his groups with nervous complexity; his characters gaze in different directions, implying a loss of repose and a lack of adjustment between person and person, a multiplicity of psychological states without any centering of attention.

The figures presented by Parmigianino are enigmatic in expression, pose, and situation. They suggest an incomplete control of a sensibility with an "excessive" or "shuttling" quality; there are signs of unexplained overresponse to unknown stimuli. And above all, the emotional implications are incongruous with the logic of the composition; that is, *the iconography does not correspond to the psychology.* In his Saint Margaret (*c.* 1528) two opposing movements are created, out of which arises a psychic tension discharged exactly where we least expect it—across the small gap between the heads of Christ and Margaret. His *chef d'oeuvre*, the Madonna dal Collo Lungo (Madonna with the Long Neck), shows in her distorted ornamental pose no "objective logic" of structure or weight, but an excited linear rhythm whose energy releases itself in vague "directions" rather than in any decisive gesture or accent. In this composition the background space is in unintelligible relation to the foreground space, and the levels of foreground and background are utterly ambiguous. The figures are also out of scale, the "prophet" in the flimsy background being absurdly tiny. More important in connection with Donne and the Jacobean drama, there is no logical focus for the composition, and the psychological relation between the figures is left suspended; they look out toward us but "evade our search for contact" and remain fixed in their psychological detachment even while they stare at us.

Throughout, there is an intense intellectualism in Parmigianino, along with a perverted originality. In his Roman period he uses classic Raphaelesque figures for strange psychological purposes. His equilibriums are uneasy, as in Saint Roch and Donor, where diagonals intersect in complicated tenuous and involved adjustments and counter-adjustments. In The Conversion of Saint Paul, Parmigianino tortures the form of the horse by an "aesthetic vivisection." His grace (*venusta* or *grazia*) is fastidious but lewd; the Madonna della Rosa (*c.* 1530) is said to have been originally painted for Pietro Aretino as a Venus and Cupid, then slightly altered for Pope Clement VII into a Virgin and Child. This sort of license reappears in Donne, whose profanity is as subtle as Parmigianino's. The Madonna with the Rose is as fleshly as it is cold in temper; and beneath her veil are revealed the breasts that are not maternal.

In his amazing Self-Portrait (1524), a *trompe-l'œil* of an unprecedented kind, Parmigianino studied himself in the distorting reflection of a convex mirror that ridiculously enlarges his hand in the foreground and leaves his face unnaturally remote in the glassy "distance." This device for self-contemplation is dramatically immediate, but preposterously contrived, like some of the self-regarding poems of Donne. Always Parmigianino's portraits show great self-awareness in the sitters, but a cautious defense against the probing of the spectator, a neutrality and skepticism, as if they were steeped in the speculations of Montaigne. Yet they suffer too from a sense of strain, with their twisted bodies, for which there seems to be no reasonable physical explanation. We are baffled by his portrait of Antea, supposedly a Roman courtesan, with her suave and patient face, her long nose, her restrained expression; her stare is catlike, as if seeking us in rigid and distrustful observation. She has no confidence in us. Antea is "engaged with the spectator in a cautious, penetrating mutual assessment of intentions." There is no release; only tension.

Mannerism is not only decorative but also expressive in a taut uneasy way, as if the figures had the resistance of the coiled spring. Yet they appear passive, suffering mutely from internal and unintelligible strain. They hold their distance even while they dramatically approach our world through an unnaturally extended hand or foot; if these people are agitated, they nevertheless have the still repressed air we see in portraits by Bronzino. It is customary to speak of the hauteur of Bronzino's people as "distinguished"; but their very lifeblood has congealed. Bronzino seems to have possessed them as they have possessed the world—by calculation and double intents.

Their tone is insolent, like that of Donne, the youth who lived at the Inns of Court "very neat, a great visiter of ladies, a great frequenter of plays, a great writer of conceited verses." We detect this insolence, and all sorts of double intentions, in Donne's verses to his mistress—or his wife, or his God:

> But since my soule, whose child love is,
> Takes limmes of flesh, and else could nothing doe,
>   More subtile than the parent is
> Love must not bee, but take a bodie too . . .
>   Then as an Angell, face and wings
> Of aire, not pure as it, yet pure doth weare,
>   So thy love may be my loves spheare;
>   Just such disparitie
> As is 'twixt Aire and Angells puritie,
> 'Twixt womens love and mens will ever bee.
>   "Aire and Angels"

So Donne is able to love his mistress twice or thrice

before he knew her face and name, and in praising her he mocks his soul, and hers, his wit playing frigidly over his passion. Donne revolted from renaissance platonism; he shifted the accents in his verse psychologically as well as metrically. We also recall that Donne wrote fervid hymns—"To God My God"—in his mortal sickness, and that before the hour of his death he summoned Nicholas Stone to draw him in his winding sheet and standing on an urn:

. . . and having put off all his clothes, had this sheet put on him, and so tied with knots at his head and feet, and his hands so placed as dead bodies are usually fitted, to be shrouded and put into their coffin or grave. Upon this urn he thus stood, with his eyes shut, and with so much of the sheet turned aside as might show his lean, pale, and death-like face, which was purposely turned towards the east, from whence he expected the second coming of his and our Savior Jesus.

He died with this image of his corruption beside his bed.

Donne the lover—Jack Donne—and Donne the zealot: there is a psychological crisis behind the mannerist poses, which may look like clichés; but the clichés hardly conceal the malaise. The insolence and calculation in mannerism do not arise from self-confidence, but are really signs of anxiety and repression. Parmigianino, we hear, was in his last days converted, like Donne, and became morbidly pious. And the French etcher Bellange chooses to express a private half-mystical religious emotion by means of nervous, graceful figures swaying and swirling with "aristocratic elegance"—an hysteric fluency. While Donne is wittily exhibiting to us his lust, his devil's advocacy of suicide, he may be goring his own thoughts and looking askance and strangely upon the truth he seeks with a devious logic.

At the very outposts of mannerist expressionism are Tintoretto and El Greco, and it is hard to avoid believing that Tintoretto's distorted fields of vision or El Greco's curved space and subjective focus are not tokens of some constraint, excitement, or, possibly, compulsion. We are told that El Greco would not go into the streets of Toledo because it would dispel his inner vision. Tintoretto's painting of Cain and Abel, a wild stabbing in quiet shadow, conveys in the hideous staring head of the slain calf a sense of primal guilt and primal pathos. We can believe that mannerism is an art of bad conscience when we see the helpless gesture of El Greco's Laocoön, who seems destined to his serpent beneath a torn sky that is like a wound in the mind. The restlessness in Michaelangelo's figures, the willful David-frown, the writhing Night, and the unfinished marbles he left in their stony anguish provoke us to ask psychoanalytic questions—the questions we are tempted to ask about El Greco's enraptured saints, Saint Teresa, the puzzled Hamlet, and the strange people in Ford's evasive play *'Tis Pity She's a Whore.*

The emotional and moral atmosphere of the period is strained. In *Measure for Measure* we can hardly believe that the Duke of dark corners really intends to close the stews in Vienna; how seriously, we might ask, did Pope Pius V intend to cleanse Rome in 1566 by compelling all prostitutes to leave the city within twelve days? According to a Roman law of this year a physician must cease treating any patient after three days unless the sick man meanwhile had confessed his sins to the Church. Since 1540 the Jesuits had been active, and a new generation of saints—Carlo Borromeo, Teresa, Filippo Neri—had in common the intensity and austerity of their religious practice and a knowledge of the practical affairs of the world. While the Inquisition, extending its powers, was taking over Spain, Philip II was fulfilling his vow to build that monastic palace The Escorial, and the censors were lengthening and strengthening the Index Purgatorius.

Characteristically, Baltasar Gracián, that Jesuit rebuked for his worldliness, was devoted to wit (*agudeza*), discretion (*prudencia*), the art of playing with words (*culteranismo*), and the art of playing with ideas (*conceptismo*). He gave some very equivocal advice in the practical maxims he finally collected in *The Oracle* (1647), these "thoughts" being a counterpart, in fact, of Saint Ignatius Loyola's *Spiritual Exercises*. With the greatest "ingenuity" Gracián revises Machiavellianism to his own smooth, and even pious, uses:

Keep your affairs in suspense. . . . Make people depend on you. . . . Avoid victories over your superior. . . . Behave sometimes disingenuously, sometimes with candor. . . . Control your imagination. . . . Know how to keep yourself to your self. . . . Know how to take and give hints. . . . Use, but do not abuse, caution. . . . Adapt yourself to your company. . . . Know how to be evasive (that is how wise men get themselves out of difficulties). . . . Know how to be all things to all men, a discreet Proteus. . . . Know how to make use of your enemies. . . . Be a man without illusions. . . . Authority in word and deed. . . . The art of getting into a rage. . . . Without lying, do not tell the whole truth. . . . Exercise restraint. . . . Do not commit yourself entirely. . . . Behave as if you were watched. . . . *In a word, be a saint.* . . .

Thus mannerism has two modes, technical and psychological. Behind the technical ingenuities of mannerist style there usually is a personal unrest, a complex psychology that agitates the form and the phrase. When we examine the strains within the mannerist structure in painting, architecture, and poetry, we inevitably become aware of the scourge—or the quicksand—within the mannerist temperament. Mannerism is experiment with many techniques of disproportion and disturbed balance; with zigzag, spiral, shuttling motion; with space like a vortex or alley; with oblique or mobile points of view and strange—even abnormal—perspectives that yield approximations rather than cer-

tainties. It deflects toward some inward focus the clear
mathematical perspective renaissance art had taken
upon the outside world. It "opens," dislocates, or disintegrates the harmonious closed order of the grand
style; it uses acid colors and half-lights that penetrate
the flesh and dissolve the dimensions of the renaissance "enclosed Eden" into transparencies. As the art
historians put it, the mannerist style has a tension
(*Spannung*) and an elasticity of forms (*Streckung*)
seen under fleeting, shimmering light (*gleitendes
Licht*).[2] Mannerist forms are sometimes noted in a
temperamental shorthand. Mannerist space is either
flimsy and shallow, concealing volumes behind a papery façade, or narrow, curving, and *coulisse*-like, a
"projection without climax" (*Raumflucht, die Flucht
ohne Ziel*). Or it stretches upward, waveringly, toward
the vertical. By means of such techniques mannerist art
holds everything in a state of dissonance, dissociation,
and doubt—*Zwiespalt*. This is the art of *Hamlet*, where
ambiguities and complexities are exploited.

II

DISTURBED BALANCE   For the renaissance artist beauty was exact proportion, clear outline, stable
relations. Ghiberti said, "Only proportion makes
beauty." Alberti repeats that beauty is a harmony, congruity, and consent of all the parts. Spenser believed
that God framed the world in a comely Pattern. Then
a spasm broke open this goodly Pattern, and religious
schisms cleft a world charged with the new forces of
the Protestant era—forces that played through politics
and commerce as well as faith, and diverted the course
of history on two continents. Luther burned the Papal
bull in 1520. Rome itself was sacked in 1527 by the

army of Emperor Charles V. The harmony between microcosm and macrocosm was untuned; "the circle was broken" when Tycho Brahe, Galileo, Kepler, found the motions of the universe to be eccentric and elliptical.

A typical "renaissance" structure in poetry is Sidney's sonnet "Heart Exchange" with its clear units, its harmonious and uncomplicated parallels, its "closed" form and decisive coda:

> My true love hath my heart and I have his,
> By just exchange, one for the other given;
> I hold his dear, and mine he cannot miss;
> There never was a better bargain driven.
> His heart in me keeps me and him in one,
> My heart in him his thoughts and senses guides;
> He loves my heart, for once it was his own;
> I cherish his because in me it bides.
> His heart his wound received from my sight;
> My heart was wounded with his wounded heart,
> For as from me on him his hurt did light,
> So still methought in me his hurt did smart;
> Both equal hurt, in this change sought our bliss:
> My true love hath my heart and I have his.

Then, by contrast, there is the loose, devious, zigzag development of that spasmodic mannerist poem "To His Coy Mistress" by Andrew Marvell, which shifts in theme and tone through three powerful dissonant passages. Under the attack of the sophisticated mannerist writer, the renaissance harmony, clarity, and unity are "disturbed." As if echoing Donne's mockery of love, the poem opens with a condescending extravagant praise of Marvell's mistress, whose eyes, forehead, and breasts deserve centuries of adoration. *But* (and the poem swivels abruptly to a sardonic perspective on himself and this coy mistress of his) her Honor and his Lyric will not be found in the grave—that fine and private place. Then Marvell, abandoning both trifling and sardonic tones, is shaken by his own sense of panic: he and this delicate, knowing mistress with her enchanting flesh must tear their pleasures, like birds of prey, from the iron gates of the tomb. The poem ends with a frantic—and suspended—jest, which betrays Marvell's own urgency to love:

> Thus, though we cannot make our Sun
> Stand still, yet we will make him run.

Marvell's sharp but unsustained attack—brilliant, sensitive, private—is like the loose and surprising adjustment and counter-adjustment of figure to figure in Parmigianino's paintings, with their evidence of subjective stress. Parmigianino relies upon an involved energy, not a closed design, and his equilibriums are always momentary and undependable.

Formal as Donne's language may be, his logic is as spasmodic as Marvell's. Eliot has remarked that Donne brings to every experience "an awareness of the apparent irrelevance and unrelatedness of things"; he has an appetite for opposite responses; he develops his poems with "hardly any attempt at organization," if we mean by organization coherent progress; he extracts every minim of emotion from each isolated situation and in so doing wrenches the accent of his verse. Yet it is wrong to think that Donne, or the Jacobean playwright either, makes hardly any attempt at organization; for the poets and dramatists of this era have a logic of their own, a rhetorical and dramatic logic that does not operate by transition and sequence but by circulating through extremes, opposites, and divergencies, digesting every sort of experience by putting sudden stress on language and gesture. It seems fair to say that Donne employs a great many logical devices but is entirely careless of the *direction* in which his logic leads him. Consequently Donne, like the Jacobean dramatists, seems "as ready to defend sophistry as truth," and in describing his art we need to have in mind a kind of logic or structure essentially different from the logic or structure of both renaissance and baroque art—the logic and structure of mannerism, devious, contradictory, shuttling, perverse, and always dramatic in an immediate intense way. Francis Bacon wrote as a mannerist when he said, "There is no excellent beauty that hath not some strangeness in the proportion."

Mannerist painters and poets alike defy rules of proportion and perspective to satisfy the needs of their subjective view of reality. One of the reasons it is difficult to define the mannerist style is that each painting, statue, façade, each poem and play, is a special case, a personal manipulation of design, material, situation, language, response. Metaphysical poetry is not original exactly in the way Eliot and other critics once supposed—that is, in "toughness" and "unified sensibility." [3] The real originality of Donne, whose wit resembles Jonson's and the Cavaliers', is his being an essentially private poet, giving each verse a personal note; thus in reading Donne we must always attend first to the tone, the inner vibration that makes each poem sound like a personal intrigue even if it is not. Webster's is a drama of obscure exploration, suggesting the private imbalance of a Hamlet. Donne, Webster, and Tourneur, Cellini, Tintoretto, and El Greco, approach everything from hidden and inward angles, and their readings are in one or another way ambiguous. It is hard for us to "read" Donne's "Extasie" or Middleton and Rowley's *The Changeling;* it is hard to "read" the façade of the Palazzo Massimi alle Colonne in Rome (Peruzzi, 1535).

Mannerism means experimental response, tentative commitment, learned but personal research, overcleverness in handling conventional forms and elements. Its style and its temperament are variable and diverse. Montaigne, in fact, speaks with the unofficial philosophic voice of mannerism: "Que sçay je?" he asks—What do I know? In his "Apology of Raymond Sebond" all absolute judgments come under his gentle but scathing regard, and he thinks of himself as willing to exist in the element of uncertainty—"the uncertainty that every man feels in himself" when he is wise at his own cost:

How variously we judge of things! How often we change our opinions! What I hold and believe today I hold and believe with my whole belief; with all my tools and all my strength I grasp that opinion; and they guarantee it with all the power at their command. . . . But has it not happened, not once, but a hundred, nay a thousand times, and every day, that, with those same implements and under the same conditions, I have embraced something else, which I have since concluded to be false?

Montaigne moves freely over the whole philosophic terrain between passion and detachment. The senses, he knows, are full of uncertainty and cannot guarantee any truth; thus we must have recourse to reason. But every reason is built upon the quaking foundation of a preceding reason: "so here we are retreating backwards to all eternity." Montaigne, too, has a "subjective" relation to his world, since our senses give us only the impressions of outside objects, and impressions and objects "are different things." Thus we must live amid appearances; and he is brought to question with Hamlet whether our mere thinking does not make it so. "There is," Montaigne placidly continues, "no permanent existence, either of our being or of that of the objects." We, our opinions, our mortal selves, "incessantly go flowing and rolling on." Meanwhile we live convinced that "truth ought to have one face, always and everywhere the same." Surely Montaigne did not have Hamlet's bad dreams, and he seems less damaged than Hamlet by his own curiosity. But he has a great deal of Hamlet's sense of insecurity brought about by living in a world without a known order; and, like Hamlet or Donne, he has glimpses of man's life as a passionate comedy:

Is it possible to imagine anything more ridiculous than that this miserable and puny creature, who is not so much as master of himself, exposed to shocks on all sides, should call himself Master and Emperor of the universe, of which it is not in his power to know the smallest part, much less to command it? . . . Who has sealed him this privilege? Let him show us his letters-patent for this great and noble charge.

Significantly, tragi-comedy is a particularly mannerist form of drama. Plays like *The Changeling* are inscrutable because the pathos and the laughter are both pressed as far as they can be in opposite directions without any attempt to reconcile, compromise, or accept the logic of either. Donne, Webster, and Tourneur do not seem to conquer their disillusions, and not being able to mediate between irreconcilables, leave us with a sense of disrelationship, ambiguity, and in general what Woelfflin calls in painting a "complexity of direction." It is symptomatic that the many prose passages in Jacobean drama gradually encroach upon verse, implying in the author a frame of mind with a minimum of formal articulation.

Donne's false and verbal (perhaps false? perhaps verbal?) resolutions—his incapacity to commit himself wholly to any one world or view—appear in his extraordinary poem on his own death, "Hymn to God the Father," resigning his soul to his Redeemer, asking whether He can forgive the sins which he has *done*, and which, he says, he deplores—although we have strongly the sense that the poet is only too convinced of the profit of each sin as a means of fulfilling his adventurous experience of life:

> When thou hast done, thou hast not done,
> 　　For I have more.
> I have a sinne of feare that when I have spunne
> My last thred, I shall perish on the shore;
> Sweare by thy selfe that at my death thy sonne
> Shall shine as he shines now, and heretofore;
> 　　And, having done that, Thou hast done,
> 　　　　I feare no more.

This calling his Judge to account, this demand for re-assurance from God, this trifling in puns with his sins in the flesh and spirit and his fear of hell, is either extreme devotion or extreme insolence; and we cannot clearly tell which. The resolution is gained, if at all, only rhetorically by a logic of the pun, not reason. But there is no doubt of Donne's fear for his soul. So in Donne's last and most cavalier pun there is the tension of mannerist techniques. In *The Duchess of Malfi* and other plays by Webster we find the same high tension of the moment together with a blurring of total mean-ing—glaring flashes of perception along with brutal acts and unexplained contradictions.

The unresolved tensions and contradictions in man-nerist art appear early in Michaelangelo's designs for the Laurentian Library anteroom and the Medici Chapel (1526–34). Michaelangelo never seems to have decided whether architecture is, or is not, simply a background for sculpture, an uncertainty revealed fully in the Medici Chapel, where his architectural plan seems to be a framework for some shocking feats in sculpture and for niches some of which, by a break-down of logic, are left vacant. Burckhardt thought the Laurentian anteroom to be "an incomprehensible joke," just as, we might add, the literary historians be-fore Grierson thought Donne's poetry a joke, and a bad joke at that. In fact, Michaelangelo was the first to turn architecture into a medium for individual ex-pression, and both the Chapel and the anteroom show us "a world of frustration" where all the forces seem ac-tive, yet frozen or paralyzed by "a highly artificial," se-vere, and uncomfortable system.[4]

As if Michaelangelo had intended to parody archi-tectural logic, the Laurentian anteroom, with its rest-less narrow proportions, its complex black moldings, columns, and pediments crowded and broken, leaves the observer everywhere in doubt about structure and function. The relations of column to wall are reversed, since the columns, being set within niches, stand not before, but *within* or even *behind,* the wall. Ungainly brackets on the *surface* of the wall "support" the *inset* doubled columns, whose weight does not bear directly on these absurd brackets, which nevertheless receive full plastic emphasis. Thus *the logic of the structure does not coincide with the structural elements.* The moldings and the frames of the door and niches are broken, or not held in one plane; the triangular pediment over the harsh narrow door is twice broken, and so heavy that it seems to press unbearably down upon the frame of the doorway. The empty niches beside the door are crowned with semicircular pediments, rasping against the pediment above the door and also against the engaged pilasters framing the niches. These pilasters taper toward the bottom—another *reductio ad absurdum* of normal support for weight. The molding is broken inward precisely above the outward-moving capitals of the inset columns, and the ugly little black tablets set below the frames of the niches only emphasize that these frames are not supported by the molding beneath them. The mass of the steps is heavy, sluggish, inert, a lumpy flow "as of lava," and while the side flights go straight upward, the central flight, rounded in the middle, then again rounded as it clashes against the balusters, lacks any convincing rhythm, volume, or weight. There is an insoluble conflict between logic and appearance, horizontal and vertical movement, motion and rest, energy and paralysis.

In mannerist façades there is a frank display of illogicality in the frequent *double functioning of members,* particularly where there appears a kind of architectural pun, a single member having a duplex use—a molding, for example, used as a sill. There is also a "principle of inversion" in mannerist façades, for the customary relation of orders is reversed by "permutations" of elements, conflicting directions, shifts in scale, or other overingenious devices that are learned but irresponsible. Often the closed units are not really bounded but placed in doubtful adjustment to the open units.

One of the decisively mannerist façades is that of the Palazzo Massimi alle Colonne in Rome (1535) which, being slightly curved, obscures the harmonious clear logic of the renaissance surface, and dramatizes the "poignant contrast between the deep darkness of the ground-floor loggia and the papery thinness and flatness of the upper parts." The façade of the Chigi Palace in the Piazza Colonna, Rome (begun in 1562 by Giacomo della Porta?), also shows the mannerist inversions and the tendency to mask the logic of the structure. At the corners the coigns are far too bulky for the flimsy-looking walls; so also is the heavy cornice casting melodramatic shadow over the plane surface beneath. This surface is kept in a restless, "interesting" movement by four stories (five, if we count the windows *above* the cornice) completely out of proportion, making us wonder what the interior structure could be. Over the thick casings of the lowest windows, shadowed by giant canopies, runs a thin string course touching the sills of the next rank of windows and serving, like a pun again, a double function as string course and continuous sill. Above the upper shallow casings are huge pediments, alternately triangular and semicircular, that are supported "wittily" by massive brackets. Immediately above these pediments runs a series of tiny absurd "horizontal" windows, over which are corresponding "vertical" windows of larger size. The whole effect is one of melodrama and levity—or demented ingenuity.

In designing both churches and palaces mannerist architects broke up the renaissance a-b-a-b symmetry in open and closed bays of naves, or in alternating tri-

angular and semicircular pediments. On the façade of
the Palazzo Bevilacqua, Verona (1530), the pediments
were planned irregularly (a-B-B-a-a-B); and in such
palaces the portals may not be symmetrically placed.
The width of bays, the handling of columns, the treatment of orders and other elements, may also be whimsical. The eye *jumps* across a mannerist façade since
there is little repose or balance; or else the balances
are false. In the Redentore, Venice (1576–92), Palladio's interpenetrating giant and minor orders make
the façade difficult and surprising to "read." Even
Inigo Jones' Banqueting House in Whitehall has certain mannerist features, for the front does not keep
the plane, the cornices are broken, the accents "move"
somewhat because the central axis is so strong, and
although the interior is one large room, the exterior
uses three levels.

The architectural symmetries wavered and broke up
as soon as the balanced, "centralized" renaissance
church was replaced by the mannerist church having
a strong medial axis because of its long nave, surmounted by a dome at the crossing, where the high
altar stands in a flare of sunlight. Except for this, the
mannerist church is dim, the chapels along the aisles
serving as nooks for private devotion, each chapel having its painting, lighted by candles. The heightened
devotional atmosphere of the mannerist church, together with its irregular architectural features and dramatic austerity, seems to betoken the "bad conscience"
also expressed in the somewhat chill yet agitated mannerist art which "contracts its material" yet gains an
effect of spirituality from its strong verticality and constraint. Certainly that typical mannerist façade of the
Gesù Church in Rome (1569–84), with its unnatural
withering of rich materials, has a false austerity, a
thwarted and puny upward motion. Deprived of repose by Vignola's and Della Porta's plans, the central

unit is of painfully narrow proportions; the small side doors are huddled up against the central door, and the double engaged pilasters move inward away from the receding wings of this façade; these wings support the shrunken awkward brackets intended to make a transition between the superior orders and the orders of the ground floor. The coherence is uncertain. The disharmony of the triangular-within-semicircular pediments over the main door is probably not due to Vignola, who is, however, responsible for the conflict between the engaged pilasters on the ground story and the columns set about the rectangular window in the upper story.

Thus the mannerist churches have a repressed elegance, an ascetic refusal to achieve baroque splendor; in this architecture there is a sign of struggle, but no fulfillment, no conquest—except for *a "tendency to excess within rigid boundaries."* The mannerist energy suddenly expends itself in surprising, illogical places. But the uncertain proportions, the wavering accents, do not reduce the mannerist tensions; neither the vertical motion nor the awkward masses give any sense of release or exuberance. The mannerist architect uses weighty volumes only with reluctance or indecision; at least the appearance of weight is denied by broken rhythms. The play of forces is checked, dissonant, perplexed. The major plastic accents do not coincide with the major structural accents. Consequently in mannerist art *the psychological effect diverges from the structural logic.* The style is "atectonic." It seems to be a response to the temper of Europe between 1520 and 1620, one of tormenting doubt and rigorous obedience to ardently felt but incoherent dogmatic principles. Mannerism is full of contradictions: rigid formality and obvious "disturbance," bareness and overelegance, mysticism and pornography, El Greco and Parmigianino.

faith & doubt struggle in man. literature

During the mannerist era prose writers broke up the classic ("tectonic") rhythms of the Ciceronian style, which in slow and orderly cadence progressed to a clear emphasis and closed the period harmoniously. One reaction against this "grand" Ciceronian style was the "curt" period with a lack of syntactical relation between members, a deliberate asymmetry of phrase, and many shifts from concrete to abstract language, alternating the "planes" of the vocabulary, so to speak.[5] The accents in this new prose "hover" and sometimes are determined by emotive stress instead of any logic of syntax. The "loose" style of the age is even more subjective, with emergent meanings, sharply phrased statements budding off into new members at will, unfolding toward an *O Altitudo*. Though the loose style willfully violates coherence, it uses many connectives; yet these connectives are of doubtful logic since the period develops by a series of dangling members introduced by a *which*, a *wherein*, a *whereto*—or by some absolute construction amounting to a *non sequitur*, a breakdown in symmetry. With their erratic tempo both kinds of style are "exploratory." In one or another way Montaigne, Bacon, Browne, and Burton all brought to bear, in curt or loose manner, a strain on their sentences beyond the capacities of syntax; one sign is their abuse of interpolation and parenthesis. Burton's language, so variable as to be freakish, with its whimsical lardings of Latin, has the "broken," eccentric, unsustained mannerist energy. In verse Donne does not "keep the accent" either, as Ben Jonson complained, for he wrenched his meter by every sort of dissonant stress, making the ear jump just as the eye jumps across a mannerist façade. The new seventeenth-century prose is called "baroque"; but it is, properly, mannerist in its explosive accent, its experimental and indecisive "hovering" order of statement.

The hovering is partly psychological. In Donne, too,

the psychological effect is not co-ordinated with the structural effect; often the metaphor does not coincide with the mood of devotion, for there is an interplay between John Donne very insolent and neat, and Dr. Donne the Dean of Saint Paul's who dreads to be damned eternally, eternally, eternally, and dropped into the flaming pit—unless he can jest his God out of His righteous anger. Donne writes of the Church in terms one usually applies to an adulteress or whore: "Show me, deare Christ, thy Spouse so bright and cleare," he begins; and then urges:

> Betray kind husband thy spouse to our sights,
> And let myne amorous soule court thy mild Dove,
> Who is most trew, and pleasing to thee, then
> When she's embrac'd, and *open to most men.*

This is witty; this has a lively stress; this shows a capacity for every range of response, an ability to assimilate opposite and diverse appetites and experiences. But it is strained, and the resolution is equivocal. If it is true that pornography is a sign of sensuousness with a bad conscience, Donne comes near betraying a bad conscience. In the same way subject and image—devotion and rhetoric—diverge in Góngora's witty religious poems. In a sense, mannerism is a reaction, after the renaissance optimism, to medieval faith; but a gulf is fixed between the two eras. The tendency of all the cinquecento art and thought is to be "rich in directions," and we must associate Donne's ability to digest heterogeneous experiences with the mannerist instability and tension in architecture, its inversion of orders, its permutations and double functions, its impulse toward austerity and the vertical—the verticality of the Gesù façade, more troubled, complex, jarring, self-conscious, and frigid than any gothic verticality. If mannerism shares some of the gothic religious spirit, it oversophisticates and overintellectualizes the gothic line. Its rationalism has lost direction.

The quasi-austerity, the wavering aspiration, are both in Donne's "Divine Poems," which use a double functioning of members, since the so-called *catena* group of sonnets interlocks the opening and closing verses of successive sonnets, although the meaning of the verse shifts constantly in tone and direction from piety to wit to hysteria to resignation to query, and every excess within artificial boundaries. A more subtle complexity is the sixth Holy Sonnet, showing the mannerist tension, dissonance, and perversion. Purportedly the verses claim that Donne does not fear death; yet the argument only conceals Donne's horror of the grave. The strain on the logic is very great, and the resolution occurs by a leap or ellipsis due to faith—or fright:

This is my playes last scene, here heavens appoint
My pilgrimages last mile; and my race
Idly, yet quickly runne, hath this last pace,
My spans last inch, my minutes latest point,
And gluttonous death, will instantly unjoynt
My body, and soule, and I shall sleepe a space,
But my'ever-waking part shall see that face,
Whose feare already shakes my every joynt:
Then, as my soule, to'heaven her first seate, takes flight,
And earth-born body, in the earth shall dwell,
So, fall my sinnes, that all may have their right,
To where they'are bred, and would presse me, to hell,
Impute me righteous, thus purg'd of evill,
For thus I leave the world, the flesh, the devill.

The clash between the psychological and rhetorical directions is audible in the wavering caesura, the sliding meter, the wrenched accents. The renaissance sonnet did not try to accommodate these strains, which suggest the curious torment in mannerist faith—and mannerist doubt.

III

The German art historians summarize the situation by saying that the mannerists reverted to an almost gothic inwardness and spirituality—*Verinnerlichung* and *Beseelung*—yet with a "private" unrest and complexity (*Unruh und Komplikation*) gothic man is unlikely to have known. There is an almost existential sense of personal extremity in Claudio's frightening speech on death in *Measure for Measure*:

> Ay, but to die, and go we know not where;
> To lie in cold obstruction, and to rot;
> This sensible warm motion to become
> A kneaded clod. . . .

In *All's Well That Ends Well* Lafeu feels the helplessness of man: they say, he remarks, that the age of miracles is past, and philosophic persons try to explain away things supernatural and causeless; "hence is it that we make trifles of terrors, ensconcing ourselves into seeming knowledge, when we should submit to an unknown fear." While he is mad Lear asks, "Is man no more than this?" Shakespeare and the Jacobean playwrights wrote with a divided mind and a sense of imminent calamity:

Standing between a belief in natural order and a growing perception of chaos, between the Renaissance enthusiasm for living and an ever-darkening disillusion, between the twin poles of Fate and Chance, of predestination and free will, they went through mental experiences of a peculiar intensity, knew the darkness and the terror all the more keenly for the light that still remained in the diminishing fragment of the heavens.[6]

Deep within himself Donne bears the mannerist sense of reprobation and helplessness before the will of a God awful in His power and unaccountable in His autocracy. He complains, "All our life is a continual burden, yet we must not groan; a continual squeezing, yet we must not pant . . ." In his sermon preached on Easter, 1619, he asks hollowly: "I know I must die that death, what care I? . . . I will find out another death, *mortem raptus*, a death of rapture, and of ecstasy." But his ecstasy is really panic, and in sermon 66 he confesses:

when I shall rely upon a moral constancy, and God shall shake, and enfeeble, and enervate, destroy and demolish that constancy; when I shall think to refresh myself in the serenity and sweet air of a good conscience . . . God shall call up the damps and vapors of hell itself, and spread a cloud of diffidence, and an impenetrable crust of desperation upon my conscience . . .

Donne's God, like Calvin's, is arbitrary, and Donne cries in dread that God will let his soul fall out of His hand into a bottomless pit, where he will be secluded eternally, eternally; he exclaims in complex prose with erratic syntax:

. . . . mine enemy is not an imaginary enemy, fortune, nor a transitory enemy, malice in great persons, but a real, and an irresistible, and an inexorable, and an everlasting enemy, the Lord of Hosts Himself, the Almighty God Himself, the Almighty God Himself only knows the weight of this affliction, and except he put in that *pondus gloriae*, that exceeding weight of an eternal glory, with his own hand into the other scale, we are weighed down, we are swallowed up, irreparably, irrevocably, irrecoverably, irremediably. (Sermon 66)

Donne has Dante's fear of hell, but without the calm of Dante's faith, without any assurance of the goodness and reliability of God's judgment.

You must obey this God, and reason about Him, but His laws operate unpredictably. The renaissance Logos-God revealed his nature and his dispensation by the regularity of a platonic Order; the mannerist God of Donne and Calvin and the Jesuits imposes his will by fiat, and his justice is despotic, inexplicable, perhaps equivocal. For the Calvinist, God's will is rationally unknowable but terribly immanent in its effects; as Calvin said, not a drop of rain falls but at the express command of God, to whose sanction man must submit himself in fear and humility. According to the *Institutes* (1535) each man has his own foreordained destiny, of which he is ignorant:

By an eternal and immutable counsel, God has once for all determined both whom he would admit to salvation, and whom he would condemn to destruction. We affirm that this counsel, as far as concerns the elect, is founded on his gratuitous mercy, totally irrespective of human merit, but that to those whom he devotes to condemnation the gate of life is closed by a just and irreprehensible, but incomprehensible, judgment.

. . . For the will of God is the highest rule of justice; so that what he wills must be considered just, for this very reason, because he wills it. When it is inquired, therefore, Why the Lord did so, the answer must be, Because He would.

John Knox, writing on *Predestination* (1560), shows how the Christian stands in a very personal and always uncertain relation to his God, which deprives him of confidence but gives a melodramatic sense of the unpredictable: "But why it pleased God to show mercy to some, and deny the same to others, because the judgments of God are a devouring depth, we enter not in reasoning with him . . ."

Is it any wonder that the sense of sin bears upon Donne and upon the seventeenth-century conscience with an incommensurate force? The neat mechanics of the renaissance Order have been disturbed by the power of a capricious divine will, whose activity means that all relationships within the soul and the universe are no longer a harmony, a congruity, an ideal proportion, but a mere possibility, or at best a probability. Everywhere one must allow for contingencies, the ul-

timate contingency being the will of God. Mannerist
art and mannerist conscience accept a principle of indetermination, for all ratios and proportions become
provisional. We have mentioned that the regular a-b-
a-b alternation of elements in renaissance architecture
was revised by the mannerists into variable and surprising patterns (a-B-B-a-a-B). This uncertain rhythm
is inherent in the mannerist cosmology. The medieval
ptolemaic system was irreparably broken when Copernicus proved that the universe is not geocentric; but
Copernicus had, after all, found a solar center for his
cosmos and a "wonderful symmetry." Then in 1588
Tycho Brahe discovered many irregular motions in the
mannerist universe; the sun was, perhaps, the center
still, but the orbits of the planets were elliptical about
the sun, which did not repose in the mathematical center, and about the planets revolved subordinate bodies each going its erratic course. Bacon sought to explain gravity as being a kind of spiraling, diagonal
movement of objects near the surface of the earth. The
motions in the mannerist cosmos were "disturbed" so
deeply that Kepler tried to reduce the disorder left by
Brahe; and through his second and third laws he managed to "save the principle" that there is a constant
Divine Cause by transferring uniformity from the
paths of the planets to the areas through which they
swept. There were also alarming sights in the sixteenth-century heavens—the new star that blazed
throughout most of the year 1572, and the flaming
comet of 1577.

The treatment of space in mannerist architecture
and painting shows this change from the "closed" renaissance world order to the "open," "loose," and devi-
ating motions in the mannerist universe. The harmony,
intelligibility, and coherence of the renaissance world
view were inherent in the symmetrical courtyards of
Italian palaces; but about 1570 Vasari used the long

corridor-like court before the Uffizi Palace, without any accent whatever on the logical focus, which falls, almost meaninglessly, within the loggia opening in an indecisive puzzling way upon the River Arno, which cannot be seen at all. Thus the "suction-like" energy generated in the narrow alley reaches no climax; yet as we look down this artificially restricted vista we feel the full force of the mannerist compulsion to "enforce movement through space within rigid boundaries"— boundaries that appear to be as arbitrary as they are artificial. Mannerist architecture tends to rely upon forms like the ellipse and the elongated rectangle, or "*coulisse*" space seen from a sharp diagonal.

Painters like Tintoretto and El Greco, too, use the parabola, the zigzag recession, the elongated forms and wavering verticality, suggesting the structural instability of the contemporary world. A glance at Tintoretto's Presentation of the Virgin in Santa Maria dell' Orto, Venice, reveals the disproportions and the compulsive movements in this "atectonic" mannerist world. The point of view, as usual, is private and arbitrary— from below (*di sotto in su*) for we enter the painting at the level of the woman standing with her back to us, pointing upward, with a twisting foreshortened swing of body and arm, to the tiny isolated figure of the Virgin, a common little girl who turns toward the top of the bright curved stairway, where the solemn priest waits with outstretched arms to bless her. The strong, almost intoxicating, spiral leads the eye inward and upward, and the climax of the motion is not actually the Virgin but the steeple projecting above the stairway into vacant space. Since the Virgin is not stressed, we have some trouble "reading" her position, not only because she is subordinated to the steeple but also because the distance between her figure and the outstretched hand of the pointing woman is uncertain. Again, the psychological and structural accents do not

coincide. The diagonals are strong, and there is a gulf
between the rank of the figures lying along the stairway to the left and the isolated figure of the second
woman, disproportionately large, standing half way up
the stairs on the right. The volumes are less dynamic
than the vacancy between them, the energy of this
painting not being conveyed in the bodies but in the
direction in which the bodies move through this fluid
"perforated" space, split open as renaissance space
was not. The heart of the composition is space itself,
in doubtful and unstable relations. The "directional"
tension is highly dramatic, especially in the third
woman on the right lower steps, facing this time outward toward the lower right, beyond the limits of the
scene. She is the only person not intent upon the
mounting Virgin, but she counts heavily and serves,
by a kind of complicated witticism, to reverse the direction illogically. The light is no longer "still" but fleeting and arbitrary, the glimmering gold stairway obscuring the figures grouped along the left incline: thus
the plasticity of these figures is waived, or denied, as
it is in Rembrandt, by the radiance dissolving the material world. The left area of the painting, disproportionately large, is spread upon a "flat" plane, very
flimsy, making the spiraling in the right-hand area
overemphatic. All movements terminate in incommensurate space. The contrast between the solidity of the
foreground figures and the weightless body of the
priest illustrates the contradictions in mannerist painting.

In his Transporting the Body of Saint Mark (Venice,
Accademia) Tintoretto drives his space into a *coulisse*
or vortex; by technical daring he fixes a central axis,
then at once twists his composition away into an acute
diagonal along the lines in the tessellated pavement,
which runs to exaggerated "distance" by hysterical
foreshortening. Meanwhile in the lower right the

heavy body of Mark is being carried off directly out of the corner, while the phantasmal figures on the other side of the square flee like wraiths among the arches of the loggia, which is denied all architectural value by the ghastly light falling upon it. The sky is rent with storm. Because of the weird light the regularly foreshortened colonnade is a mere transparency, a screen for infinity. This world is shaken with tempest, wracked by the Lear-hurricane, and gives us a nightmare-glimpse into a chaos that swallows up puny but violent human effort. The figures change scale without warning and crowd the frame with urgent pressures. Even before its borders were clipped, this painting must have shown the mannerist frantic activity within constricted boundaries.

If the "schizothym" mannerist world is no longer organized in stable relationships, then possibility, probability, or, better, contingency, becomes the prevailing law. It is the law of the mannerist soul, too, whether man was subject to Calvin's willful God or the system of casuistry evolved by the Jesuit order, approved in 1540. Granted that the Jesuits were more concerned with ends than with means, nevertheless the followers of Saint Ignatius are too much blamed for using casuistry, which is a strategy of exacting penance by treating each sinner as an exceptional case. Thus the casuist could "loosen" or "adapt" the law to suit the particular person involved in a particular instance, here and now, immediately. Casuistry is the Jesuit method of submitting to the uncertainties and flexibilities in the mannerist world, which required a pliable and provisional law of pro and contra, like the agile logic in Donne. The Jesuits simply utilized the *play* in the mannerist world, where things fitted together with great tolerance. The structure of the mannerist universe is not wholly determinate; it is open and shifting, and the equivocations in casuistry are a special tactic of mannerist conscience, just as an extremely elastic logic is the special tactic of mannerist art, or as the double meaning, the ambiguity, is the tactic of mannerist verse.

The evil effects of casuistry later provoked Pascal to write his bitter *Provincial Letters* attacking the Jesuits as dishonest and opportunist. Though Pascal is no mannerist, his satire on Jesuit tactics of equivocation and contingency gives us our best definition of the mannerist psychology and conscience. Pascal hates the mannerist "double probability" of pro and con, which is always striving to adjust contradictions verbally, and, surprisingly, as in Donne's "Hymn to God My God" or his sonnet on death, does reconcile them—verbally. The strain within the mannerist or Jesuitical conscience, and in Donne's sensibility, is reduced by a legalistic wit, a juggling with opposites, by taking advantage of the doubt in the elliptical, shuttling system of things—in short, by *accommodation*. Pascal's Jesuit explains, with calm audacity, the mannerist adroitness in absolving sin: "The grand project of our Society, for the good of religion, is never to repulse anyone, let him be what he may, and so avoid driving people to despair." If God is arbitrary, then the Jesuit will be nimble. The answer to Calvin's terrifying system of arbitrary predestination was furnished by the casuist, who yields suavely to the eccentricities of God by his system of pro and contra and exploits uncertainty for his own benefit. The casuist is arbitrary, too, and manipulates contingencies *ad hoc* in a universe where "the circle is broken," where coherence is gone, where one must go about and about to seek truth, as Donne has it. Thus in different ways Calvin and the casuists allow for the incommensurate: Calvin making everything contingent upon the despotic personal will of God, and the Jesuit making everything contingent upon the occasion.

By applying the laws of penance ambiguously, with a "double functioning" of principles, the Jesuits provided a squinting absolution for all sorts of persons— for benefactors, for rich men, for the poor, for commercial men, for the devout, for the married and irregular people, as Pascal's Jesuit explains. "In short," says this Jesuit, "nothing has escaped their foresight." Every situation becomes a special case; there are few certainties but many approximations. This law of contingency opens a broad path for the sophist and the cynic, and Donne, who had a Jesuit education, is able to argue pro and contra upon suicide, upon love, death, and hell. "But do you know," asks Pascal of the Jesuit, "what is to be done when no equivocal words can be got?" Yes, replies the Jesuit—there is always the mental reservation, or "telling the truth in a low key."

The mannerist usually tells the truth in a key pitched so high it is hysteria or ecstasy, or else in a key so low it is nearly inaudible. Manipulating the truth in every way, Shakespeare's *Measure for Measure* is a very mannerist drama concerned with evasions, for in Vienna "Some rise by sin, and some by virtue fall." The whole action is, as Angelo and Isabella find, "At war 'twixt will and will not," presenting the high-pitched Isabella and the high-pitched prenzie Angelo; and opposite them are the ineffectual Claudio and Escalus, and the equivocating Duke of dark corners, whose truths are spoken in a very small voice indeed, hardly to be heard above the riot in Vienna, where everyone adapts the law to his own uses. The world of this play is "disintegrated" and its atmosphere foul, touching the "lowest depths of Jacobean negation." [7] The Duke saves the situation, of course, where everyone "smells of calumny," by a tactic of mental reservation, and strains the quality of mercy until justice is something like an accommodation, but hardly measure dealt for measure. While every legal equation is breaking down, the Duke reassures us: "Put not yourself into amazement how these things should be. All difficulties are but easy when they are known."

If the key is low enough, the truth becomes a lie. Therefore the Jesuit found use for the "artifice of devotion" and particularly the sacrament of easy penance, which maintains the appearance of righteousness even while the truth may be deeply reserved or only loosely approximated. In *Measure for Measure* Angelo is saved from the scale of justice by a convenient marriage to Mariana, which is an approximation and an artifice of devotion. And Donne's "Hymn to God" is among the extraordinary artifices of English devotion —as Pascal's Jesuit would say, Devotion Made Easy by punning upon the name of the poet, who when he is done is not Donne. "Whence it follows," explains Pascal's Jesuit, "that opinions probable in speculation may be followed with a safe conscience in practice." Mannerism is *practiced* in using approximations and accommodations, double functions, inversions, techniques of ambiguity, and variable accents. The mannerist directions are, indeed, as Pevsner once said, *problemreich* —"rich in problems."

IV

THE DRAMATIC ARTIFICE   No drama is better able to accommodate these problems than the Jacobean, behind which are a strange "spiritual uncertainty" and a "world of chaotic thought." The Jacobean drama "of infirm orientation" operates upon a principle of indetermination and uses a technique of contingency; it holds its actions "in the loose of question," as Angelo puts it in *Measure for Measure*. Perhaps *because* it could no longer arrive at moral certainties this drama presented the foreground of experience, here and now, with great intensity. Elizabethan drama has been said to be a product of "the mentality of crisis," a condition that occurs whenever there is vagueness or inconsistency in ideals together with a vivid awareness of one's immediate situation and a proclivity to act on the stimulus of that awareness. A mentality of crisis develops when thinking about large first principles is confused although there is great clarity about single unrelated concepts—an unthinking clarity that leads to ferocious action precisely while the reasons for that action are open to doubt: in brief, uncertainty as to the ultimate but extreme certainty and commitment as to the immediate. The moral premises behind *The Merchant of Venice* or *Measure for Measure*, for example, are all obscure or debatable, though the motives and the acts in these plays seem decisive. Of course this kind of situation is compellingly dramatic, and the mentality of crisis is a typically mannerist (not simply an Elizabethan) mode of psychology. Among Jacobean playwrights the state of tension is the more severe because their world view is insecure, and their immediate impressions are set down with overexcitement. The dramatic experience is not the less effective because it depends upon mere probabilities and approximations instead of certainties; the very uncertainty of God's will brings into Calvinist religion a dramatic vision of the self in peril. When the position of man is unsafe, religiously or theatrically, fate does not so much bring resignation to what is Inevitable as it does a maximum shock of Surprise, or Qualm. Acting under the full force of this uncertainty principle, the characters of *The Changeling*, or those in plays by Webster and Tourneur, behave according to some psychology of "indetermination," as if they were subject to seizure by irresistible but aimless impulses. This capacity for the sudden act in crisis appears along with the rather mechanistic "faculty" psychology of the Jacobean stage, making man a prey to the onset of violent passion that cannot be explained by any consistent or coherent motivation.

Such dramatic irregularity is a sign of a mentality of crisis with its techniques of accommodation and approximation suitable in a world where, as Donne fears, the sun and stars run in cozening lines, where motions are not one inch direct. The very wrenching of accent in Donne's meter expresses the disturbed sensibility of a poet who holds all in the loose of question and accepts the shock tactics of drama as a means of representing experience. "Then, as my soule, to heaven her first seate, takes flight" is a line governed by metrical approximations and accommodations, like many other irregular but strangely dramatic lines in Donne:

The ends crowne our workes, bút thou crown'st our ends. . . .

If yet I have not all thy love,
Deare, I shall never have it all. . . .

'Twas so; But this, all pleasures fancies bee.
If ever any beauty I did see,
Which I desir'd, and got, 'twas but a dreame of thee. . . .
And now good morrow to our waking soules . . .

The dramatic irregularity of accent reappears in Tintoretto and El Greco, and makes their style "anti-classical"; the anatomical distortions in mannerist painting betoken a dissociated view of reality.

In Tintoretto's Leda in the Uffizi there are all the anomalies of mannerist psychology and action. Here the space is so crowded that it is hardly adequate to contain the magnificent, lyrical, sleek body of the Leda, whose nudity is as resplendent as any in Titian, but lengthened suavely into a knowing suppleness; yet this sophisticated and seductive flesh is ascetically pale and of an austere transparence. Leda turns outward to the right as she reaches downward toward the swan, though her head is reversed toward her maid (who has just released the creature from a wooden cage?). The maid, with one of Tintoretto's most subtle recoils, bends her body in an arc, her hand, her head, and her right foot pointing outward, forming an abrupt contrast with the diagonal of the cage. Since the maid is clothed, she emphasizes the nakedness of Leda, who lies abandoned before the dim splendid curtains, which are like some mysterious aspect of reality. Again the spatial relations are confusing: we cannot measure the interval between Leda and the maid or the cage, even if Leda's foot and the maid's almost touch. The point of contact is implied, not stated. Psychologically there are conflicts: Leda accepts the sinuous eager creature, but her face is held frigidly in the impersonal masklike neutrality of all Tintoretto's female nudes (for whom, it is said, the models were either men or lay figures). Here, by a dramatic *tour de force* the *attention is transferred to the maid,* who, instead of Leda, becomes the center of psychological gravity as she intently watches the swan; the sexual tension shifts toward this commonplace servant who gives us a shock because she is so like one of the literal people in any Flemish portrait group. In spite of her lustrous flesh Leda has no convincing weight, and becomes a pure and floating attitude. The maid stands heavily, with an impact of weight exactly where we least expect it, upon her left foot.

One of the most dramatic devices of mannerist painting is using the "Sprecher" (the "speaker"), like the man in the left-hand corner of Tintoretto's Presentation of the Virgin—a sharply accented foreground figure who faces outward toward the spectator, yet twirls inward, gesturing or glancing toward the action behind him. The Sprecher is a mannerist mode of direct address corresponding to the intimate soliloquy in Jacobean drama, a form of brusque communication between actor and audience that tends to violate dramatic distance. The figure of the Sprecher appears here and there in earlier painting, but not with the urgency of those who invoke us in Tintoretto. By his outright psychological attack the Sprecher puts the picture and the spectator in immediate but equivocal relation, as do the intensely personal soliloquies in *Hamlet;* both venture to pass from one context to another, from the theatric situation on the stage to the non-theatric world outside. The Sprecher solicits us— at times assaults us—in our own world, frontally, melodramatically, illegitimately, and involves us in introspective space, which is different from aesthetic space. We yield to his solicitation, but soon find that the problem of adjusting the two worlds, art and life, is not really met but left in heightened ambiguity. The Sprecher is a daring psychological exploit of mannerist art, a case of unsustained but very energetic theatrical logic, a logic operating under the stress of crisis. The Sprecher is a kind of opportunist.

So Donne dramatizes his lyrics by taking toward the reader some position or tone like that of the Sprecher in painting; he involves us, by direct address, almost by shock tactics, in the pressure of his own experience, thus shortening the aesthetic distance between us and his poem: "For God's sake," he opens a lyric, "hold your tongue and let me love." Or "Go and catch a falling star." By making this attack Donne reverses the perspective of the poem as Rembrandt reverses his perspective in the Syndics of the Cloth Guild (1662), a picture in which the vanishing point is fixed, by implication, somewhere outside the composition in *our* space; for we seem to have broken into a conversation among the six figures who suddenly, questioningly, almost accusingly, turn their scrutiny upon the spectator himself. As with the Sprecher, this reversed perspective creates a new pictorial value of introspective

rather than aesthetic space. In both Rembrandt's painting and Donne's poem the attention is unexpectedly
transferred, and since the focal point for the energies
of the composition is outside the composition itself, the
psychological accent does not correspond to the structural accent. The center of psychological gravity has
been displaced, and when the force of the poem or
painting has been diverted toward us, we are com-
pelled, willy-nilly, to make a double adjustment: first,
to meet the shock of the diversion, and second, to re-
gain some aesthetic distance and disengage ourselves
from the situation in which we have been involved.
The "logical" vanishing point in renaissance style did
not require this special adjustment to the aesthetic representation. Donne, like Hamlet or the Syndics, raises
the question of his relation to us and also to his experience. The mannerist composition has a psychological
focus, perhaps, rather than any stated structural focus,
for we are not concerned with Love but Donne's attitude toward his mistress; not Death but Donne's
moods while dying; not the events in Denmark but
Hamlet's consciousness of them.

In spite of its maximum psychological attack, mannerist art strikes us as being bleak as soon as we are
aware that the attack is calculated. Bronzino and
Parmigianino present us with a "frozen" type of figure,
people who assume striking poses without in the least
seeming to feel them, since an artful formality obscures
or conceals their nature; or else there is some dissociation of their gesture from their feeling. Surely there is
some repression in Bronzino's taut, still Bartolommeo
Panciatichi; his left hand is too strained. At times Hamlet seems to be this kind of hysteric, detached mannerist figure; his sensitivity to Ophelia and his insensitiv-
ity to Ophelia's death show this disrelationship, and it
is impossible to reconcile his generosity with his Mach-
iavellian scheming. The mannerist drama suspends

the laws of probability, and in the mannerist theater all responses seem to be unconditioned. T. S. Eliot proves, after all, to be correct in saying that Hamlet is dominated by an emotion which is inexpressible; the Prince's responses do really seem in excess of the facts as they appear, for the negligible figure of Gertrude could hardly cause the Hamlet-obsession. The activity in this play is introspective. Eliot's remark would apply equally well to the apparently unmotivated excitement of many figures in Tintoretto—the man, for instance, who frantically reaches outward, grasping the curtain, in the lower left corner of Transporting the Body of Saint Mark. In one of El Greco's earlier works, The Martyrdom of Saint Maurice, there is an utter dissociation between the horror of the beheadings going on in the background and the placid conversation being carried on in the foreground among a group of passive, effeminate, overbred gentry whose self-possessed gestures, gracious, artificial, and leisurely, apparently have meanings entirely apart from the savage executions and curiously irrelevant to the normal range of response. The mannerist figure seems to obey forces that operate outside natural law.

In mannerist painting, drama, and poetry conflicting or unrelated modes of feeling and conduct are brought together side by side and left unreconciled, as if one phase of activity had nothing to do whatever with another phase of activity in which the same persons take part. Thus the mannerist composition employs a kind of *parapsychology*, an adjustment by disrelationship. We know that the Elizabethan dramatist anatomized the passions using a psycho-physical mechanism of "humors" and "rhetoric" to give each character its proper decorum. But the Jacobean playwrights have a psychology of *dis*-continuity more intense than the earlier anatomy of passion. They accept two or three different scales of value at the same time and fill their scenes with virgins and lechers moved irrationally and violently by unrelated motives like Bosola's. At the heart of Hamlet's mystery lies this dissociating parapsychology, which causes an extreme diversity of response but at the same time leaves everything in suspension or paralysis.

Mannerist art, in fact, already shows the disturbing disrelationship of mind and body which became a major problem in Descartes, who never succeeded in explaining how mind acts on flesh or flesh on mind. The best he and his followers could do was to accept a psychology of "occasionalism" assuming that the body itself has no power to move but is controlled in even its slightest action by God, who, as the philosopher Malebranche thinks, "wills incessantly" to animate the flesh and desires of man instant by instant. We ourselves are completely "impotent" and every gesture we make is an act of God: "All creatures are united to God alone in an immediate union. They depend essentially and directly upon Him. Being all alike equally impotent, they cannot be in reciprocal dependence upon one another." The mannerist world was depolarized except to the fiat of a willful God; and the Jacobean stage accepts a desperate concept of human action so disoriented it can swing erratically through a complete circle of responses like an imperfectly magnetized needle.

El Greco's famous Burial of Count Orgaz is parapsychological in this sense, showing disrelationships, not coherence. What are we to make of the calm with which the delicate body is being laid at rest amid the flamelike agitated upward movement of the composition, the excitement in Heaven above that self-satisfied gathering of Spanish grandees with their impeccable ruffs, their well-bred piety, their effete graces? Here the figure of the Sprecher uses the most artificial mannerist gestures: the priest at the right with his fastidi-

ous outspread hands, and the boy and the monk at
the left with their mechanical reverence. Most of the
spectators appear to be entirely detached; yet clearly
there is some devotional crisis at the instant of this
burial—a crisis transferred to the heavenly host. The
crowding of the figures simply emphasizes the lack of
psychological relation between person and person and
also heightens the dramatic urgency. As usual the angle of vision is arbitrary, and the main action is kept
off center, for the axis is shifted to the left. The space
in heaven has an uneasy discord, since neither the
winding nor the diagonal motions seem logical against
the flimsy plane of the clouds. Everywhere there is
double statement: mystic vision, and an extremely
facile notation of concrete details—the shimmer of bro-
cade, the flicker of torches, the exquisite transparency
of vestments, the muscles of the hand, the direct stare
into the world as it is where *we* are.

Sometimes the mannerist world has the appearance
of delirium, as if the too-too solid flesh had really
melted, thawed, and resolved itself. In his frescoes in
the Scuola di San Rocco Tintoretto uses his "white
writing" to outline his background figures, and even
rocks and trees—mere quick chalky lines that evapo-
rate things into a ghostly calligraphy. His Magi come to
worship like pale wraiths, and his Saint Catherine is
martyred in a flame that consumes the earth to a fierce
orange; his green Arcadian landscape, into which his
Saint George rides like a maniac, eats away space with
acid color. El Greco's Toledo is seen as if it were under
the glare of the Last Day. Hamlet takes this double
view of reality, which is often dream—a bad dream.

For Hamlet, existing in a mannerist world, takes,
along with the characters of the Jacobean theater, a
radically dramatic view of reality. We cannot say it is
merely a theatrical view because the motives and acts
of Hamlet and De Flores seem somehow to be answer-

able to ordinary experience; yet these characters, driven by some obsessive psychology that disturbs us because it is so powerful, exist outside any satisfactory moral context. Take the action in Tourneur's *Revenger's Tragedy,* which ranges over extreme limits of moral values: Vendice's mistress has been violated, then killed, by the Duke, whose lascivious wife loves his bastard son Spurio. Vendice and his brother Hippolito, in disguise, act as panders to the Duke's son Lussurioso, who intends to enjoy Vendice's sister Castiza. Although Castiza remains pure, her mother, Gratiana, wishes her to sell herself. Vendice arranges for the Duke an assignation at midnight and contrives that he kiss the skull of his late mistress, on which poison has been smeared; as the Duke's face is eaten away, he is made to see his bastard Spurio and his wife in their incestuous pleasure. At dagger's point Vendice converts his mother Gratiana to virtue, and the play ends with the death of all the Duke's sons, the insanity of the Duchess, and the arrest of Vendice and Hippolito for murder. All this activity is both mechanical and passionate.

Tourneur's play, crowding its plot to bursting with macabre episodes, is not simple melodrama like Marlowe's *Jew of Malta;* there is an overheated moral atmosphere about this exertion, yet we cannot say that the morality is consistent or that it deals with our ordinary human condition. Can we find this play's relation to life by asking what kind of katharsis it is able to give?

The answer is implied in Muriel C. Bradbrook's *Themes and Conventions of Elizabethan Tragedy,* which speaks of this kind of play as seeking a maximum emotional response; therefore Tourneur's scale of moral values is always being adjusted to the needs of the immediate dramatic crisis. This means that the motives and the actions need not be consistent with

any one scheme of morality, but effective only for the
instant. So, also, in Webster the behavior of the characters is determined by the demands of particular moments in the play. Thus occurs a dissociation of dramatic from moral relevance. Nor does the violence of
the characters mean that any emotion is intimately or
necessarily identified with the character who displays
the emotion; the characters are "depersonalized" in so
far as they are manipulated *for the sake of the intrigue
in which they are engaged.* Consequently a consuming
emotion may *play through* a character at a certain instant but may not seem to *belong* personally to that
character, who behaves as an instrument to convey a
dramatic effect. The Jacobean playwright used this sort
of "occasionalism" in his dramas: the passion may be
furious while the character may be rather mechanically possessed by it, as if from without. And moral values are exploited in the interest of dramatic shock.
This is the only way we can account for Gratiana's sudden conversion from vice to virtue at the point of Vendice's dagger.

The responses in Donne's poems are often violent
but depersonalized in this manner, since Donne, especially when in love, manipulates his emotions for the
sake of engaging himself in intrigue. That is why his
reactions seem discontinuous, irreducible to a logic of
personality, incoherent and diverse. This depersonalization also explains the lack of psychological relation
between figure and figure in mannerist paintings.
However private his feelings may be in quality, Donne
exploits them to gain a dramatic effect. While he sur-
renders to the drama of a situation, he watches himself, almost experimentally, as if he himself were a lay
figure to express an emotion, not really possessing his
responses but utilizing them to attain a crisis. So also
in El Greco's Martyrdom of Saint Maurice there are
the gestures of the lay figure manipulated for maxi-

mum effect. Donne has a taste for the maximum dramatic response without at all trusting the validity of this response. Hamlet has maximum reactions in many different directions, these reactions having, really, little to do with the stimuli acting upon him. Dissociated as his psychology is, Hamlet is undeniably dramatic in his capacity to represent emotion.

Donne's double personality, like the double personality of Hamlet, Gratiana, or Vendice, operates within a moral framework of extreme values: pure and impure, vicious and virtuous, profane and saintly. Yet these polarities do not firmly orient the action playing between them largely because the mannerist drama first of all seeks excitation; it uses an ethic of dramatic expediency, and any moral value can be invoked to sharpen the psychological stress. At any given moment a character may, to meet the need for a striking pose, be deflected from one moral extreme to another unpredictably, erratically, illogically. Since opposite responses are available, Donne swings from one moral or emotional pole to another, not modulating his attitudes but swerving, as it were, irresponsibly from one excitement to another. His irony is heavily charged but ambiguous because his reversals occur (as they do not occur in Racine) capriciously, casually, without logic or necessity. He allows himself to respond sensitively but irritably, with an irony that is unregulated because it is intermittent. When Donne, like Vendice, Gratiana, or Hamlet, leaps from one pole of sensibility to another, his will does not seem to be his own; he seems to be possessed by forces operating outside our usual world. On this account we might speak of the mannerist depersonalization or frigidity as lacking an appearance of humanity although the sensitivity to experience is extreme. This kind of drama is powerful but mechanical and fitful, a performance due to incommensurate stimulus, then incommensurate, sudden, reaction. When Gratiana, with Vendice's sword at her throat, renounces her lewdness and seeks grace, she assumes the pose of the Magdalen, the archetype of mannerist penitent, whose conversion can be explained by this para-morality:

I wonder now what fury did transport me!
I feel good thoughts to settle in me . . .

O you Heavens! take this infectious spot out of my soul.
I'll rinse it in seven waters of mine eyes!
Make my tears salt enough to taste of grace,
To weep is to our sex naturally given;
But to weep truly, that's a gift of Heaven.

Gratiana's conversion is a dramatic "act of accommodation" contingent on the crisis in which she is placed. The motives in this sort of play are often conventional, although the characters appear realistic. Similarly, the mannerist pose is sometimes a cliché although the features are very personal.

Any conventional character will look strange when it is situated within the ambiguous contexts of Jacobean drama; perhaps the figure of the "good" Duke in *Measure for Measure* puzzles us because of the fluid moral situation in which he is put. Does not the Duke resemble those figures in mannerist painting who are conventionally posed but situated in an illogically constructed space receding in zigzags or spirals about them, their presence seeming dramatic but unnatural? Can it be that the Duke practices a consistent morality while the moral values of the play, pliable according to the demands of the instant, are manipulated for dramatic immediacy alone? Furthermore, since in mannerist art there frequently is a disrelationship between character and the situation in which it appears, we cannot assign any certain moral valency to the many dubious episodes like substituting soiled maids in virginal beds, as happens with Mariana in *Measure for Measure*. Equivocation—the operation of a universe by

1

RUBENS (WITH
JAN BREUGHEL
Adam and Eve
*Mauritshuis,
Hague*

2
Pietà d'Avignon
Louvre, Paris

3a Rucellai Palace, Florence, façade

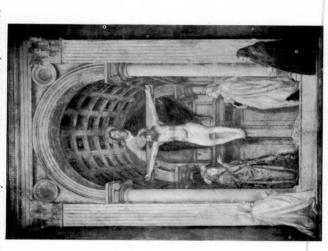

3b MASACCIO: Trinity *Santa Maria Novella, Florence*

4
Pazzi Chapel
Florence, interior

5

RAPHAEL
School of Athens
Vatican, Rome

6

BOTTICELLI

Birth of Venus

Uffizi, Florence

7
GIOVANNI BELLINI
Allegory of
Purgatory
Uffizi, Florence

8a San Francesco, Rimini, façade

8b Palazzo Massimi alle Colonne, Rome, façade

9a　Chigi Palace, Rome, façade

9b　Gesù Church, Rome, façade

10 PARMIGIANINO: Madonna dal Collo Lungo

Pitti, Florence

II   EL GRECO: Laocoön   *National Gallery, Washington*

12
Laurentian Library
Florence, anteroom

13

TINTORETTO

Presentation of the Virgin

Santa Maria dell' Orto, Venice

14   TINTORETTO: Transporting the Body of Saint Mark
Accademia, Venice

15   TINTORETTO: Leda and the Swan   *Uffizi, Florence*

16 BRONZINO: Bartolommeo Panciatichi *Uffizi, Florence*

17 EL GRECO: Burial of Count Orgaz   *San Tomé, Toledo*

18 CARAVAGGIO: Call to Saint Matthew

San Luigi dei Francesi, Rome

19b CELLINI: Deliverance of Andromeda

Bargello, Florence

19a CELLINI: Nymph of Fontainebleau *Louvre, Paris*

20a

BERNINI

Vision of Saint
Teresa
*Santa Maria
della Vittoria, Rome*

20b

BERNINI

Saint Longinus
St. Peter's, Rome

21a
San Carlo
alle Quattro Fontane
Rome, façade

21b
San Carlo
alle Quattro Fontane
Rome, interior

22   Sant'Andrea della Valle, Rome, façade

23 Sant'Agnese in Agone, Rome, façade

24   GUERCINO: Vision of Saint Bruno   *Bologna*

25a
RENI
Samson
Bologna

25b
BERNINI
Scala Regia
*Vatican Palace
Rome*

26

POZZO

Ceiling of Sant'Ignazio
Rome

27

Spanish Steps

Rome

28a Church of the Invalides, Paris, façade

28b San Carlo al Corso, Rome, façade

29
POUSSIN
Funeral of Phocian
Louvre, Paris

30

POUSSIN

Shepherds in Arcadia

Louvre, Paris

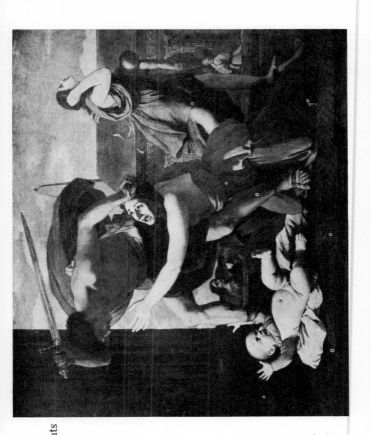

31

POUSSIN

Massacre of the Innocents

Musée Condé, Chantilly

32a   Chapel at Versailles, interior

32b   Santa Croce in Gerusalemme, Rome, façade

laws of <u>pro and contra,</u> when there must be many accommodations—makes it difficult to set any action within a stable moral context. The result is that mannerist drama utilizes sensational acting even if the actor is not placed within any "logical framework of events." In painting, the dissociation of figures from the space about them makes possible every kind of dramatic ingenuity; it has been conjectured, for example, that El Greco's "secret" is using curved elongated figures against a background of flat, shallow, unconvincing space.

Decisiveness of gesture within a fluid or dissonant context: this is one source of ambiguity in mannerist tragi-comedies, one of the strangest being *The Changeling,* in which there is an illusion of parallel actions. In the major action Beatrice is unwillingly pledged to Piracquo, and in order to wed Alsemero she asks the repulsive De Flores to kill Piracquo; which act being done, Beatrice finds herself emotionally as well as criminally committed to De Flores. In the comic plot Isabella is wedded to Alibius, keeper of a madhouse, and in order to enjoy her lover Antonio she enlists the services of the foul Lollio, her servant, who, like De Flores, claims his right to "lay his hand upon a thing of pleasure":

> . . . My share, that's all;
> I'll have my fool's part with you.

Structurally the two plots are parallel; but the comic values of the subplot gradually consume the tragic values of the main plot, and the parallel is obscured as soon as the madmen and fools are invited to caper at the wedding of Beatrice and Alsemero "to make a frightful pleasure." Then the moral focus shifts, and De Flores and Beatrice find themselves in a hideous comedy, strained, duplex, dramatically and morally impure. There is the horrible jest of De Flores offering Beatrice, for proof of his murder, Piracquo's finger with the ring on it; it should have been the ring alone, but "finger and all shall off," because the ring is so fast on. When Beatrice protests that she cannot "with any modesty" give herself to De Flores, he replies:

> . . . Pish! you forget yourself;
> A woman dipped in blood, and talk of modesty!

This is when Beatrice says, "I'm in a labyrinth." The action with its tragi-comic involution is a labyrinth—as when Franciscus is about to be whipped among the madmen while he sings to Isabella his perverted lyric:

> . . . Sweet love, pity me,
> Give me leave to lie with thee.

Antonio in his fool's disguise says to her, "This shape of folly shrouds your dearest love." Immediately we think of Beatrice. De Flores is a comic, pitiful, repulsive, morbid creature: "Her fingers touch'd me! She smells all amber. . . . 'Tis half an act of pleasure, To hear her talk thus to me." Beatrice abuses him; but De Flores is not deceived about "the danger in her mind":

> . . . O my blood!
> Methinks I feel her in mine arms already;
> Her wanton fingers combing out this beard,
> And, being pleased, praising this sad face.
> Hunger and pleasure, they'll commend sometimes
> Slovenly dishes, and feed heartily on 'em.
> Nay, which is stranger, refuse daintier for 'em;
> Some women are odd feeders.

The entirely dramatic and irresponsible morality of Jacobean plays is brought to bear when De Flores foretells that once Beatrice sins she will forever be committed to her lusts; for he predicts, with an excited calculation, that if a woman only once

> Fly from one point, from him she makes her husband,
> She spreads and mounts then like arithmetic;
> One, ten, a hundred, a thousand, ten thousand,
> Proves in time sutler to an army royal.

One, ten, a hundred, a thousand, ten thousand—De Flores reckons this increment in sin not by any usual arithmetic, but by the erratic and feverish logic of mannerist drama, of mannerist conscience. So throughout this play the proportions are unreliable; there is a displacement of tragic and comic values, of pruriency and virtue. There are similar frightful pleasures in other Jacobean plays of adultery or incest, *The White Devil, The Atheist's Tragedy, 'Tis Pity She's a Whore.*

The disproportion is most frightful in *Lear,* where the tragi-comic King is stripped, suddenly, of his followers at a stroke: from a hundred to fifty, to twenty-five, to ten, five, one, none. The computation is as elliptical and vicious as was De Flores'. Before the first scene of this unnatural play is done, Lear has fulfilled his darker purpose and begun to crawl toward death in an action that appears to be a parody of tragic justice cruelly exacted in a world where nature is scourged, where "all's cheerless, dark, and deadly," where man is cut to the brains. In this crazy world only the Fool is wise; and the gods kill men for sport. Even the tragic action is distorted, for Lear's progress towards death is a slow anguishing recognition, a protracted "discovery" that reveals only the outer darkness. The play opens at the normal tragic "turning point" and then descends ruthlessly through a "falling action" to chaos. In *Lear* the ratios are all confused, for this is a play of monstrous excess in which all probabilities break down under the power of some black fate that would be comic were it not so terrifying. The Lear-world is a tumult of mighty discords.

V

THE REVOLVING VIEW   To Hamlet the world seems weary, flat, and stale, as doubtless it did to Shakespeare also when he wrote that mannerist sonnet

> The expense of spirit in a waste of shame
> Is lust in action . . .

This sweet Prince feels the heartache and the thousand shocks that mannerist flesh is heir to. "I could accuse me of such things," he tells Ophelia, "that it were better my mother had not borne me." Hamlet is paralyzed by introspection; he knows his "weakness and his melancholy," yet has "something in him dangerous":

> . . . Now whether it be
> Bestial oblivion, or some craven scruple
> Of thinking too precisely on th'event—
> A thought which, quartered, hath but one part wisdom
> And ever three parts coward—I do not know
> Why yet I live to say "This thing's to do"
> Sith I have cause and will and strength and means
> To do't. . . .

Ironically, Polonius has reason to say that my Lord Hamlet walks too much at large and that his vows are mere implorators of unholy suits, breathing like sanctified and pious bawds. Denmark is a rotten world, to be sure; but the instability in this play is Hamlet's own —personal, temperamental, mercurial.

If we try to decide what Hamlet's nature really "is," we find that we must take one of two incompatible points of view: we must either take a quite arbitrary, narrow approach and consider Hamlet as a "revenger," or we must look at him from many angles as if we circulated about this figure. The mannerist artist is always experimenting with points of view and approaches.

If we take a "revolving view" of this mannerist hero, as we are surely tempted to do, he corresponds to Michaelangelo's *figura serpentinata* in sculpture. Lomazzo's treatise on painting (1584) reports how Michaelangelo gave the following advice to his pupil Marco da Siena:

. . . that he should always make his figures pyramidal, serpent-like, and multiplied by one, two, and three . . . For the greatest charm and grace that a figure may have is to seem to move, which painters call the "fury" of the figure. And there is no form more fit to express this motion than that of the flame of fire. . . . Figures will never look graceful unless they have this serpentine arrangement . . . and unless the face is turned either in the direction required by the emotion it is meant to express or else towards the action of the hands.

Wrested into foreshortenings, overlappings, and spirals, the mannerist flamelike statue cannot be satisfactorily seen from any one point of view; the space about this serpentine figure is fluid, and since we cannot rest content with any one impression we must circulate about its changing contours and supplement our immediate view of it by imagining other available views of this uneasy image with its mobile proportions. Panofsky describes the "form" of the mannerist figure as follows:

The *figura serpentinata* of the mannerists, presenting what I have called a "revolving-view," seems to consist of a soft substance which can be stretched to any length and twisted in any direction. It conveys the impression of an insecure, unstable situation, which however could be transformed into classic equilibrium if the aimless versatility of the figures were directed by a stabilizing and controlling force. *Studies in Iconology*

Michaelangelo's own titanic statues are disturbed in another way; although they have no interior vitality, they are subjected to a gigantic, almost Egyptian-like volumetric system and bear an *aspect* of suffering an interminable inner conflict expressed by "brutal distortions, incongruous proportions, and discordant composition." The gigantic volumes make the languid Michaelangelo-figure unhappy on a monumental scale. The mannerist figure is disturbed, elastic, and uneasy, but not monumental; rather, the unrest in the slender, wavering mannerist image rises from its being placed in "accidental and conditional" circumstances, and from its "aimless versatility."

Cellini's pliable figures lack the heroic volumes of Michaelangelo's David or his Slaves, and the resistance of the Medici statues. Instead they have the aimless versatility we associate with Hamlet's action and temperament. The Bargello model for Perseus is more slender, lithe, and insecure than the finished hero standing in the Loggia dei Lanzi with his "classic" body, his impassive face, the inwound limbs of the bleeding corpse. Yet we must take a revolving-view of either version of this Cellini-action, where horror is treated with too much sophistication—perhaps like Hamlet's murder of Rosencrantz and Guildenstern, whose deaths "are not near his conscience." There is a sinister carelessness about this triumph with its cruelty, ingenuity, and grace, its ease and severity, the indifference in Perseus' attitude as he offers us the dread Medusa-head. The figure is too casual to be engaged in this enterprise. There is an air of crisis, but also of inscrutable repose, of sadist calm. Like Hamlet, Cellini's Perseus exists in the climate of danger. And like Hamlet he is "mobile"; he illustrates Michaelangelo's theory that the body has no stable proportions, for all its members change in breadth and length during motion. The space about this figure is fluid, too, as Perseus holds aloft, languidly, the dripping head and sets his foot easily on Medusa's body. The position of Hamlet is also uncertain since we cannot place him in stable relation to anyone in the play except, possibly, Horatio.

A more thoroughly mannerist performance—suave, constrained, too facile in its study of anatomy—is the Cellini Nymph of Fontainebleau, now in the Louvre, the elongated bronze nude who almost falls out of the low hemicycle in which she lies so casually. Like Michaelangelo's figures on the Medici sarcophagi she has a disturbing immediacy because she is put in an unten-

able position. This Nymph is as dramatically naked as
Tintoretto's Leda. Her body has a lyrical grace, slender and dainty proportions; yet seems male. Her knees
are bony, her arms and legs are angular, and her belly
droops a little; her flesh is no longer virginal. And over
her calm *mondain* head project, unpleasantly, the distorted horns of the stag. The state of tension, the pose
of languor: this is also the contradiction in El Greco,
whose figures seem shaken by some powerful alien motion as they writhe, slim, ascetic, passive, helpless;
the tortured Laocoön (Washington) holds the serpent
at his head with a strengthless gesture, and there is a
strange lack of internal vitality among the victims who
are suffering in this incandescent landscape. The strain
in Cellini's Nymph would be eased if we could pass
behind her, if we could take the revolving-view. As it
is, we are frustrated by having a two-dimensional view
of a situation conceived in three dimensions.

To interpret a poem by Donne we need to take a
revolving-view, for he approaches a situation with an
aimless versatility, going about and about his responses. The course of his "Anniversary" is tentative,
circulating, shuttling. The poem is a tribute to his mistress and opens with his usual strong attack, a triumphant assurance of their fidelity to each other:

> All kings, and all their favorites,
> All glory of honors, beauties, wits,
> The Sun it selfe, which makes times, as they passe,
> Is elder by a yeare, now, than it was
> When thou and I first one another saw:
> All other things to their destruction draw,
>   Only our love hath no decay;
> This, no to morrow hath, nor yesterday,
> Running it never runs from us away,
> But truly keeps his first, last, everlasting day.

But there is also the grave; and Donne, by one of his
capricious dissociations of mood, like the discontinuous
logic of the Jacobean stage, begins the next stanza:

> Two graves must hide thine and my corse,
> If one might, death were no divorce.

The jest, however, does not work; the grave is too frightening:

> Alas, as well as other princes, wee . . .
> Must leave at last in death, these eyes, and eares,
> Oft fed with true oathes, and with sweet salt teares.

Now love can transcend the grave; and his sense of conquest returns, for his devotion is not of eye or ear, but of soul:

> But soules where nothing dwells but love
> (All other thoughts being inmates) then shall prove
> This, or a love increased, there above,
> When bodies to their graves, soules from their graves remove.

So the final stanza recovers his assurance, but with a reservation:

> And then wee shall be thoroughly blest,
> But wee no more than all the rest;

and he returns to the guaranteed pleasure of his lust:

> Here upon earth, we'are kings . . .

Yet lust is a danger, too; and at last he admits his secret fear, which he turns off with a sally that betrays—very casually—his insecurity:

> . . . and none but wee
> Can be such kings, nor of such subjects bee.
> Who is so safe as wee? where none can doe
> Treason to us, *except one of us two.*

The climax is discord—unresolved—for his cynicism destroys his triumph, and his tribute to his mistress is precautionary, or almost incidental to his doubt:

> *True and false* feares let us refraine,
> Let us love nobly, and live, and adde againe
> Yeares and yeares unto yeares, till wee attaine
> To write threescore: *this is the second of our raigne.*

In spite of his many ingenious approaches to the problems of love, Donne yields to a fatality he does not wish to acknowledge without screening it in a witticism.

The atmosphere of crisis, the ultimate passivity; the seizure by forces which are too powerful, but to which one cannot be resigned any more than one can be securely resigned to the irresistible will of Calvin's God—this mannerist situation may lead to either desperate faith or desperate cynicism, neither tenable for long. Perhaps Hamlet could be played upon, he says, if one knew all his stops; yet we cannot pluck out the heart of his mystery, his uncontrolled responses driving him toward irreconcilable extremes, as if by accident. He yields to Providence only after feeling strange "excitements of my reason and my blood."

The mannerist situation is inherently "rich in directions," in discontinuities. In *The Duchess of Malfi* Bosola suffers unexplained reversals: "My trade," he says as he comes with hangmen to murder the Duchess, "is to flatter the dead, not the living; I am a tombmaker." Then after she is strangled, he is moved by some obscure mechanism of pro and contra and endures a reversal:

> These tears, I am very certain, never grew
> In my mother's milk; my estate is sunk
> Below the degree of fear; where were
> These penitent fountains while she was living?

The mad cruel Ferdinand, too, when he sees his dead sister suffers a reversal, and moved by some parapsychology, exclaims:

> Cover her face; mine eyes dazzle; she died young.

Donne's conversion from lust to holiness must have happened in some such way. Hamlet loves Ophelia so, we can hardly say how: fitfully, with divided mind, a puritan mind obsessed with the fatness of the flesh and

the rank sweat of enseamed beds. This is Hamlet's
madness. It may also have been El Greco's.

VI

UNRESOLVED TENSIONS   For art critics mannerism is a moment of dualism—a *Spannung,* a strain
not decisively resolved. That is why mannerist psychology and art are dramatic; because *the dramatic
act can accommodate opposites as logic cannot.* When
Donne stands upon his urn to be drawn in his shroud,
when Hamlet leaps into Ophelia's grave to struggle with
Laertes and to mouth, there is a vivid accommodation
of opposites by stagecraft without assuming the full
responsibility for a logical, moral, or spiritual resolution.

The task of the Council of Trent was to meet the
crisis in the mannerist conscience by a tactic of accommodation and artifice; to counter the challenge of Protestantism, to cleanse corruption within, and to attack
heresy. So the Council adopted a twofold program,
first, reaffirming certain dogmas, second, encouraging
the use of sacraments and rituals of piety such as the
veneration of images. There is this difference between
medieval and Counter-Reformation theology: the system of Aquinas was an argument and an exposition;
by contrast, Trent did not try to erect a coherent system of thought but to make a dogmatic statement of
the very premises of theology, requiring the faithful
to take a certain point of view arbitrarily defined by
the Church. The policy at Trent was to use *ex cathedra*
authority; its special technique was to pronounce
anathema. To support the Council, Pius IV in 1564 pro-
mulgated the Tridentine Profession of Faith, which
uses argument in the form of imperative, demanding

that the Christian believe *as follows*. After reaffirming
the Nicene Creed, the Profession continues: "nor will I
ever receive and interpret the Scripture except according to the unanimous consent of the Fathers." The
Council adjourned its sessions in 1563 with a solemn
invective against heretics—"Anathema, anathema!"
The first tactic of the Council, then, was to create an
effective program, not a theology. The Jesuits were entirely at one with this *ex cathedra* tactic, for Loyola
had urged in his *Spiritual Exercises* "That we may be
altogether of the same mind and in conformity with
the Church herself, if she shall have defined anything
to be black which to our eyes appears to be white, we
ought in like manner to pronounce it to be black."

According to this Jesuit policy, we must approach
God from the angle prescribed by the Church. If we do
so, we have a "sufficient" vision of truth. Tridentine
faith was, so to speak, as daringly controlled by a feat
of authority, an arbitrary perspective, as Tintoretto's
compositions, which create a very powerful illusion by
sweeping us along a diagonal into a pictorial world
where there is maximum dramatic shock but where, if
we think of it, things stand in shifting, unstable, or distorted relations. The more oblique, or dogmatic, the
angle of vision, the more dramatic can be the accommodation of situations that can hardly be adjusted
by logic. Mannerist dramas like *The Merchant of Venice*
are approached from a very arbitrary angle indeed to
accommodate Shylock the monster and Shylock the
injured Jew who asks, "If you prick us, do we not
bleed?" Logically the two Shylocks cannot be adjusted
to each other; dramatically they can—provided we look
at the situation in Venice and Belmont from certain
narrowly limited premises. If we stop to think, of
course, or try to bring consistency into such a vivid
dramatic accommodation of irreconcilables, the illusion vanishes. The accommodations one can make from

an arbitrary perspective and suspended premises certainly are no disadvantage for the dramatist or painter, whose purpose is to gain a certain kind of illusion; but they may prove a treacherous aid to faith, and medieval theology did not rely heavily upon any such dogmatic approach.

To foster piety the Council during its Session XXV approved the use of images for the invocation and veneration of saints and the Virgin; and in general it tried to give a dramatic immediacy to rituals of penance, contrition, confession, and absolution. Session XXII endorsed an essentially dramatic view of the Eucharist, the primal sacrament:

And whereas such is the nature of man, that, without external helps he cannot be easily upraised to the meditation of divine things: on this account has holy Mother Church instituted certain rites, to wit that certain things be pronounced in the mass in a softened, and others in a raised, tone. She has likewise made use of ceremonies, such as mystic benedictions, lights, fumigations of incense, vestments, and many other things of this kind . . . whereby both the majesty of so great a sacrifice might be recommended, and the minds of the faithful be excited, by these visible signs of religion and piety, to the contemplation of those most sublime things which lie hidden in this sacrifice.

For the performance of the Mass, too, can be a dramatic accommodation, like the venerating of images.

These rites seem to require exercising the sort of "concrete" imagination Donne employed in writing his verse, which has been defined as a poetry of extremely material image. Among metaphysical poets, it is said, a thought "terminates in the senses," and the state of a poet's sensibility is expressed by his reference to a physical object (an "objective correlative" as Eliot has it). But we misunderstand the nature of both Tridentine piety and metaphysical poetry if we think that either really does fulfill itself, or terminate, in the activity of the senses. Although Tridentine piety and metaphysical poetry both utilize, or *exploit*, the senses, there is no final resolution of the tensions of experience, for either, in sense experience alone. If the inward unrest of mannerist poetry and faith could really be released in the concrete image, then the tensions would be reduced by that image. We shall postpone discussing poetry, but must observe at once that the Council of Trent *distrusted* the very images it sanctioned, and cautioned strongly against worshiping the image itself: that would be idolatry. The warning is emphatic: images are "good and useful," and

due honor and veneration are to be awarded them; not that any divinity or virtue is believed to be in them, on account of which they are to be worshipped; or that anything is to be asked of them; or that confidence is to be reposed in images . . .; but because the honor which is shown unto them is referred to the prototypes which they represent.

To terminate worship in any activity of the senses is a perversion of piety; after all, the Council knew better than anyone that the senses are treacherous. In short, however convincing the image may be, the act of worship cannot be performed by adoring the icon. At another level of mannerist consciousness, John Donne discovered that sense experience is incomplete experience, that "no contact possible to flesh" allayed the fever of his love; and the concrete images seized by his imagination could not assuage, or even represent, the vexation of his spirit. Trent sanctioned the image only as a dramatic expediency.

The drama of Tridentine faith is a conflict between sense and soul—another half-medieval crisis in the mannerist situation. In Saint Teresa and Saint Ignatius Loyola the tension between soul and sense is as tight as it is in Donne's poems. Loyola's *Exercises* require "daily particular examinations of conscience"; the discipline of the conscience, however, demands that the exercitant "use the five senses" to stimulate a dramatic mode of prayer during which he exploits the faculties of sight, smell, taste, hearing, and touch. During its most ardent exertions the spirit must use the fleshly imagination, vividly "realizing" and "representing" the situations on which it must focus. The fifth exercise of the First Week is a meditation on hell, requiring the exercitant

to see in imagination the length, breadth, and depth of hell . . . the vast fires, and the souls enclosed, as it were, in bodies of fire, to hear the wailing, the howling, cries, and blasphemies; . . . with the sense of smell to perceive the smoke, the sulphur, the filth, and corruption, to taste the bitterness of tears . . .; with the sense of touch to feel the flames which envelop and burn the souls.

The fifth contemplation of the Second Week is an "application of the senses":

This consists in seeing in imagination the persons and in contemplating and meditating in detail the circumstances in which they are . . . to hear what they are saying, or what they might say . . . to smell the infinite fragrance and taste the infinite sweetness of the divinity. Likewise to apply these senses to the soul and its virtues . . . to apply the sense of touch, for example, by embracing and kissing the place where the persons stand or are seated. . . .

This intensely dramatic realization Saint Ignatius calls "the composition," as if the mind of the exercitant were a *camera obscura*. It is followed by a "colloquy"— an effort to talk with saints personally, to enter the heavenly world as if one walked upon a stage. There is a contemplation on the Nativity, imagined on the first day of the Second Week, representing Our Lady about nine months with child, seated on an ass and setting out from Nazareth:

This is a mental representation of the place. It will consist here in seeing in imagination the way from Nazareth to Bethlehem. Consider its length, its breadth; whether level, or through valleys and over hills. Observe also the place or cave where Christ is born; whether big or little; whether high or low; and how it is arranged; . . . seeing the persons, namely, Our Lady, Saint Joseph, the maid, and the Child Jesus after his birth. I will make myself a poor little unworthy slave, and as though present, look upon them, contemplate them, and serve them in their needs with all possible homage and reverence; . . . consider, observe, and contemplate what the persons are saying . . . what they are doing. . . . Close with a colloquy.

Always, Saint Ignatius warns, the exercises must be "suited and adapted to the needs of a soul disturbed" and to the condition of him engaging in them, that is, to his age, education, talent, and the degree of perfection he would attain.

The tension is more severe in Saint Teresa, who says that we are unlike angels because we have bodies. At times it seems as if her religious experience culminates in the senses. An angel appears "in bodily form" to wound her with a golden spear, causing an anguish like death, a "sharp and delightful" pain:

It pleased the Lord that I should see this Angel in the following way. He was not tall, but short, and very beautiful, his face so aflame that he appeared to be one of the highest types of angel who seem to be all afire. They must be those who are called cherubim. . . . In his hands I saw a long golden spear and at the end of an iron tip I seemed to see a point of fire. With this he seemed to pierce my heart several times so that it penetrated to my entrails. When he drew it out, I thought he was drawing them out with it and he left me completely afire with a great love of God. The pain was so sharp that it made me utter several moans; and so excessive was the sweetness caused me by the intense pain that one can never wish to lose it.

When her eyes are shut there comes the vision of the white Christ in the resurrected flesh, bleeding with thorns, and her soul exclaims, "O true Lover!" Yet, she protests, her flaming love "is *purely* spiritual, and has apparently nothing to do with sensuality or the tenderness of our nature." The body dies. Ignatius and

Teresa attain ecstasy by exploiting the sensorium; yet
however enthralling the experience of the senses may
be, the activity of the soul cannot culminate in the
senses. Their rapture is precarious, and can be sanctified only by discipline, scruple, and unceasing self-examination.

This is the Tridentine crisis of conscience. In 1599
the critic Guarini, speaking of tragedy, said that man
lives two lives, "one of the intellect and the other of
the senses." The vacillation between flesh and spirit is
the true metaphysical tension; and there is no resolution beyond a dramatic accommodation. In the ambiguity of the harshly dramatic act the mannerist psychology expresses what it cannot by other means represent.

Hence the irritability of Donne at the level of the
sensorium. The torment in Donne, like the torment in
Teresa, is that the senses do not suffice to consummate
experience yet are the medium of compelling experience—a mannerist dilemma. In "The Extasie" Donne
achieves rapture while he and his mistress lie upon a
bank, their hands cemented by a fast balm, their eye-
beams twisted, their souls gone out of their flesh to
hang between them:

> And whil'st our soules negotiate there,
> Wee like sepulchrall statues lay;
> All day, the same our postures were,
> And wee said nothing all the day.

For the instant, their love is grown—like renaissance
platonic love—all mind, and their sensibility is "unper-
plexed" by the interinanimating of their souls. Then
the poem closes with the old dualism of flesh and spirit;
the platonism fails, and when their love again speaks
the language of the flesh, the mannerist tension tight-
ens the old perplexities:

> Our bodies why doe wee forbeare?
> *They are ours, though they are not wee,* Wee are
> The intelligences, they the spheare. . . .

> So must pure lovers soules descend
> T'affections and to faculties,
> Which sense may reach and apprehend,
> Else a great prince in prison lies.
> T'our bodies turne wee then, that so
> Weake men on love reveal'd may looke;
> Loves mysteries in soules doe growe,
> But yet the body is his booke.

But Donne cannot, any more than Hamlet, rest at the level of the too-too solid flesh. He is caught either way: the body will not suffice, the soul will not suffice, to consummate experience. To his frustration, Donne finds that sense does not reach and apprehend love's mysteries. His ecstasy is jeopardy; his transcendent love begins and ends in the flesh; but the flesh is false, and there is no resolution. There is only the dramatic moment, in isolation, and a desperate conclusion that

> Love is a growing, or full constant light;
> And his first minute, after noone, is night.

The tension in George Herbert is between the poet's calm, assured piety and his agitated awareness of things in the world. He depends for his metaphors, as if he had drawn them from Caesar Ripa's *Iconology* (that manual for Counter-Reformation rhetoric), upon pulleys, glasses, floors, chests, perfumes, jewels, and every other ordinary object thrown into a succession of images quickly collected; then comes a sudden dramatic resolution that cannot be expressed in the senses, and which has nothing to do with the images piled up in the poem. Again, if the poem exploits the senses, it is not resolved within the medium of the senses.

Yet mannerist art has a "passionate naturalism" (*naturalisme passionné* says Focillon)—not only Cellini's, but also in Saint Teresa, Saint Ignatius, Donne, and Hamlet, who wishes to hold the mirror up to nature. Now that we know more of Caravaggio's development, we can trace the stages by which he used, at first, a

flimsy sort of genre-technique, then a "harsh and dras-
tic theatricality" that has been compared to Webster's,
and finally, in The Raising of Lazarus, an astonishing
expressionism. By turning away from the intellectual
formulas of the renaissance, Caravaggio created an ar-
resting somber drama played out brutally amid vulgar
scenes. In so doing he inspired a group of "tenebrist"
painters whose naturalism is closer to actualities than
Cellini's. But the mannerist actualities never really look
like actualities, whether in Caravaggio, Louis Le Nain,
or the still forms of Georges de la Tour. To be sure
Caravaggio makes his apostles and saints look like
peasants, and treats the "sacred" motif of the Call to
Saint Matthew as a sordid episode in a countinghouse;
his Martyrdom of Saint Matthew is a shocking execution, and in his Deposition the intensely painted body
of Christ is lowered into a grave by common workmen
while some disreputable women stand crowding and
gesticulating with uncouth grief. The same common
folk gather about the body of Mary in The Death of
the Virgin, the corpse looking as if Caravaggio "had
portrayed a courtesan" with bloated legs (the clergy
had the painting removed from the church of Santa
Maria della Scala in Rome because of this lack
of "decorum"). All these compositions are daring experiments in transforming the densest actualities by a
calculated arbitrary light that finally reduces Caravaggio's style to a savagely dramatic shorthand, one figure
in The Seven Works of Mercy being only "an ear and a
leg." The Call to Saint Matthew is not the less portentous because it happens at a counting (or gaming?)
table; the shock is heightened by the fierce glare upon
these shabby persons. The naturalism in Donne's poem
"The Dream" is of this passionate and scandalous sort,
his mistress having come to him at midnight, and unexpectedly, like some figure from a tenebrist painting:

Deare love, for nothing lesse than thee
Would I have broke this happy dreame,
　　It was a theame
For reason, much too strong for phantasie. . . .
Enter these armes, for since thou thought'st it best
Not to dreame all my dreame, let's act the rest.

This is like Hamlet's outrageous public jesting with
Ophelia. Yet this seduction (or adultery) is poetic because it is seen, as if with Caravaggio's lurid eye, from
the violent angle of Donne's perplexed, exploited, and
curiously mechanical egoism, which foreshortens the
"actualities" of his world by a willful perspective. Mannerist naturalism always carries a psychological charge.

VII

SHIFTING PLANES OF REALITY　　From the
arbitrary dramatic angle, actualities often appear to be
illusions. Take the intense actuality in Velázquez'
Maids of Honor (1656), a belated mannerist composition to which the beholder must at once adjust himself
as if he had opened the wrong door—right there before
us is the great edge of Velázquez' own canvas, the
painter himself staring at us, as we glance at the hesi-
tating little Princess and her maids, and at the painter's
"brother" turning toward us in the light beyond the
doorway. Suddenly we realize that we must be looking
at the scene through the eyes of the King and Queen,
who are there, like ourselves, by the theatrical implication of the mirror dimly reflecting the royal presence. No composition could better suggest how mannerist painters, by inverting perspective, transformed
aesthetic to introspective space. Presently we do adapt
our vision as we do when a curtain rises in a theater;
but we know, too, that things will in a moment change;

Velázquez will go on painting, and his brother will step from the doorway and revise all the spatial relations in this world. The most "actual" mannerist worlds paradoxically deny the stability of the world. We half expect Velázquez' Rokeby Venus to *turn around*. Rembrandt, in a mannerist moment, has caught his Syndics just as they have been taken off guard by some question from the floor. Bronzino's sitters glance at us only by chance. The light will soon change the structure of a Pieter de Hooch interior. In mannerist art there is no Being, but only Becoming; it has passed outside the aesthetic realm of renaissance art and discovered the existential. We could say of Velázquez or Vermeer what the critics say of Donne: the actuality of his images energizes the mind to higher levels of perception. The most mysterious Velázquez-world is probably The Tapestry Weavers ("The Spinners"), which is also his most ordinary world.

In Shakespeare's last plays, we are told, the planes of reality shift. *Cymbeline*, for instance, accommodates two or three different worlds in multiple perspective: the vicious world of Italian intrigue ruled by the yellow Iachimo; the political-historical world of Cymbeline's court ruled by the evasive Queen and her stinking, bestial son Cloten; the fanciful "mountainous country with a cave" where live Belarius and his sons who guard the innocent Imogen. When the illusion is so complex, it is possible for Cloten to woo Imogen with that crystal lyric "Hark, hark the lark at heaven's gate sings"; and for Imogen to find Cloten's headless body and embrace it. In *The Tempest* the many planes of reality dissolve into each other until Prospero's world seems to be the stuff of dreams. Yet this insubstantial pageant can accommodate the murderous Antonio, the brutal Caliban, and the sottish Trinculo as well as Miranda and sage Gonzalo. It is a world where Caliban can seek for grace and hear sweet airs and twangling instruments that make him cry to dream again. It is a world of sea-change, where each man is most himself when he is not his own.

Mannerism completes the transformations that had begun to take place in renaissance arts, and brings the aesthetic world into more complex, variable relations with the world where we live. What is the relation between *Hamlet* and life? We cannot fix this play within any one context, just as we cannot hold Cellini's relief of Perseus Delivering Andromeda within any one spatial scheme, for the figure of Perseus emerges to enter our own space; Andromeda is already there, beyond him, her arm extended directly toward us. Quite like the mannerist playwright, Cervantes complicates his perspectives—improvising, swerving, yielding to the moment—not satirically always but with awareness that the world can be looked at from above and below, as romance and pathos, by Sancho and Don Quixote. Like Montaigne, Cervantes is neutral. The reality of madness and the madness of reality; we never know which Cervantes is presenting. Quixote says to the Duchess, "God knows whether Dulcinea exists on earth or no, or whether she is fantastic or not fantastic. These are not matters whose verification can be carried out to the full." But he insists that "love and fancy easily blind the eyes of the understanding, which are so necessary for choosing one's estate." And he has Hamlet's suspicion that his mind may be tainted: "I most certainly know that I am enchanted." What does Hamlet mean when he says to Ophelia, "Go to, it hath made me mad"? Like Parmigianino or Velázquez, Cervantes deliberately raises the question about the reality of his fiction: "When the translator of this history comes to write this fifth chapter, he declares that he considers it apocryphal, because in it Sancho's style is much superior to what one would expect of his limited understanding, and his remarks so subtle that they seem beyond the

range of his intelligence." Shakespeare, too, reminds his
audience in *Midsummer Night's Dream* that "the best
in this kind are but shadows."

The distances between life and art are all uncertain
in *Lycidas, perhaps the greatest mannerist poem*, and
one where the planes of reality are so interchanging
and complex that we shall never be able to "read" it
better than we "read" *Hamlet*. In *Lycidas* the young
Milton is using in a very personal willful way the traditional elegy, just as Michaelangelo, earlier, used the
traditional orders of architecture in a willful personal
way in the anteroom of the Laurentian Library. Edward King is dead, and Milton, too self-consciously,
must exhibit his talent prematurely; this striking self-
awareness gives to the elegiac formula with its *mondain* air of sophisticated and vocal grief a very private
and expressive accent. Lycidas must not float unwept:
but clearly this poetic occasion does not account for
Milton's disturbance any more than Gertrude accounts
for Hamlet's. First, the ceremonial lament, the backward glance at Old Damoetas, the resumption of the
pose of grief with appeals to those bloodless Nymphs,
those austere Muses, and the abstract Universal Nature
—figurines like the thin, chill, elegant forms painted by
the School of Fontainebleau. Then, amid these learned
and classic niceties, the hideous roar as the gory visage
of Orpheus is borne down the swift Hebrus; and the
urgent question whether it were not better to sport
with Amaryllis or with Neaera's hair; and the desperate
fear that the blind Fury may slit the thin-spun life—the
young Milton's life! After a brief appeal to the waves
and felon winds comes the inexplicably stern outburst
of the dread Puritan voice, the onslaught against blind
mouths, the menace of the two-handed engine. This is
hot anger and contempt, very private, entirely out of
context. Without any transition whatever, Milton again
shifts perspective:

> . . . return Sicilian muse,
> And call the vales, and bid them hither cast
> Their bells and flowrets of a thousand hues. . . .

The line "Throw hither all your quaint enameled eyes"
shows how Spenser's illustrative art was transformed
under the stress of Milton's powerful psychological accent. There is no accounting, either, for the inscrutable
pathos of "Look homeward angel, now, and melt with
ruth." Then the false and formal inflation of the celestial triumph with solemn troops and sweet societies.
The gentle modulation of the closing landscape might
have been imagined by Claude Lorrain; it belongs in
another style, the picturesque:

> And now the sun had stretched out all the hills,
> And now was dropt into the western bay.

Finally, and possibly most disconcerting of all the shifts,
there is Milton's youthful eagerness, this lament done,
to turn to fresh woods and pastures new. All this, we
remind ourselves, is supposedly about Edward King.
What could possibly account for this erratic performance with its frigidity, its discouragement and tenderness, its rage, its callow hope, and its pictorial harmony? The world of *Lycidas* is as complex as that of
Cymbeline.

The poem reveals that the strangeness and power of
mannerist art are in its intervals and discontinuities—
not its co-ordinations—and in its irregular stresses and
wrenched accents. The phrases of a mannerist poem
gain dramatic force when they are isolated: then they
exist vibrantly and poetically, deprived of context:

> A bracelet of bright hair about the bone . . .

> I shall be made thy musique as I come. . . .

> And now good morrow to our waking soules. . . .

> So close the ground, and 'bout her shade
> Black curtains draw, my bride is laid . . .

Similarly, one of the mannerist devices in portrait groups is to isolate the figures, at a moment of dramatic tension, against a black or green plane; this explains the "attack" of Giambattista Moroni's rather mechanical single figures, and Bronzino's. In the Titian-Giorgione *Concert* the sympathetic and tense figures, held in suspended relations that can only be called potential, are arrested amid a strongly implied but wholly unwritten drama. Apparently the mannerist painter did not feel the need of providing a context for the psychological language of the mannerist hero. Nor did Shakespeare in *Hamlet*.

The power of the isolated phrase is a mark of the "disintegration" occurring in mannerist art, as is also the constantly shifted level of statement from extreme concreteness to abstraction, as we find it not alone in *Lycidas* but in a less complex poem like Herbert's "Prayer":

> Prayer, the Church's banquet, angel's age,
> God's breath in man returning to his birth,
> The soul in paraphrase, heart in pilgrimage,
> The Christian plummet sounding heaven and earth.
> Engine against th'Almightie, sinner's towre,
> Reversed thunder, Christ-side-piercing speare,
> The six-day's-world-transposing in an houre,
> A kind of tune, which all things heare and feare.
> Softness, and peace, and joye, and love, and blisse,
> Exalted manna, gladnesse of the best,
> Heaven in ordinarie, man well drest,
> The milkie way, the bird of Paradise,
> Church-bells beyond the starres heard, the soul's blood,
> The land of spices, something understood.

The leaps from concrete to conceptual statement in Sir Thomas Browne's prose may partly be due to the author's belief that man is "that great and true amphibium, whose nature is disposed to live, not only like other creatures in divers elements, but in divided and distinguished worlds: for though there be but one to sense, there are two to reason, the one visible, the other invisible." In the nature of man, Browne advises us, there are united "incompatible distances." Thus in his "Valediction" John Donne can express his love most spiritually by using images of gold to airy thinness beat, and of stiff twin compasses. Webster reaches his full tragic dimension by using the nausea-image of the dying Duchess of Malfi:

> . . . Come violent death,
> Serve for mandragora, to make me sleep!——
> Go, tell my brothers, when I am laid out,
> *They then may feed in quiet.*

These intervals open only in a world that does not cohere; they are almost mysterious in Donne's "Nocturnall Upon S. Lucie's Day," a poem that moves across incompatible distances:

> But I am none; nor will my sunne renew.
> You lovers, for whose sake the lesser sunne
> At this time to the Goat is runne
> To fetch new lust, and give it you,
>   Enjoy your summer all;
> Since shee enjoyes her long night's festivall,
> Let mee prepare towards her, and let mee call
> This hour her vigill, and her eve, since this
> Both the yeares, and the dayes deep midnight is.

The cruel plot of *The Duchess of Malfi* develops in some darkness where the love of the Duchess and Antonio seems not to belong to the world into which they are cast. Antonio says despairingly:

> Heaven fashioned us of nothing, and we strive
> To bring ourselves to nothing. . . .

Tintoretto must have had some such vision when he painted on the wall of the Ducal Palace in Venice a Paradise that has the dissonance of hell; its white souls dance wildly within the ultimate night.

Nowhere in mannerist painting are the intervals more vibrant than in the great Crucifixion in the Scuola

di San Rocco, Venice, where Tintoretto dissolved the
world in space as Rembrandt was presently to dissolve
it in light: the double wedge of space about the giant
cross which trembles in its rising; the oval of the middle
ground vanishing in two reversed semicircles, one
opening upward, the other downward; the rectangle of
the enclosing group broken into smaller oblongs and
triangles; the masses at the left unbalanced by the diagonal pressures at the right. This composition is
phrased in the doubtful mannerist language—a dialogue (*Zwiesprache*) Pevsner calls it; and all is suspended (*alles bleibt in der Schwebe*). The tensions are
not relieved even by the ascetic gray tonality of which
the painter Fuseli wrote that it engulfed "the whole in
one mass of ominous twilight, an eclipse, or what pre-
cedes a storm or hurricane or earthquake." The tempest
eventually broke, we might say, in Lear's thought-ex-
ecuting fires that cracked nature's mold, spilled nature's germens, and left man a poor forked animal
unable to carry the affliction and the fear. This eclipse
darkened Tintoretto's world—a world which opens in
oblique directions, and is constructed along some daring curve of probability. But a feverish drama can be
played there.

NOTES

*1. It would be hard to overstress the importance of Sidney
J. Freedberg's meticulous analysis in his* Parmigianino *for
anyone who wishes to understand the spirit and technique
of mannerism. Although Freedberg takes a strictly historical
approach to his subject and scrupulously limits his interpretation of mannerist "psychology," his comment is indispensable to literary criticism, and in the following paragraphs I have not hesitated to adopt his terminology and
extend his implications while summarizing his views. To understand the psychoanalytic implications of mannerist style,
which can be seen as a distortion of renaissance forms and
a reaction against the unconsciously repressed forces of renaissance art, see Anton Ehrenzweig:* Psycho-Analysis of

Artistic Vision and Hearing, *1953, chaps. 9, 12, and 16.*

2. Of the many Continental art historians who have written on mannerism I have relied chiefly in the following discussion upon Erwin Panofsky (Idea), *Nikolaus Pevsner* (Barockmalerei in den Romanischen Laendern), *Walter Friedlaender ("Die Entstehung des Antiklassischen Stiles,"* Repertorium fuer Kunstwissenschaft, *1925*), *and Hans Hoffmann* (Hochrenaissance, Manierismus, Fruehbarock). *On this account I have preserved the German terminology that is sometimes hard to translate adequately.*

3. Rosemond Tuve's Elizabethan and Metaphysical Imagery *proves that metaphysical poetry is not so "unconventional" as was once supposed. However, I have stressed the perhaps more balanced opinion of J. B. Leishman, whose* Monarch of Wit *emphasizes the personal tone of Donne's verses, their "inner vibration." Similarly, in talking about Jacobean drama I have accepted Clifford Leech's opinion that Webster makes an "exploration of the individual" in his plays of "infirm orientation" with many "blurred meanings" and "a minimum of formal articulation"* (John Webster, 1951).

4. My remarks of Michaelangelo here and in the next paragraphs, and on the asymmetrical techniques in mannerism generally, are drawn largely from Pevsner (Outline of European Architecture) *and his article on "The Architecture of Mannerism"* (The Mint); *also from an invaluable article by Wittkower, "Michaelangelo's Biblioteca Laurenziana"* (Art Bulletin, 1934), *reviewing the methods of mannerist architecture.*

5. The account of these changes in English prose style in the seventeenth century summarizes Morris W. Croll's article "The Baroque Style in Prose" (Studies in Honor of Frederick Klaeber).

6. Clifford Leech: Shakespeare's Tragedies, *1950, p. 44.*

7. Una Ellis-Fermor takes this view of the play in Jacobean Drama.

BAROQUE

I

REINTEGRATION   As John Donne well knew, renaissance humanism had not succeeded in exorcising all the devils that can worry the Christian soul. The Council of Trent hoped to banish such devils by its resolute optimism, "having this aim always before its eyes, that errors may be removed" if Christians obey its holy and ecumenical decrees. Seeking to vanquish Protestants, skeptics, and heretics, the Council urged the priest to avoid raising "the more difficult and subtler questions which do not tend to edification" and to reaffirm the essentials of sound doctrines "believed, held, taught, and everywhere preached." When it closed in 1563, it had given new sanctions to dogma and inspired new and moving rites of piety. Even while cautioning against worldliness, it was willing to exercise temporal authority—the authority soon to be claimed outright in Cardinal Bellarmine's tract *De Potestate summi Pontificis in rebus temporalibus* (Concerning the Supreme Sovereignty of the Pope in Temporal Affairs, 1610). Thus the Council, which had convened in a climate of mannerist doubt, laid the foundations for a settlement in theology and a reintegration of style in the arts, the baroque acceptance of secular pomp and the sufficiency of the flesh. When the Council had done its work, the arts moved with gathering momentum toward full declarations of power and glory expressed, during the abundant years of piety between 1620 and 1680, in Roman churches by Borromini, Cortona, and Carlo Rainaldi, in sculpture and architecture by Bernini, in painting by Rubens, who was nourished upon the harmonies of Titian and the facility of Tintoretto. Counteracting the mannerist instability, baroque asserts its "gigantic excelsior" in the façades of Sant' Agnese in Agone, San Carlo alle Quattro Fontane, and Santa Maria della Pace, and in Bernini's Piazza San Pietro and his Saint Teresa sculpture in Santa Maria della Vittoria. This art speaks with the voluminous tones of a new orthodoxy, for the Council of Trent announced its decrees with majestic voice; it overwhelmed heresy by splendor; it did not argue, but proclaimed; it brought conviction to the doubter by the very scale of its grandeurs; it guaranteed truth by magniloquence. The baroque style reaches its decisions through spectacle. It resolves the uncertainties in mannerist art by overstatement in the flesh, energy, mass, space, height, color, and light. After the bloodless and shrunken mannerist forms, the baroque is a style of plenitude, capable of absorbing, and robustly transforming to grandeur, every sort of realism. It is an art given to superlatives.

For another reason, also, the Council of Trent is a watershed in the cultural history of Western Europe: it controlled the last epoch of Italian (in this event, Roman) dominance in architecture, sculpture, and, perhaps, painting. During the years following the Council, the Italians gradually yielded, amid the glory of baroque itself, the ascendancy in painting to the transalpine artists who, having little more to learn from Italy, returned northward, where Rubens brought baroque to its pictorial maturity. Meanwhile El Greco and Velázquez were carrying mannerist painting through its Spanish phase, while Rembrandt, continuing Tintoretto's experiment with flickering light, reached a final iridescence of vision. Baroque architecture, having triumphed in Rome, was presently to be revised in France and England toward more academic forms—the forms of a late-baroque style. In literature the North had never conceded anything to Italy even during the renaissance and mannerist eras; and if the supreme baroque architecture and sculpture are attained in Rome, the supreme baroque literature appears not in Tasso, who lacks the full baroque energy, but in Milton's *Paradise Lost* and *Samson Agonistes*. We can hardly find an adequate analogy to these baroque poems unless we look to the architecture of Bernini or to the Roman churches like Sant' Agnese in Agone. Even while Milton remains stubbornly anti-papist and Puritan by doctrine, these two poems represent the fruition of a Counter-Reformation style in literature.

Further, we must recall what an amazing century was the seventeenth, producing not only Cervantes, the ripe Shakespeare, and Donne, but also Milton, Dryden, Corneille, Molière, and Racine; not only Caravaggio, Velázquez, and Vermeer, but also Rubens, Rembrandt, Bernini, Borromini, François Mansart, Le Nôtre, and Wren, along with the Poussins and Claude Lorrain; not only Descartes and Pascal, Spinoza and Locke, but also Galileo and Newton. It is indeed "a century of genius." In the arts it encompassed not one style, or two styles, but the astonishing total of three—the height of mannerism, baroque, and late-baroque—or four, or five, if we choose to trace rococo and picturesque to their origins. Considering the fertility of this era, we can understand how the Council of Trent presided over two distinct phases of western-European consciousness and style: a mannerist phase and a baroque phase, a phase of disintegration and of reintegration in techniques. Is it to be wondered that the artists of this century should sometimes practice, simultaneously, more than one style, or reveal a development through successive phases; from mannerism to baroque, to, in some instances, late-baroque styles? Just as Milton passes from the renaissance calm and equilibrium of *Comus* through the mannerist agitations of *Lycidas* to the baroque diapason of *Paradise Lost,* so also architects like Vignola, Maderna, and Bernini pass through an early mannerist phase to the splendors of high-baroque structures like Saint Peter's; and Caravaggio, like Rembrandt, has a mannerist and a baroque aspect.

Both mannerism and baroque are authentic styles; yet we must always have in mind that baroque art often derives directly from the "grand style" of the high-renaissance and also has a kinship with that form of art known as "academic." Indeed, baroque accepts from the art of the high-renaissance—from Raphael's School of Athens, for example—a classic tradition and form, the influence of which is apparent through late-baroque style. More often than not the distinction formerly made between baroque and academic or "eclectic" art seems unwise, for reasons we shall presently consider. Painters like Paolo Veronese generate a baroque style within the conventions of high-renaissance art; and Rubens, however indebted to Tintoretto and other mannerists, surely is equally an heir of Michaelangelo and Titian and the later renaissance. From this point of view mannerism looks like a momentary deviation from the major current of style running from the high-renaissance through baroque to late-baroque. In any case we must not assume that a mannerist phase always intervenes between renaissance and baroque styles. In Guido Reni's painting, for instance, where Raphael's "classicism" reappears in titanic scale, the continuity between renaissance and baroque is obvious, just as it is obvious between *Comus* and *Paradise Lost.* Then too, certain art historians faced with the problems of Caravaggio's troubled but monumental paintings treat late forms of mannerism as being "early-baroque." In spite of these affiliations between renaissance and baroque, between late-mannerism and early-baroque, and between baroque and academism, baroque art is, in general, a reaction against the unstable, involved, and over-ingenious structures of mannerism, and is a distinct style with its own laws of composition.

Occasionally literary critics speak of baroque as if it were simply a reckless burst of energy, an emotional explosion; as if baroque were not a style with a formal canon of structure. Rather, Geoffrey Scott is more accurate when he says that baroque "remains subject rigidly to the laws of scale and composition. . . . It enlarged the classic formula . . . the movement is logical. For baroque architecture is always logical." We should expect as much, considering that baroque, if not *always* logical, is the orthodox style of the Counter Reformation, and that the Counter Reformation was based upon the well-defined neoscholasticism of the Council of Trent. Mannerist art had its own structural laws: diagonal or mobile point of view, disproportion, imbalance, thwarted verticality, funnel space, double functioning of members, contraction of materials, excess within rigid boundaries, shifting levels of statement, uncertain intervals, and tensions that were accommodated rather than resolved. The controlling laws of baroque are especially significant as a counteraction to the dissonant forces in mannerist art; for baroque style openly and *formally* resolves the mannerist tensions in dense masses of material, redundant statement, kinetic energy, an elevated center of gravity, a broadening and consolidating of the foreground plane, a monumental academic balance, and flashing color and light. Baroque is indeed an extravagant style; but it is no mere explosion. There is a "law for exuberance," so to speak, and having fixed his point of view, the baroque artist adopts a tactic of, first, negation, then strong affirmation, which gives a special illusion of release into "distance" and "infinity." It becomes increasingly clear that there is no necessary opposition between baroque and academic art, since both academism and baroque obey many of the same laws of structure.

In general, then, baroque art has an effect of decision, release, and fulfillment, and resonantly declares the glories of heaven and earth. After the crisis in mannerist conscience, with its repressions, defections, complexities, and double evasive answers, its dissonant, involved contours, baroque performs a mighty katharsis by spectacle, by an expressive power. The baroque canon of style does not depend upon mannerist contingencies, but upon assurances and certainties—certainties lacking the mannerist subtlety and discrimination. These certainties, confidently affirmed, are exhilarating to the eye even if they are not wholly convincing to the mind. But then, baroque is able to win assent from the spirit through its power over the sensorium alone.

II

RESOLUTION IN THE FLESH Passionate as was the naturalism of mannerist art—in Cellini, in Donne, in Webster, in Tintoretto—it was troubled and constrained, and yielded none of that healthy amplitude we feel in Rubens' Garden of Love or Borromini's interior of Sant' Agnese in Agone. For baroque has a plastic abundance, and takes delight in the potency of the material (Woelfflin's useful phrase is *die Freude an der Stoffgewalt*).[1] About a century after Vignola's awkwardly restrained plan for the Gesù façade (*c.* 1569) comes Rainaldi's invigorating façade of Santa Maria in Campitelli (*c.* 1656–65) having two stories of harmoniously grouped columns supporting mighty pediments. One of the most characteristic baroque devices is redundance, clustering columns and pilasters, compounding orders, setting a triangular within a semi-

circular pediment, or doubling the dome, as in Saint
Cecilia's chapel in San Carlo ai Catinari, where voluptuous brackets on the lower half-dome support, or
seem to support, a smaller oval dome, the surfaces of
both domes being encrusted with *putti* and angels
clambering over the balconies of the higher dome in
waves, giving the whole structure a licentious Rubens-
like pulsation.

Baroque forms have a corporeality (*Koerperlichkeit*)
partly because the baroque artist does not carve his
material, but models it. Renaissance sculpture gave a
carved effect even when it was as colossal as Michaelangelo's; but baroque expands its volumes from within,
so that the cartouche is a basic baroque motif. When we
contrast renaissance painting by Piero della Francesca
and Mantegna, who are often called "sculptural," with
painting by Rubens, we recognize that Piero's and
Mantegna's figures are really "carved," whereas those
in Rubens are "modeled" as if the color and volume
were built up by an accretion of pigment about an
armature. By means of this pictorial increment Rubens
is able to "expand" his forms in a wealth of "fat" textures. Much baroque painting, and almost all baroque
architecture and sculpture, are vigorously "haptic," giving us a maximum tactile value and being "felt" in the
viscera and the finger-ends as well as on the retina.
The coarse, but convincing, baroque forms are sur-
charged with the density of the medium, which the
artist spends generously. Through this ability to model,
baroque art gains one of its most powerful illusions,
for so prodigally does it accumulate its materials that
it gives an impression of transvaluing matter to expanding force. When Bernini designed the baldachino over
the high altar in Saint Peter's, he used swelling tortile
columns as a means of resisting the weight of the huge
space at the crossing where this canopy stands, ex-
pending its golden energy freely in lavish curves which

are repeated in the giant rhythms of the surrounding sculptures. The baroque statue, also, bulges into the space about it. Space itself can be modeled by the baroque artist, as Bernini demonstrates outside, in the Piazza San Pietro, where the void before the basilica expands into a heroic theater bounded by the mighty doubled arcades.

The materialism of baroque art is justified theologically by certain recommendations and doctrines of the Council of Trent, notably the permission to use images, and the dogma of transubstantiation. We know that the Council had a good many scruples about the veneration of images, warning the devout at every turn that the image itself is not to be taken as "substantial" of the spiritual reality behind the image; "confidence" was not to be placed in the icon as such. We know, too, that mannerist piety was tormented by a tension between experience in the flesh and experience in the soul. Thus the mannerist consciousness dealt equivocally, if vividly, with the body, and the ascetic, constrained, troubled forms of mannerist art and piety testify that neither Saint Teresa, El Greco, nor Donne could be satisfied by the physical sensation.

However, by sanctioning the veneration of images and by its emphasis upon transubstantiation the Council, in effect, gave the pious a confidence in sensory experience and offered a means of reducing the anxiety in mannerist consciousness, relaxing the tension between body and soul. For baroque piety and art are able to consolidate and fulfill experience at the level of the flesh, and they do so ardently, triumphantly, unthinkingly. If the image is sufficiently powerful, if the physical sensation is adequately enriched, the crisis in mannerist conscience can be resolved in the external, material world, and by the "visible signs of religion and piety." The act of faith can be performed and terminated, literally, in the senses. Besides, in Session XIII the Council had reformulated the dogma of transubstantiation, according to which the bread and wine consecrated during the Mass become the very body and blood of Christ, which are eaten and drunk in performing the sacrament. At the consecration of the host, the Council insisted, "a conversion takes place of the whole substance of the wine into the substance of His blood," and "Christ whole and entire is under the species (appearance) of the bread, and under any part whatsoever of that species; likewise the whole Christ is under the species of wine and under its parts." Without intending to equivocate, the Council declared that Christ's actual body and blood are consumed; when the conversion takes place, the spirit becomes flesh, and the material of the bread and wine becomes spiritual food. During this ceremony, therefore, the spiritual experience can be represented and consummated at the level of the flesh. Indeed, according to the new "baroque scholasticism" of Suarez and the Counter-Reformation theologians, essence and existence cannot be distinguished; for when existence is given, essence is implied, and in essence actual existence is included. The dualism of body and soul is thus reconciled.

Of course the Council did not wish to sanction materialism by either its theory of transubstantiation or its tolerance of images. Yet baroque piety and baroque art alike modified, or corrupted, the doctrine of transubstantiation; the flesh did not become spiritual—the spiritual became fleshly. As soon as 1600 in Italy the early-baroque painters, sculptors, and architects were reacting against the asceticism in mannerist art; the "anti-mannerist" Italian painters turned from the bloodless, spare, strained, and contorted mannerist forms toward an art capable of representing the solidity of the body. The new anti-mannerist naturalism appears in the early Caravaggio, who shows, in spite of his tenebrist somber vision, a concern to get back to "reality." This reaction against mannerism expressed itself as a "secularizing of the transcendental" (Walter Friedlaender's phrase is *die Verweltlichen des Transzendenten*). No phrase could better describe what was happening in baroque art and piety, which often transfused the spirit with the flesh instead of transfusing the flesh with the spirit. Presently the transcendent was to be secularized by accepting the material image, the physical sensation, as sufficient. Then both religion and art can really terminate in the senses, and thought does really become a physical experience.

Crashaw may be the most characteristic poet of baroque piety; and Crashaw gives to the conceit, and to wit, a sensuousness more ornate and voluptuous than appears in the other English devotional poets like George Herbert. Crashaw yields easily to his ardor, which expresses itself in recurrent images of tears, sighs, fragrance, and harmony; his prevailing tone is one of fulfillment, surrender, relaxation, and dissolution in joys—"Sweetness so sad, sadness so sweet." After the tensions in high-gothic art there was a moment of *détente;* after the double-mindedness of mannerism, its severities, Crashaw's saints die delicious deaths:

> Like a soft lump of incense, hasted
> By too hot a fire, and wasted,
> Into perfuming clouds: so fast
> Shalt thou exhale to heaven at last
> In a dissolving sigh.

The very titles of his poems suggest how they illustrate the iconography of painters like Guido Reni: "Upon the Crown of Thorns," "Upon the Bleeding Crucifix," "Upon the Body of Our Blessed Lord," "Saint Mary Magdalene, or The Weeper," "Sancta Maria Dolorum." The name of Jesus is itself a "display of bright joys," "an universal synod of all sweets," a balmy shower, a nectarean fragrance:

> Sweet name, in Thy each syllable
> A thousand blest Arabias dwell;
> A thousand hills of frankincense;
> Mountains of myrrh, and beds of spices,
> And ten thousand Paradises.

His translation of the Jesuit Strada's poem on the nightingale, "Music's Duel," is a flood of liquid melody, a tender warbling harmony that swells to "a tide of streaming sweetness," a whirlwind peal, a torrent of a voice that expires in "a full-mouth diapason" and a ravishing death of song. At the full range of his delight Crashaw attains, for one instant, the fierceness of Saint Teresa's vision and enters the fiery kingdom of intellectual day, where the bowl of desire is "brim-filled." But ordinarily Crashaw does not burn away the flesh in flaming revelation, and is able to enjoy, instead, more imaginable spectacles of heavenly bliss, which satiate, if they do not consume, and glitter cheerfully in an aromatic radiance where

> . . . a sovereign ray
> Beats bright upon the burning faces
> Of souls, which in that Name's sweet graces
> Find everlasting smiles.

This revolution from mannerist distrust of the flesh to baroque release in the flesh marks the shift from the art of Donne and *Hamlet* to the art of *Paradise Lost*. In speaking of that essentially mannerist play *Hamlet*, T. S. Eliot aptly said that the Prince's reactions are continually "in excess of the facts as they appear." That is, Hamlet overresponds to the situation in which he is put, and therefore the drama is played inside his consciousness in a theater with a subjective focus; it cannot be fully played in the external world of Denmark. So also the mannerist painter "operates from within" by having some sort of subjective focus, a *disegno interno*. In *Hamlet*, says Eliot, there is no adequate theatrical "objective correlative" for expressing the

Prince's emotions. Eliot defines an "objective correlative" as being "a set of objects, a situation, a chain of events which shall be the formula of that *particular* emotion; such that when the external facts, which must terminate in sensory experience, are given, the emotion is immediately evoked." Any such formula gives us proof of "the complete adequacy of the external to the emotion." To be sure, there is not in this mannerist drama any "accumulation of imagined sensory impressions" to "objectify" Hamlet's excessive disgust; the play does indeed lack any theatrical objective formula to "project" its meaning unequivocally.

Unwittingly Eliot is indicating that in the realm of mannerist art satisfactory objective correlatives are not provided. Few of the mannerist "formulas" (that is, images or acts) are adequate to express the emotions that gather about them. Donne's most famous poetic image—in "A Valediction: forbidding Mourning" when the poet speaks of himself and his mistress as being the legs of a compass, the inner leg being his lady, he being the outer leg—is surely not an adequate formula to express the gentle meanings or to resolve the internal tensions. Material, actualized, as the compass-metaphor is, neither the object nor the logic represents the quality of the poet's response or his view of his situation; indeed, a double strain arises when it becomes apparent that Donne *himself* is aware of the incongruity and inadequacy of his strained image, and has used it as a provoking understatement of his feeling rather than as an adequate formula for that feeling. Donne "reserves," as it were, his mood, and tantalizes us by his image. Thus the compass is a typical "metaphysical" (mannerist) image precisely *because* it is an ambiguous and paradoxical objective correlative for the love or other values associated with it or embodied in it. Its intellectualism diverges from the poet's emotional direction. We are surprised at the degree by which Donne's affection exceeds his mechanical metaphor, and the disparity between the rational-material image and the lyrical feeling is left, impudently, unmediated. In the language of the art critic, Donne has willfully "contracted his material" in this metaphor until the compass serves as an objective correlative only by wrenching the logic and feeling. Obviously Donne uses this compass-image with a consciousness of its limitations. He is not *committed* to his image.

The situation in Milton's *Lycidas* is not dissimilar, and this elegy has no adequate objective correlative, in either the death of Edward King or its pastoral mechanics, by which to project Milton's own severe rebellion, his fear, his hope. Paradoxically, this "exercise" in a very pagan form is used to express one of Milton's most strongly felt religious crises. By contrast with this unexpectedly private and thinking poem, *Paradise Lost*—ostensibly a work of Puritan piety—is coarse and secular, and more obviously "projected."

That is, unlike *Lycidas, Paradise Lost* finds its objective correlative, its formula of images, action, and characters that insure a complete adequacy of the external situation to the emotion. *Paradise Lost* makes its resolutions sweepingly at the level of "an accumulation of sensory impressions." It is an "inevitable" poem in Eliot's sense that when these material images and vistas are before us, they immediately evoke "that particular emotion" for which they provide a sufficient representation. Remembering Donne's compass-image, and the unresolved tensions in *Lycidas,* let us glance at Adam and Eve in their connubial paradise, a gorgeous fleshly spectacle to which Milton is fully and rather unthinkingly committed, and which *creates* a confidence by its very overplus, its abundant corporeality (*Koerperlichkeit*):

> Thus talking hand in hand alone they pass'd
> On to thir blissful bower; it was a place

> Chos'n by the sovran Planter, when he fram'd
> All things to man's delightful use; the roofe
> Of thickest covert was inwoven shade
> Laurel and mirtle, and what higher grew
> Of firm and fragrant leaf; on either side
> Acanthus, and each odorous bushie shrub
> Fenc'd up the verdant wall; each beauteous flour,
> Iris all hues, roses, and gessamin,
> Rear'd high thir flourist heads between . . .
> . . . Here in close recess
> With flowers, garlands, and sweet-smelling herbs,
> Espoused Eve deckt first her nuptial bed,
> And heav'nly quires the hymenaean sung
> What day the genial Angel to our Sire
> Brought her in naked beauty, more adorn'd,
> More lovely then Pandora, whom the gods
> Endow'd with all thir gifts . . .
> . . . into thir inmost bowre
> Handed they went; and eas'd the putting off
> These troublesom disguises which wee wear,
> Strait side by side were laid, nor turn'd I weene
> Adam from his fair spouse, nor Eve the rites
> Mysterious of connubial love refus'd . . .

Such is the plenitude of baroque. The plastic realization more than suffices to express the rather naive sexual
response Milton entertains on this occasion. If we are
seeking evidence of a "unified sensibility" in poetry,
we shall find it in this sort of Miltonic passage, not in
Donne and the metaphysicals.[2]

Milton, we feel, *relies* on this profuse scene, about
which, for the moment at least, he has no reservations.
Indeed, he would probably be unwilling to admit to
what degree he has committed himself, emotionally
and poetically; but his abandon is indicated by the
verse rhythms with their repletions. In this scene Milton accepts his sensory impressions, poetically, as
Donne could not, or as he himself could not in *Lycidas*,
where his meanings seem to be suspended at some distance from his sensuous imagination. Immediately the
appropriate emotion is evoked by this generous em-

bodiment of Adam and Eve—a statement so effectual in its way that it gives Milton, and us, a kind of guarantee mannerist art cannot give. The constraint and the suspended statement of *Lycidas* are gone, for the lushness of Milton's imagined Eden resolves his tensions.

Of course the irony is, artistically, that these rites of love in Eden are not at all mysterious; they are, in fact, rather more familiar and available than Donne's vexed and vexing lust for his mistresses. In Eve Milton has found an intoxicating material image and surrendered to it; like Adam he submits his will and his reason, in effect, to the cogency of the flesh. Donne did not surrender so naively to his images, nor did Milton in *Lycidas,* where the tenor is far withdrawn from the poetic vehicle, the elegy. However "pure" this wedded love may be, Milton is seduced by his own vision of Eve; in this Adamic experience in the flesh nothing can be, poetically or ethically, reserved. Unlike Gertrude in *Hamlet,* Milton's Eve is all too capable of representing a particular emotion; the poet has, against his scruples about impurity, been able to project into her his own warm sexuality. Adam's love, and Eve's, is consummated in their bower; it terminates in the senses. But it is no inexpressible passion; it is unsophisticated intercourse.

During this phase Milton brings to his art an overpowering accumulation of sensory impressions, a capacity to realize the magnificent Body, Act, and Scene. The center of his poetic activity has been shifted from the internal mannerist design to the external, showing how baroque sought to reach the spirit through the senses. Consequently Milton's images gain ascendancy against his own intellectual tenets, and his mind capitulates to his sensory imagination. Intellectually and theologically Milton holds the ideal of temperance; but "poetically" the baroque image of Eve is so potent that his ethic and theology seem almost irrelevant. If this particular dissociation does not appear in other baroque artists, the reason for Milton's curious dilemma is not hard to find: he was living in an era of baroque artistic vision, but he had a Puritan (possibly a mannerist) distrust of the sensorium. *Paradise Lost,* it happens, is the point at which his Counter-Reformation poetic imagination submerges his *anti-*Counter-Reformation ethic. As poet he is the maker of resplendent images; as Puritan he is a mighty image-breaker—*Eikonoklastes.* This Miltonic dissociation, however, is not like Donne's mannerist dissociation, for Donne is always aware of the conflicts within him at each instant, thus suffering the tensions of the discordant mannerist self. Milton, on the contrary, is here so enthralled by the wealth of his haptic imagination that he does not appear to be fully awake to the contradictions between his baroque sensuousness and his Puritanism. Thus occurs the discrepancy between Milton's pictorial and conceptual thinking.[3]

So Milton's capacity for "magniloquence" led him into an artistic situation curiously untenable, since his magnificent spectacles, his splendid corporeal representations, express precisely those impulses in his temperament that his intelligence cannot approve. His most fully "realized" scenes—the pastoral wedded love in Eden, the fury of the battle in Heaven, the violent suicide of Samson—represent a kind of intemperance and tragic rebellion of his Adamic and Satanic self. In such scenes Milton's baroque vision betrays his "right reason"; thus the majestic close of *Paradise Lost* makes man seem nobler than God and qualifies the theology of the poem:

> The world was all before them, where to choose
> Thir place of rest, and Providence thir guide:
> They hand in hand with wand'ring steps and slow
> Through Eden took thir solitarie way.

It is doubtful if Milton's epic does justify the ways of

God to men, although the dramatic, the tragic, action
is pictorially convincing. And the figure of Eve grows
to classic stature, although according to Milton's masculine logic Eve is unworthy, created deficient, destined to rely on Adam's will. Above her weakness and
her folly she rises, as poetic image, to a tragic recognition of guilt, a tragic gesture and suffering, grander
than Adam's when she says to him:

> . . . both have sinn'd, but thou
> Against God onely, I against God and thee,
> And to the place of judgment will return,
> There with my cries importune heaven, that all
> The sentence from thy head remov'd may light
> On mee, sole cause to thee of all this woe,
> Mee, mee onely just object of his ire.

Eve's self-discipline is richer than Adam's, and cannot
be accommodated within the theological concepts behind this epic, for measured on that scale, Eve is not
a responsible agent. Throughout *Paradise Lost* Milton
encounters the Counter-Reformation risk of trying to
solve a crisis of conscience in the theater of the sensorium.

Early as it is, *Comus* is a summary statement of Milton's lifelong moral code, a platonic-puritan-renais-
sance discipline for those who can live by the sober
dictate of spare temperance:

> And that which is not good, is not delicious
> To a wel-govern'd and wise appetite.

Accepting this ideal in his *Areopagitica*, Milton exclaims, "How great a virtue is temperance, how much
of moment through the whole life of man!" This ethic
of moderation, indebted to mannerist as well as renaissance thought, is averse to the veneration of images and
relics; it is the Puritan reply to the Council of Trent
and the externalizing of piety in worship and art. "Believe it, wondrous doctors," urges Milton, attacking
prelacy, "all corporeal resemblances of inward holiness

and beauty are now past." Milton is the iconoclastic Protestant when he argues:

And thus prelaty, both in her fleshly supportments, in her carnal doctrine of ceremony and tradition, in her violent and secular power, going quite counter to the prime end of Christ's coming in the flesh, that is, to reveal his truth, his glory, and his might, in a clean contrary manner than prelaty seeks to do, thwarting and defeating the great mystery of God; I do not conclude that prelaty is antichristian, for what need I? The things themselves conclude it.

For Milton the Puritan, every sacrament should be an inward act, the Papists erring "when they attribute to the outward sign the power of bestowing salvation or grace by virtue of the mere *opus operatum;* seeing that sacraments can neither impart salvation nor grace of themselves. . . ." Therefore Milton will hold to the unwritten scripture, the austere unseen paradise in the hearts of believers, nobler than Eden itself.

Yet the ascetic Comus-action, the constraint of *Lycidas,* will not suffice for *Paradise Lost,* which needs the sumptuous kind of arena Bernini created for Roman piety. Milton's mature baroque imagination was founded upon the materialism of his *Christian Doctrine,* which admits, "It is clear then that the world was framed out of matter of some kind or other . . . ; it was necessary that something should have previously existed capable of receiving passively the exertion of the divine efficacy." Though Milton adopts this classic premise from Aristotle, he also has an exuberant baroque "delight in the power of the material"—*Freude an der Stoffgewalt:*

Since therefore, both Scripture and reason concur in pronouncing that all these things were made, not out of nothing, but out of matter, it necessarily follows, that matter must either have always existed independently of God, or have originated from God at some particular point of time. . . .

If it is inconceivable that matter should always have existed, Milton concludes that it is divinely made, "that all things are of God"—or, as baroque scholasticism would have it (the very Tridentine theologians whom Milton opposed!), when actual existence is given, essence is implied, and in essence existence is included. (We must also recall that in 1584 Bruno had written in his Fourth Dialogue how "the matter of corporeal and incorporeal things is one.") Once having chosen this explanation, Milton moves toward Spinozism and a quasi-pantheism: matter must be the stuff of God, and the soul of man is not made of two substances, but is one indivisible nature—"the whole man is soul, and the soul man, that is to say, a body, or substance." Without debating his logic, we see that Milton the Puritan has out-prelated the Council of Trent and sanctioned the veneration of the image of man with a truly baroque "enthusiasm for the material." This is Milton's own queer version of the doctrine of transubstantiation: for him, spirit is flesh. As a result, *Paradise Lost* is more successful as a poem than as theology, for it is a noble act of worship of the Counter-Reformation image—not the image of saints, but of man and woman in their most human condition.

For *Paradise Lost* secularizes, in a grave and special way, the transcendental. The conflict between Satan and God is the transcendental theme of the poem; but Adam and Eve assuming the burden of the self is the secular theme. Thus there are really two sorts of myth: the transcendent or theological epic, a cosmic war between good and evil; and the secular tragedy of Adam and Eve undertaking to risk the dangers of their will and gaining by their experience in the flesh a "knowledge of good bought dear by knowing ill." The tragic, secular action seems more moving than the epic action. Adam makes a Recognition that is radically baroque when he sees that the *body* of Eve is his fate:

> . . . Flesh of Flesh,
> Bone of my bone thou art, and from thy state
> Mine never shall be parted, bliss or woe.

Both piety and drama can employ the Great Image. Some Great Images are sacred: Isis, Artemis, Diana, Hecuba, and Mary. Some are tragic figures "larger than life": Antigone, Electra, Alcestis, and Cleopatra. The mythology of Trent was devoted to the Virgin and the Magdalen. In Eden's tragic scene Eve is convincing enough to secularize the transcendental and make Raphael the Angel frown "with contracted brow." Adam knows that Eve brings him into the situation of existing under the liability of will and guilt:

> . . . here passion first I felt,
> Commotion strange, in all enjoyments else
> Superiour and unmov'd, here onely weake
> Against the charm of Beauties powerful glance.
> Or nature faild in mee, and left some part
> Not proof enough such object to sustain,
> Or from my side subducting, took perhaps
> More then enough; at least on her bestow'd
> Too much of ornament, in outward shew
> Elaborate, of inward less exact. . . .
> . . . yet when I approach
> Her loveliness, so absolute she seems
> And in her self compleat, so well to know
> Her own, that what she wills to do or say,
> Seems wisest, vertuousest, discreetest, best;
> All higher knowledge in her presence falls
> Degraded . . .

According to the epic structure of *Paradise Lost* the figure of Eve is negligible, a mere occasion for Adam's downfall; but tragically she humanizes the action:

> . . . Whence haile to thee
> Eve rightly call'd, mother of all mankind,
> Mother of all things living, since by thee
> Man is to live, and all things live for man.

Artistically speaking, Milton's "original sin" is his allowing himself to conceive the image of Eve in its full

baroque potency and freedom. By creating Eve
through his "delight in the material," Milton commits,
as Puritan, a primal offense more evil than Satan's rebellion. Eve is hazardous—not theologically, but as the
most seductive baroque icon, more irresistible than any
of the images sanctioned by the Fathers at Trent. Milton the Puritan image-breaker expresses his Counter-
Reformation self in this ample theater of Eden, where
the image of man is realized in its full plastic value,
which is its full baroque and fleshly humanity. If he
cannot justify God, he places man at the center of the
most abundant world ever imagined, where deity
seems, at times, of the machine only.

Thus the dilemmas of the mannerist conscience are
resolved in the external world, where the baroque
image is overpowering. An historical irony is implicit
in Milton and all baroque: while confidence in theological systems was being shaken during the seventeenth century, confidence in the images of faith in-
creased until the image seemed capable of sustaining
the faith: or, at the very least, to be self-sustaining.
Baroque religion projected its adoration into a worship of the convincing image. If one's mind was unsettled, one could, at worst, trust the senses. The theater
of high-baroque faith is the profuse world of Counter-
Reformation art, where dogma is affirmed by satisfy-
ing eye and ear. If Donne's vision was *mondain,* the
complexity of Donne's drama was inward; but the great
baroque dramas of conscience are played openly and
amid the splendors that secularize the transcendent. If
the scene of Shakespeare's *Measure for Measure* is the
private labyrinth of the mannerist conscience, *Othello,*
written during the same year, displays a rich and luxurious world, a "downright violence and storm of for-
tunes," a sufficiency of image and power of gesture
like Samson's pulling down the temple of the Philis-

tines. Samson resolves his terrible anguish by the public
act.

III

RESOLUTION IN ENERGY The art critics speak
of the baroque ability to "think in masses" and of baroque "rhythmical movement" in contrast to the "metrical movement" of renaissance art; and they have
held that baroque is not only Image and Body, but also
Energy: *Koerperlichkeit und Energie.* Baroque performs the feat of "activating" its mightiest bodies, so
that "masses in motion" (Woelfflin's *Massigkeit und
Bewegung*) are an index of this style. The concepts of
dynamic force, of inertia, of weight, mass, and motion,
entered physics with Galileo, who measured the velocity of balls moving up and down inclined planes.
When he died in 1642, the year of Isaac Newton's birth,
he had found that matter is endowed with power, that
bodies do not need to be kept moving by Aristotle's
Unmoved Mover, but that once set in motion they behave according to certain laws of force. Newton gave
these baroque laws of force their threefold definition,
distinguishing between mass and weight, and formu-
lating the dynamics of action and reaction, direction,
and momentum. The rhythmical movement—the momentum, so to speak—in baroque style is analogous to
the play of forces in baroque physics, matter having
"mass" as well as "weight," and obeying a principle of
"motion compounded." In baroque architecture the
heaviest walls "move" and "swing" as they do in San
Carlo alle Quattro Fontane, Rome (1638–68), a small
but powerful church completed chiefly under Borromini, with a façade activated throughout its two stories
of half-engaged columns. Here the motion is broken

by a sharp cornice between the stories; but the elliptical plaque pushes the upper balustrade into a daring cadence, a triumphal upsurge. The interior, a complicated ellipse, gives a similar impression of great masses in motion; enormous white columns are so densely grouped that they appear to be doubled; at the same time they majestically bound and emphasize the oval arms which are the chapels. Borromini has succeeded in endowing insignificant space with the aspect of containing massive forces in full play. Dwarfed as its scale actually is, this church has the high-baroque momentum. But to see baroque masses at full energy we need only to enter Saint Peter's, or the piazza before it, where the doubled arcades and columns of Bernini's great theater open before us like an expanding wall embracing the façade of the basilica.

The tumultuous rhetoric of baroque architecture is often developed by reduplicated columns, used in extravagant statement and counterstatement, as in the façade of Sant' Andrea della Valle, Rome (1591–1665), an authoritarian display with redundant masses everywhere: the eight matching pairs of columns in the two stories; the alternately triangular and semicircular pediments over portal, windows, niches; the masculine double pediment above the order of the second story. The architrave is emphasized by a broken cornice and by the weighty upper order, which yet does not seem to press disproportionately down upon the cornice or the lower order.

Recently art historians have come to the conclusion that baroque means not only mass and energy but, more exactly, "space and volume" treated in certain special relations.[4] During the earliest phase of baroque the masses are compressed or concentrated, and the tendency of an early-baroque nave is to "drive" us compulsively along the axis of the church toward the altar, which gives a strong psychological and structural accent. Doubtless the mannerist constriction of energy influences this compulsive movement. In high-baroque the masses are more open, as in Saint Peter's, and in Lanfranco's paintings inside the dome of Sant' Andrea della Valle, where heavy forms circulate with tremendous activity. When this motion reaches a climax in Giacinto Brandi's painting of the Martyrdom of Saint Blaise, there seems to be a headlong "waste of energy." In short, if early-baroque concentrates its masses and energies in one powerful rhythm, high-baroque art tends to expand by ample movements bursting into jubilant rhetoric.

Without dogmatizing about the periods within baroque, we can see how Milton's art changes between the writing of *Lycidas* and the writing of *Paradise Lost* and *Samson Agonistes*. The energies in *Lycidas* have a compulsive "direction," although none of the forces has free play and the power does not expend itself in any satisfactory climax. In contrast, the energies in *Samson*, which are as compulsive as those in *Lycidas*, are finally released, almost wastefully, in the hero's devastating outburst at the end—in "some great act." When we first hear Samson speak, he is tormented, almost like some mannerist figure, by swarming deadly thoughts of his humiliation: "what once I was, and what am now." Yet during his blind anguish Samson insists that at his birth there was given the promise of "some great act/Or benefit revealed to Abraham's race":

> Why was my breeding order'd and prescrib'd
> As of a person separate to God,
> Design'd for great exploits . . . ?

So in the midst of his massive despair Samson feels himself moved, profoundly, by irresistible impulses gathering momentum as his strength swells within him:

Be of good courage, I begin to feel
Some rouzing motions in me which dispose
To something extraordinary my thoughts . . .
This day will be remarkable in my life
By some great act, or of my days the last.

"Great exploit . . . some great act": this is the baroque principle of expenditure, of giant mass in motion, in complete release, in dynamic fulfillment. If the energies in *Lycidas* are potential, the energies in *Samson,* and in the heavenly war in *Paradise Lost,* are kinetic. If Shakespeare feels the mannerist paralysis in *Measure for Measure* (where everyone is "at war 'twixt will and will not") he also allows himself the baroque release in Othello's terrifying outburst:

. . . Like to the Pontic Sea,
Whose icy current and compulsive course
Ne'er feels retiring ebb, but keeps due on
To the Propontic and the Hellespont,
Even so my bloody thoughts, with violent pace,
Shall ne'er look back, ne'er ebb to humble love,
Till that a capable and wide revenge
Swallow them up.

In his barbaric simple way Othello is as torn as Donne or Hamlet; but he cannot, like a mannerist hero, exist in the climate of exsufflicate and blown surmises, quartering his thoughts. He cannot equivocate or accommodate, for "To be once in doubt is once to be resolved." So he must murder.

Once the high-baroque rhythm has started, it must be carried to the katharsis of a resolute gesture like Samson's pulling down the temple:

MANOAH: . . . what hideous noise was that!
            Horribly loud unlike the former shout.
CHORUS: Noise call you it or universal groan
            As if the whole inhabitation perish'd,
            Blood, death, and deathful deeds are in that
                noise,
            Ruin, destruction at the utmost point.

Baroque energies are effectively discharged. Othello's great act is a discharge destructive as Samson's, and with as great a waste of power. These baroque rhythms, like an upsurge of the will, seem to be engendered in the more violent forms of renaissance art, in Marlowe's Tamburlaine, in Michaelangelo's painting and sculpture. But Marlowe lacked the expansive and fleshly imagination of high-baroque, and Michaelangelo, except in his gigantic mad Last Judgment, never released his fury in a "total" gesture, so that his art gives no katharsis but is held in the troubled sloth of the Medici-tomb sculptures.

One great achievement of the baroque artist is the imaginative use of power; specifically, he learned how to express power through mass. The renaissance artist at his grandest style did not achieve this conquest. Full-baroque discovered the *artistic* properties of mass because it transformed the static effect of its greatest volumes by endowing them with resilience and abundant power. Whereas early-baroque sculptors—even Bernini in his first phase—rendered volumes expressive by generating, then frustrating, the forces within them, the full-baroque, as in Bernini's statue of Saint Longinus in Saint Peter's, releases these energies in "triumphant action," with an "intrepid exhibition" of vigor. In *Paradise Lost* Milton put his heaviest masses, his most plastic and monumental images, into grandiose motion, releasing the bulk of his material into outflowing waves of energy. This resolution of mass into motion is performed in his sustained verse paragraphs with their wasteful reduplication of phrase, their accumulation of grandiloquent names into strong cadences that break open the metrical closures into a "total" rhythm:

His eye might there command wherever stood
City of old or modern fame, the seat
Of mightiest empire, from the destind walls

Of Cambalu, seat of Cathaian Can
And Samarchand by Oxus, Temirs throne
To Paquin of Sinaean kings, and thence
To Agra and Lahor of great Mogul
Down to the golden Chersonese, or where
The Persian in Ecbatan sate, or since
In Hispahan, or where the Russian Ksar
In Mosco, or the Sultan in Bizance,
Turchestan-born; nor could his eye not ken
Th'empire of Negus to his utmost port
Ercoco and the less Maritine kings
Mombaza, and Quiloa, and Melind,
And Sophala thought Ophir, to the realme
Of Congo, and Angola, fardest south;
Or thence from Niger flood to Atlas mount
The kingdoms of Almansor, Fez, and Sus,
Marocco, and Algiers, and Tremisen;
On Europe thence, and where Rome was to sway . . .

                                    (XI)

"And thence . . . ," "nor could his eye not ken . . . ,"
"or thence . . . ," "On Europe thence . . . ," "To Paquin . . . ," "To Agra . . .": the same torrential overstatement appears in the giant columns of the façade of
Sant' Andrea della Valle. With these repetitions the
verse "swings" into an "open composition" having the
copious overflow of Milton's prose. The baroque façade
treats columns and pilasters not as mere "engaged"
decoration but as a bursting out of the surface. Milton's
latinized vocabulary and his colossal periods, his swollen phrases and truculent tone, are an idiom of power
magnified by redundancy:

These are the pretty responsories, these are the dear an-
tiphonies, that so bewitched of late our prelates and their
chaplains with the goodly echo they made; and besotted
us to the gay imitation of a lordly Imprimatur, one from
Lambeth House, another from the west end of Paul's; so
apishly Romanizing, that the word of command was still
set down in Latin; as if the learned grammatical pen that
wrote it would cast no ink without Latin; or perhaps, as
they thought, because no vulgar tongue was worthy to express the pure conceit of an Imprimatur; but rather, as I

hope, for that our English, the language of men ever famous and foremost in the achievements of liberty, will not easily find servile letters enow to spell such a dictatory presumption English. (*Areopagitica*)

Like the baroque architect or sculptor, Milton in this rhetoric has discovered the artistic properties of mass. Baroque is a style marked by dense materialism, but there is no inertia.

Baroque power expresses itself most authentically as an exercise of the will. At the heart of Milton's humanism is the problem of the will, for, as his *Christian Doctrine* says, "In assigning the gift of free will, God suffered both men and angels to stand or fall at their own uncontrolled choice." The tragedy of Samson is his struggle to repossess and exert his will, and the figure of Milton's Satan stands at the center of baroque art when he asks,

> . . . What though the field be lost?
> All is not lost; the unconquerable will,
> And study of revenge, immortal hate,
> And courage never to submit or yield:
> And what is else not to be overcome?

Spengler chose baroque art to represent the disposition of the modern "faustian" soul, creating its "will-culture," and without being "Spenglerian" we can verify that baroque is a dynamic style because the instrument of baroque imagination is the will. Wherever baroque does not convince us that it is a triumphant release of the will, there is left only the materialism that is an incomplete record of this style.

Both Milton and Hobbes are materialists, and it is another irony of the seventeenth century that Hobbes, who like Milton opposed prelacy, should have accepted the materialism implied in the doctrines of the Council of Trent and Counter-Reformation piety. But Milton gains a baroque resolution, which Hobbes does not, because Milton treats power imaginatively and thus is able to energize matter and transform it into a vehicle for the will. Hobbes the materialist thinks the imagination to be mere "decaying sense" and therefore deprives the baroque imagination of its creative power to dominate matter and employ it as an agency of will. Consequently Hobbes is left with an inert materialism.

It is worth a moment to explain how Hobbes, who lays such stress upon the will, fails to achieve the baroque resolution in exultant power. According to his materialism, life is only a motion of the limbs, and the original of all our knowledge is sense; thus Hobbes, like Milton, accepts the baroque premise that irreducible reality is the body:

The world (I mean not the Earth only . . . but the Universe, that is, the whole mass of all things that are) is corporeal, that is to say, body; and hath the dimensions of magnitude, namely length, breadth, and depth; also every part of body is likewise body, and hath the like dimensions; and consequently every part of the universe is body; and that which is not body, is no part of the universe; and because the Universe is all, that which is no part of it is nothing; and consequently no where. Nor does it follow from hence, that spirits are nothing; for they have dimensions, and are therefore really bodies. (*Leviathan*, IV, 46)

However, Hobbes never believed in the efficacy of the will, as did Milton; that is, he never sufficiently believed that matter can be impelled until it serves as an idiom of force. Of course he implies that life itself is an activity of passion and will: "I put for a general inclination of all mankind, a perpetual and restless desire of power after power that ceaseth only in death." If life is will, passion, energy, then Hobbes should not also say that "life is but a motion of limbs" and that man is an "artificial animal" moving like other "automata" or engines "by springs and wheels as doth a watch. For what is the heart but a spring," he asks, "and the nerves but so many strings?" Thus for Hobbes will, energy, and *detective*

passion are only "names," and "force" is only a figment. If, then, the will is merely a "name," it cannot perform the overpowering decisive act. Clearly Hobbes does not really believe in the supremacy of the will or energy, and his dense material universe cannot be successfully put into motion. Hence he is the baroque philosopher *manqué*. Since the body is a machine and the will, which is life itself, is a figment, Hobbes cannot use matter to symbolize energy, as can Milton the poet, who believes that the self communicates its vitality through the flesh; this is an artistic power. If Hobbes' man has only an artificial mechanical life, so also his state—Leviathan—is "but an artificial man," a mere "covenant," lacking the sovereign baroque authority. In his poetry Milton achieved the baroque triumph Hobbes was too timid to claim. The art critic would say that Hobbes failed to *activate* his masses.

Through the exertion of his imagination Milton transvalues matter to energy in *Paradise Lost* and thus transcends the weight of his medium. His baroque bodies and action are an idiom of incorrigible will, an assertion at the epic and the tragic level of the baroque disposition to conceive life as power. At the epic level the terrible warfare between Satan and God transfigures the collision of monstrous bodies into a conflict of opposing wills:

> . . . Him the almighty power
> Hurld headlong flaming from th'etherial skie
> With hideous ruine and combustion down
> To bottomless perdition . . .

A titanomachy on this scale was never painted by baroque artists except in Michaelangelo's Last Judgment where, as in Milton, the imagination expresses itself as an activity of the will:

> Light as the lightning glimps they ran, they flew,
> From thir foundations loosning to and fro
> They pluckt the seated hills with all thir load,

Rocks, waters, woods, and by the shaggie tops
Up lifting bore them in thir hands . . .

To see how the violence of the baroque imagination—
which is no mere "decaying sense" but a rebound of
the will itself—can create its own myth by transforming
matter to released energy, we must turn to the spectacle of the Son of God, that Michaelangelesque image
from The Last Judgment, advancing irresistibly, with
baroque momentum, upon the rebel archangels:

. . . forth rush'd with whirlwind sound
The chariot of paternal deitie
Flashing thick flames, wheele within wheele undrawn,
It selfe instinct with spirit, but convoyd
By four cherubic shapes . . .
Hee on his impious foes right onward drove,
Gloomie as night; under his burning wheeles
The stedfast empyrean shook throughout,
All but the throne it selfe of God. Full soon
Among them he arriv'd; in his right hand
Grasping ten thousand thunders, which he sent
Before him . . .

At the tragic level of Paradise Lost the eating of the
apple is not only experience in the flesh; it is also the
moment at which the primitive innocent bodies of
Adam and Eve are activated by the dynamics of the
human will, which inevitably means alienation from
the will of God:

They trespass, authors to themselves in all
Both what they judge and what they choose; for so
I formd them free, and free they must remain,
Till they enthrall themselves . . .

When Adam and Eve take their solitary way, hand in
hand, out of Eden, that sensuous Counter-Reformation
paradise, they have possessed their own freely elected
fate, which is their entrance into the human condition
of assuming the consequences of the human act.

So we return to the notion that baroque is mass and
motion (Massigkeit und Bewegung); or mass in mo-

tion, which is the province of Milton's imagination in *Paradise Lost* and *Samson.* Baroque art knows no contradiction between matter and energy. Because of his strong will the baroque artist can employ titanism convincingly, and can consolidate experience at the level of the senses. The audacious baroque materialism reduces the planes of reality to a uniform texture, density, and mass. The many levels of "realization" in *Lycidas,* the shifting planes of vision and statement, are synthesized in *Paradise Lost* into a heavy baroque texture of fleshly experience. Milton creates his magnificent Counter-Reformation spectacles by a kind of "tactile perspective":

> Anon out of the earth a fabrick huge
> Rose like an exhalation, with the sound
> Of dulcet symphonies and voices sweet,
> Built like a temple, where pilasters round
> Were set, and Doric pillars overlaid
> With golden architrave; nor did there want
> Cornice or freeze, with bossy sculptures graven,
> The roof was fretted gold. . . .
> . . . Th'ascending pile
> Stood fixt her stately highth, and strait the dores
> Op'ning thir brazen foulds discover wide
> Within, her ample spaces, o'er the smooth
> And level pavement . . .

In this vision of Pandemonium we behold the principle of transubstantiation operating in Milton's art: the poetic essence is in the material. But, ironically, this baroque palace is built in Hell; for Milton had visited Rome and seen the richest displays of baroque piety— Rome, where, he boasts, he did no observance to the splendors of prelacy. His homage to these baroque splendors was not done in Rome, or in his own rites of piety, but, instead, in his poetry, which represents in the experience of the senses the power of the will.

IV

RESOLUTION IN SPACE   If baroque resolves
matter in energy, it also resolves energy in space; baroque masses "spill over," and figures in baroque paintings move in a "great imagined space." Usually we hear
that baroque space is simply an explosion into infinity
—*das Ausserordentliche*—and Woelfflin himself inter-
preted baroque as somewhat "formless" because the
"edges" or "corners" of baroque forms are broken and
the "inner structure" is weakened by a "puffiness" (*das
Wulstige*). All this formlessness, however, belongs to
mannerist rather than to baroque art, which observes,
surprisingly, an almost academic canon of regularity.

Far from being an uncontrolled explosion into infinity, baroque art has its own governing law of dynamics,
which is, in brief, a technique of, first, closure, then expansion or expulsion into space. Without this prelimi-
nary closure baroque cannot gain its special illusion of
distance, release, and triumph. The energies in Milton's Samson, we recall, are first thwarted, then released in his giant, cleansing act.

The principle is illustrated in two or three characteristic baroque works, the Saint Teresa group by
Bernini in Santa Maria della Vittoria (1646), and the
Piazza San Pietro (1657 ff.). Each is a coherent structure, like that typical baroque façade of Sant' Agnese
in Agone, Rome, even if the masses are set vigorously
in motion. The Saint Teresa group is so tightly framed
by the lavish doubled columns enclosing its niche that
we come almost face to face with it before we see it at
all; inside this depth, the two figures are flooded
with a strong yellow light bursting over them from a
concealed window above, a light that unifies the composition by saturating it in a mellow golden atmos-

phere. The strong diagonals of this group are not mannerist, because the slender upright angel is in counterposition with Teresa, repeating in "looser" rhythm the zigzag of the half-reclining saint whose luxurious robes cascade down about her naked foot, which, in turn, balances the swaying head of the angel at the opposite corner of the parallelogram. Behind these eloquent figures is the glory of the sunburst. So also Bernini heightens the spatial drama of the approach to Saint Peter's by admitting us first into his elliptical forecourt, the equilibrium of this area being controlled by the central obelisk and the play of water from two equidistant fountains; then as the doubled arcades of this forecourt draw together, the ellipse opens into the widening expanse between the colonnades flanking the giant façade of the basilica. There is the same effect of release through, or beyond, a regularly enclosed space when we stand at the foot of Bernini's Scala Regia (1663–66) looking upward to the high window at the top, through a tunnel vault arching over the great columns that lose themselves in gloom, then are again seen shining in brilliant light from a hidden window halfway up. Always we have this sense of enclosure, then release, when we stand beneath the baroque domes of Roman churches, where some painted architecture on the lower surface of the dome suddenly breaks open into a blaze of light and space in which float angelic shapes that seem to disembody weight. The dome of Saint Cecilia's Chapel in San Carlo ai Catinari is a double ellipse, the lower bearing stout brackets to "support" the upper cupola, where light showers in exultantly.

Thus the "secret" of baroque space is not its infinity; rather this illusion of infinity is due to a special access to "farther" space that occurs whenever we seem to break through, or pass beyond, hugely defined boundaries; whenever, that is, a *negation* of space is immediately followed by an *affirmation* of space. The tactic of closure, then expansion or expulsion beyond this enclosure, enhances our sense of release to "distance," and authentic baroque space arises from a contradiction: first, setting monumental limits, then, immediately, denying these limits by melodramatically opening a vista beyond them, thus seeming to perform a heroic feat of liberation. Infinity is the boldest baroque spatial illusion. Actually, however, baroque encloses its areas firmly—even symmetrically—at the same time it breaks through its huge confines. This contradiction accounts for our spatial experience inside Saint Peter's, where we are shut in by massive and dense Roman walls, arches, and vaults; at the same instant we feel engulfed in infinitely extended spaciousness. Bernini performs this baroque feat in the baldachino in Saint Peter's when he gives an already huge space a powerful increment *through* the volumes and balance of the giant columns rising about the high altar. The baroque tactic is used before the Campidoglio, where the approach to the high piazza is rigorously defined by the steps up which we mount; then, by contrast with this channeled approach, the piazza itself becomes an operatic space which is further activated by the diagonal stairs running with violent counterenergies up the face of the palace.

This piazza has been called a stage for heroes, and the baroque artist had the power "to free the forces contained in ponderous volume, and to disguise the unwieldy nature of mass" because he intended "to exceed the bounds of a determined space." In painting the dome of Sant' Andrea della Valle, Lanfranco worked a high-baroque enchantment; he accepts the surface of the dome, then denies this surface by painting three concentric rings of freely moving figures that appear to be "released" from the architectural confines to soar into a spatial diapason. Bellori wrote that "this painting has rightly been likened to a full choir, in which all the sounds together make up the harmony." The tactic of breaking through mighty boundaries is a triumph of pietistic art, for we seem to emerge from our worldly space to be projected into "another" realm. The reckless and overpowering expulsion achieves an "undefinable sense of spaciousness."

The "faustian" will-to-power can express itself in this sort of space, which differs from mannerist and renaissance space. Spengler has observed that the renaissance used a logic of static space, pure and restful, like a *"dream* of classical existence." We know that mannerists like Tintoretto disturbed this calm dream of classic existence by dissolving the logic of the plane and giving to space a troubled directional energy, a compulsive and oblique "drive." It was necessary for the baroque architect and painter to reorganize and govern mannerist space, to make "direction" express a triumphant will breaking through stately boundaries. In Spengler's opinion baroque space is "not mere extension, but efficient extension into the distance, as an overcoming of the merely sensuous . . . as a spiritual will-to-power." He adds, "The enigmatic Something in the soul-image that is called 'will,' *the passion of the third dimension,* is therefore quite specially a creation of the Baroque." This baroque "physical concept of space-energy" is "brought to expression in the depth-perspective of oil-painting which makes the space-field of the picture, conceived as infinite, dependent on the observer, who *in choosing his distance, asserts his dominion.*" That is, the baroque perspective creates infinity.

To explain: if renaissance space was conceived and ordered by a theory of "the visual cone," if mannerist space opened in oblique and wavering directions, baroque space is a majestic reorganization and conquest of space by impelling will. The calm space of the renaissance "dream" was really an effort to recover the classic space established inside the ancient Pantheon, with its "cruel" light falling sternly, steadily, from above into a vast interior. The Roman architect imperially enclosed this space by massive walls, columns, and dome; but he did not attempt any illusion of "escape" into the "beyond"; he did not negate his enclosure by any release into infinity. The small aperture at the apex of the dome in the Pantheon does not inspire us to soar into the distance. The Pantheon-architect had, in effect, small sense of infinity since he lacked the "faustian" will; his low dome does not have the daring baroque height, and his heavy entablature below the dome flattens the vast interior space, which is distributed metrically in clear units by niches and columns. Space in the Pantheon, like space inside Brunelleschi's Pazzi Chapel, does not have the baroque power to expand. Renaissance space is a nostalgic and theoretic version of the Pantheon-space, usually in slighter proportions. The willful *coulisse* space of mannerism lacks the monumental baroque symmetry and logic, the mighty enclosure, the academic regularity. Nor must we think of the "romantic" space of the nineteenth century as being baroque, for romantic infinity keeps only the baroque feeling for remoteness without the baroque confines to be broken through. Thus "romantic" space, compared to baroque, is only a vague unoriented "extension" into the "boundless." While making a romantic "flight to the infinite" the artist does not clearly "choose his distance" and thus cannot enjoy the baroque triumph because there are no coherent limits for the romantic to "pass beyond" in asserting the dominance of his will. Consequently, Shelley's Prometheus Unbound is a figure "pinnacled dim in the intense inane."

By contrast, *Paradise Lost* is a formal expression of the baroque will-to-space or will-to-infinity. The whole poem is organized, so to speak, in baroque space because it sets up huge "classical" boundaries and then exceeds them. The firmly defined local areas of Milton's universe open into, or are surrounded by, "chaos." In fact the spatial relations in Milton's cosmos are illusory in the technical baroque sense:

> Mean while upon the firm opacous globe
> Of this round world, whose first convex divides
> The luminous inferior orbs, enclos'd
> From Chaos and th'inroad of Darkness old,
> Satan alighted walks; a Globe farr off
> It seem'd, now seems a boundless continent
> Dark, waste, and wild, under the frown of night,
> Starless expos'd, and ever-threatening storms
> Of Chaos blustring round, inclement skie;
> Save on that side which from the wall of Heav'n
> Though distant farr some small reflection gaines
> Of glimmering air less vext with tempest loud:
> Here walk'd the Fiend at large in spacious field.

Beyond the enclosed areas like Heaven and Hell and Paradise there is the ominous dominion of outer darkness which only the baroque perspective could suggest. Milton's passion for the third dimension is no mere romantic feeling for the boundless, because he creates his depth-perspective by "choosing his distance" so that there is an effect of giant power seemingly contained by laws and limits, then transcending them. No doubt Milton's organization of space may partly be due to his hesitation to use in epic poetry the system of a Copernican universe; but the structure of his baroque vision, as well as the state of contemporary science, must have caused him to imagine such a bounded-boundless cosmos.

At least he could not avoid expressing his feeling for "chaos" and wild night and the dark wastes immeasurable extending beyond the frontiers of Heaven and Hell and Earth. When Sin opens the gates of Hell, she releases Satan into baroque space, the hazardous,

unexplored gloom outside the ponderous bastions of
the nether kingdom:

> . . . the gates wide op'n stood,
> That with extended wings a bannerd host
> Under spread ensigns marching might pass through
> With horse and chariots rankt in loose array;
> So wide they stood, and like a furnace mouth
> Cast forth redounding smoak and ruddy flame.
> Before thir eyes in sudden view appear
> The secrets of the hoarie deep, a dark
> Illimitable ocean without bound,
> Without dimension, where length, breadth, and highth,
> And time and place are lost; where eldest Night
> And chaos, ancestors of nature, hold
> Eternal anarchie, amidst the noise
> Of endless warrs, and by confusion stand . . .

Across this deep Milton's Satanic self must soar with
the rebel archangel, and conquer its distances, for his
vision must expend itself in dynamic "space-energy."

The symbolic values of Milton's will-to-space—his
baroque passion to command the third dimension—appear in that somber passage when Adam and Eve,
playing the great drama of the will of man, which asserts itself beyond the restrictions set by God, are ex-
iled from the Garden and enter the arena of human
experience in the landscape "outside" Eden:

> In either hand the hastning Angel caught
> Our lingring Parents, and to th'Eastern gate
> Led them direct, and down the cliff as fast
> To the subjected plaine; then disappeer'd.
> They looking back, all th'Eastern side beheld
> Of Paradise, so late thir happy seat,
> Wav'd over by that flaming brand, the Gate
> With dreadful faces throng'd and fierie armes:
> Som natural teares they dropt, but wip'd them soon;
> The world was all before them, where to choose
> Thir place of rest.

The immense epic structure of the poem—conforming to academic conventions and the proportions of the

renaissance grand style, its huge equilibriums like those of the façade of Sant' Agnese in Agone—cannot contain Milton's vista, his power to transcend the formal limits of his learned composition. He must attempt to know what is "beyond"—the silent black chaos, the wide kingdoms of man's history, the blinding light of glory. All these are in the distance.

V

BAROQUE AND ACADEMIC The formal boundaries erected by the baroque imagination prove that there is no inherent contradiction between the "regularity" of academic art and the "expressiveness" of baroque. The symmetry of the baroque structure proves, too, how lineally baroque derives from the grand style of the renaissance. *Paradise Lost* is academic and classic, but no less baroque for that reason. This is surprising, for it has often been presumed that academic and baroque styles in the seventeenth century are irreconcilable trends. Yet that typically baroque façade of Sant' Agnese in Agone has a very systematic, though huge, design: the central concave wall with its great columns and doorway embraced by two majestic towers rising symmetrically before the masculine dome. Both Milton's poem and Borromini's façade are "tectonic" structures, having a mighty decorum.

Art historians have come to question the usefulness of drawing sharp distinctions between so-called baroque and so-called academic ("eclectic") forms of Roman painting and architecture. Traditionally it has been said that during the Counter-Reformation period two separate currents, especially in painting, ran through Roman art, an "expressive" baroque current and a restrained, idealizing academic-eclectic current.

According to this view Bernini and Baciccio (Gaulli) are supposed to use an expressive baroque technique, together with Caravaggio, perhaps; and the Carracci, Sacchi, and Domenichino are supposed to use an academic technique leading toward Poussin's painting. However, there seems actually to be no separate "classicist current in baroque art"; there is only baroque art, certain of its aspects manifesting themselves as academism.[5] Perhaps one should say that baroque is an expressionist movement within the neo-grand style of high Counter-Reformation art. Annibale Carracci and Caravaggio, appearing in Rome at almost the same instant, about 1600, within a few years of each other evolved an early-baroque form of painting differing only in details of idiom, not in syntax and meaning. Besides, the young Caravaggio, like other early-baroque artists, betrays certain mannerist traits. Both the Carracci and Caravaggio derive from the traditions of antique statuary and the idealized forms of high-renissance painting, which they both use with great expressiveness; in both we see classical generalized figures of heroic size. The full-baroque painters can hardly be termed less classic than the academic-eclectic painters; they idealized their compositions almost as thoroughly. Domenichino, for example, painted alternately in "baroque" and "academic" fashion, and Caravaggio, as his paintings in San Luigi dei Francesi prove, shifted from mannerist techniques toward a grandeur and simplification we ordinarily associate with Cortona and Lanfranco; and yet in his final period he returned to an expressionist shorthand. In effect, we are now inclined to accept the view that painters at the opening of the seventeenth century in Italy revolted in several ways against mannerist complication and thinness by returning to the simplified forms of the high-renaissance and the solidity and volume of the "natural" figure.

The most telling argument that we cannot sharply divide academism from baroque in this anti-mannerist period is the evolution of Guercino's painting, which shows that others besides the Carracci were "eclectic" and "academic." [6] Under the pressure of Monsignor Giovanni Battista Agucchi's theories of beauty, Guercino changed his "dark" and cryptic north-Italian manner and learned to use a Roman "classicism," holding his composition in one plane and giving up diagonals, corkscrew movements, and zigzags. Thus about 1626 Guercino was painting in a classic-baroque style; he stabilized his design in simple horizontals and verticals, solidified his forms, and used light to define his structure. Certainly the contradiction between "naturalism" (Caravaggismo) and "classicism" (Carraccismo) has been overstated. This is apparent in a painting like Guercino's Saint Bruno (Bologna). If Guercino stabilized and simplified his expressive baroque art, painters like Domenichino often tried to dramatize emotion through expressive gestures. Similarly, Annibale Carracci's extravagant paintings in the Farnese gallery are a "living classicism" within the baroque tradition; for baroque art unites idealism and naturalism, expressionism and classicism, power and regularity of design. Clearly too much has been made of Caravaggio's "dark" naturalism at the expense of his interest in formal structure and volume, his academic and classic language. In general, then, we find that after 1600 began a reaction against mannerism in the form of a classic-baroque, or academic-baroque, art, a reaction that simplified and regularized composition in both painting and architecture and re-established the plane in painting. This art is widely and learnedly eclectic, and raises the "grand style" of the high-renaissance to a more sovereign power.

Nothing could be more suggestive for interpreting Milton's academic-baroque-eclectic performances, like

Paradise Lost and *Samson Agonistes,* than these re-
appraisals of Italian art history, for now we can think
that if baroque means release and expressive energy,
as indeed it does, it also means august equilibrium,
restabilized masses, idealized forms, and grand simplified planes—an academic co-ordination on an impressive scale. Milton's baroque energy and expressiveness
can at last be reconciled with his decorum and with
the learned structure of his great epic and drama. The
Miltonic Adam is the sort of classic-baroque figure
much admired by Agucchi and that dictator among
the academic critics of this era, Giovanni Pietro Bellori. Adam is impersonal and Roman, unlike the agitated mannerist figures, and he brings idealism into
accord with naturalism; he is endowed with sculptural
solidity and poise, and prolongs the high-renaissance
"grand style" in the techniques of Counter-Reformation art:

> Mean while our primitive great sire, to meet
> His godlike guest, walks forth, without more train
> Accompani'd then with his own compleat
> Perfections, in himself was all his state,
> More solemn then the tedious pomp that waits
> On princes, when thir rich retinue long
> Of horses led, and grooms besmeard with gold
> Dazles the croud, and sets them all agape.
> Neerer his presence Adam though not awd,
> Yet with submiss approach, and reverence meek,
> As to a superior nature, bowing low,
> Thus said. . . .

Adam is presented with the measure, the simplicity,
the "breadth" and decorum Raphael achieved in creating those eclectic figures in renaissance painting who
acknowledge Giotto and Masaccio for parentage. These
ideal figures move within the grand spaces of Raphael's
School of Athens, and they inspire baroque painters.
Almost like Annibale Carracci, Milton derives his figures in *Paradise Lost* from the tradition of antique

sculpture; and Samson would correspond to some of
the more unruly figures Carracci must have adapted
from Michaelangelo. If Adam is an academic-Raphael-
esque form, Milton's Satan has resemblance to the more
"naturalistic" lurid figures in Caravaggio, who has great
expressive force also transmitted, presumably, from
Michaelangelo. Satan lies under the ghastly light of
Hell like the giant foreshortened shapes in the foreground plane of Caravaggio's theatrical altarpieces:

> Thus Satan talking to his neerest mate
> With head uplift above the wave, and eyes
> That sparkling blaz'd, his other parts besides
> Prone on the flood, extended long and large
> Lay floating many a rood, in bulk as huge
> As whom the fables name of monstrous size . . .
> So stretcht out huge in length the arch-fiend lay
> Chain'd on the burning lake . . .

The light of Hell is no wan mannerist flicker, but a melodramatic abyss of night from which emerge, expres-
sively, the flaring volumes Caravaggio roughed out in
his later "shorthand":

> The dismal situation waste and wilde,
> A dungeon horrible, on all sides round
> As one great furnace flamd, yet from those flames
> No light, but rather darkness visible . . .

The baroque expressiveness of *Paradise Lost* is, if
anything, magnified by its academic mechanism, its
regularity of form that by any usual meaning of the
term would be called classical. Milton's epic structure
is disciplined in the most scholarly sense: the unified
action beginning in the "middle" and returning to pre-
vious events through Raphael's narrative of the war in
Heaven, the double fable involving both gods and men,
the balance of episodes, the extended speeches and
similies, the allegorical figures, the dream and
prophecy, the moral gravity. This poem is thoroughly
studied and eclectic, and has none of the mannerist

improvisation and instability. So also is *Samson Ago-nistes* a "regular" tragedy in its design, holding the unities of time, character, and place, and employing a chorus and a messenger to deal with offstage disaster; the hero is elevated, and the tragic language is nobly "embellished." Here the renaissance grand style is developed to its ultimate dignity and range. Both poems are none the less baroque; for in each the pressures of the will are so formidable that the figures and action can hardly be controlled by the conventions Milton has used with an overbearing and severe learning.

These poems crowd their great academic framework almost as Michaelangelo's proto-baroque paintings in the Sistine Chapel imperil the learned design that encloses them. The mannerist painters and architects also crowded their framework; but the framework itself was irregular, and the pressure of internal forces was neither so resolute nor sustained as the baroque energies. And these forces were not resolved. Geoffrey Scott observes that baroque amplified the classical formulas by volume, mass, and movement, and used the theater with "massive finality." Baroque art employs a bold and unqualified logic.

VI

THE IMAGE IN SPACE   At this point we need a more precise analysis of baroque space and how forms are situated within it. Mannerist space was distorted, shifting, incoherent; some of the mannerist painters used a shallow flat space into which they awkwardly gathered frail agitated figures; or else there opened a funnel, vortex, or *coulisse* through which movement was diagonal, swirling, and compelling but capricious or illogical. Motion through baroque space is more "regular," for usually baroque encloses its areas symmetrically, fixing a strong central axis or obviously balancing its foreground masses, which are presented in lavish statement, as at San Carlo alle Quattro Fontane or Sant' Andrea della Valle. The façade of Santa Susanna in Rome (1597–1603) has a dynamic motion because of the heavy doubled columns and pilasters, the great triangular pediment, and the generous treatment of portal and window, but, unlike mannerist façades, it has equilibrium and defines its units so clearly that it seems almost academic in ordonnance. This equilibrium also belongs to baroque painting, which consolidates its frontal plane, its façade, so to speak, by means of heroic volumes and contours, and by dense textures; then behind this solidly realized frontal plane opens a "distance" releasing us into "infinity" and causing that special baroque forward-and-backward motion (Woelfflin's *Vor-und-Zuruecktreten*). Often the middle ground is weak. Baroque is "broad" as well as "deep"; it frankly accepts the renaissance conflict between the near and the far—indeed, vigorously insists upon it.

An heroic baroque painting is Guido Reni's huge Samson (Bologna): the sinuous but portentous figure is mounted in superhuman scale, at a slightly raised angle, upon the surface plane, and behind this gigantic apparition expands an undefined space. In his Martyrdom of Saint Agnes (Bologna) Domenichino writes his foreground action in a learned immense script; again the background is vaguely indicated. This crowding of the surface with robust, if not coarse, figures and contours gives the foreground action an impressiveness and sometimes a violence less nuanced, more stagy, than the mannerist action; the gestures are decisive; their meaning proclaims itself at once and in full without any of the mannerist ambiguity. The activity in a baroque foreground immediately and irresistibly reaches a climax; it gains unity by a display of power; the declaration is unequivocal. More fully to exploit his foreground the baroque painter often places his giant hero in the midst of a group of supernumerary figures and makes him conspicuous by stressing his mighty exertion. In any case baroque exhibits its full eloquence in the foreground, which it devotes to majestic volumes, broad strokes, forcible action; it consolidates its "façades" with authority and strength. It is, in fact, an art of the façade.

Throughout *Paradise Lost* Milton relies upon the breadth and wealth of the baroque foreground, and upon the exertions of his conspicuous heroes, figures who are presented in augmented scale amid a crowded scene. The image of Satan in Hell occupies a baroque position in space:

> . . . the superiour Fiend
> Was moving toward the shore; his ponderous shield
> Ethereal temper, massy, large, and round,
> Behind him cast; the broad circumference
> Hung on his shoulders like the moon, whose orb
> Through optic glass the Tuscan artist views
> At evening from the top of Fesole,
> Or in Valdarno, to descry new lands,
> Rivers or mountains in her spotty globe.
> His spear, to equal which the tallest pine
> Hewn on Norwegian hills, to be the mast
> Of some great ammiral, were but a wand . . .

The Council in Hell is also composed in baroque space, with Satan dominating the infernal hosts. Occasionally Satan appears among those giant allegorical figures so characteristic of academic-baroque art, as when he confronts Sin and Death before Hell's portals, beyond which extends Chaos; mass is balanced against mass, in classic equilibrium:

> . . . Before the gates there sat
> On either side a formidable shape;
> The one seem'd woman to the waste and fair,

> But ended foul in many a scaly fould
> Voluminous and vast, a Serpent arm'd
> With mortal sting: about her middle round
> A cry of hell-hounds never ceasing bark'd
> With wide cerberean mouths full loud, and rung
> A hideous peal . . .
> . . . the other shape,
> If shape it might be call'd that shape had none
> Distinguishable in member, joynt, or limb,
> Or substance might be call'd, that shadow seem'd,
> For each seem'd either; black it stood as night,
> Fierce as ten furies, terrible as hell,
> And shook a dreadful dart . . .

The passage shows how Milton's baroque vision amplified the renaissance art of Spenser, making it portentous, realizing to the full the splendors that were only intimated in the sweet clear music of *The Faerie Queene*. Almost anywhere in *Paradise Lost* we behold mighty figures opposing each other in the broad foreground of baroque space: the conflict between Satan and Christ in Heaven, the dialogue between Raphael and Adam in the Garden, the promenade of Adam and Eve, the encounter of Satan with the Archangel outside Eden, the exile of Man and Woman from the gates of Paradise. The gestures in this epic are writ large.

However inwardly Samson may be stung by Puritan remorse of conscience, the intrepid figure of Milton's hero occupies—indeed, dominates—the foreground plane of the half-academic drama. Although Samson's psychology still bears the scars of mannerist torment, the structure of this "classic" tragedy is genuinely baroque. One by one Samson, the "conspicuous" hero, confronts his enemies—Dalila, Harapha, and finally the Philistines in their "spacious theater" which we never see but which is there in the background like an evil dimension. The presence of the chorus helps to keep Samson in the foreground of the action, which has the deliberate movement and equipoise of Sophocles' drama. But "classic" as the design may be, there is none of the Greek spirit of "moderation" or *sophrosyne* in this Miltonic poem; Samson's superhuman pain and hatred increase until he purges his violence of soul in his "one great act." If we are to seek a kindred mood among the Greeks, it must not be in the more "classic" plays of Aeschylus or Sophocles, but in *The Trachinian Maidens* with its maddened Heracles, or in the excesses of Euripides. Only the structure of Milton's play is classic, not the temper. Samson knows himself, like any baroque hero, to be pre-eminent:

> . . . in strength
> All mortals I excell'd, and great in hopes
> With youthful courage and magnanimous thoughts
> Of birth from Heav'n foretold and high exploits
> Full of divine instinct, after some proof
> Of acts indeed heroic, far beyond
> The sons of Anac, famous now and blaz'd,
> Fearless of danger, like a petty god
> I walk'd about admir'd of all and dreaded
> On hostile ground, none daring my affront . . .

Of course this is classic "pride" (*hubris*); but it is also the surging of the baroque will. Milton's "argument" prefacing the poem indicates the baroque plan of the action, pitting Samson against a procession of enemies: the hero, blind and captive, comes forth from his prison to sit in the open air and bemoan his condition:

> I was no private, but a person rais'd
> With strength sufficient and command from Heav'n
> To free my countrey; if their servile minds
> Me their deliverer sent would not receive,
> But to thir masters gave me up for nought,
> Th'unworthier they.

This image with its threat of explosion suits the titanic and expressive academism of baroque art; for Milton, unlike Sophocles or Aeschylus, is himself enthralled by the awful power of his hero.

Self-regarding as Samson may be, his is not the intimate, undirected, casual psychology of Donne. His wrath is public, grand, and fatal. Samson's conflict with himself is as severe as Donne's; but the scale of passion is heroic and impersonal; he is a mythical, archetypal Captive, Sufferer, and Contestant. His psychological vocabulary is not the fastidious, evasive, language of Hamlet, who gives himself over, sicklied with thought, to the intrigue of the metaphysical mind with its own responses, random, exploratory, indecisive. Samson's remorse is grim, and his fury like the whirlwind; but he is not a victim of the capricious feelings that play through the mannerist characters, unpredictably, in Tourneur, Middleton, and Webster. A baroque psychology has reduced and simplified Samson's emotions, which are magnified to epic pain and epic wrath; his strength his bane, his violence projected luridly against the darkness in his mind and in the world into which he has been cast, without hope of day. Again, there is no contradiction in saying that Samson's responses are at once academic and baroque—strongly defined but hardly mastered, and of massive power. Samson's baroque action is "total" in gesture and energy, ruinous and final as is the fall of Satan or the exile from the Garden.

Samson concentrates in his passionate, but naive, soul all the baroque force of will, which is here divided against itself, and the cause of his tragedy:

> . . . of what now I suffer
> She was not the prime cause, but I my self.

The full momentum of the baroque personality is Samson's, the vigor and rebellion; the image of man creating and accepting his own fate makes God's judgment of only minor interest, as it is in *Othello*:

> Appoint not heavenly disposition, Father,
> Nothing of all these evils hath befall'n me

> But justly; I my self have brought them on,
> Sole author I, sole cause.

The humanism of the renaissance speaks with solemn
voice in the tragic Samson, who exists deep within the
gulf of his own disaster, and who uses the "total"
language of passion, resembling the language of the
mad, abused, blinded Othello:

> Out, out, hyena; these are thy wonted arts,
> And arts of every woman false like thee,
> To break all faith, all vows, deceive, betray.

In destroying the temple Samson illustrates how far
baroque simplified—or coarsened, perhaps—the intricate mannerist psychology that sustained but could not
resolve its tensions. Samson is torn between the kind
of polar moods that impel the credulous, brutal
Othello: arrogance and humility, willfulness and frustration, trust and distrust, piety and insolence. These
contraries had also played through Donne, but fitfully,
irregularly, puzzling and paralyzing the metaphysicals
and Hamlet. Since the impulses in the mannerist temperament were always being diverted or thwarted,
mannerist drama could not provide a discharge or pur-
gation in some inevitable event. The mannerist action
ended in dissonance, irresolution, not in decision; the
tenor of the mannerist act was never entirely clear.
In baroque the impulses and values are clarified: contrary forces, colliding powerfully, are discharged in
some great act. In such a conflict we do not doubt what
is "right" and "wrong" because the fluid, shifting contexts of mannerist art have been steadied by fully declared meanings. The premises of the action are secure;
the moral and tragic focus is stabilized. After these
clarifications, we can yield ourselves, unthinkingly, to
an overcharged action that bursts into extravagant
conclusive gesture, guaranteeing a katharsis. At the
end of The Duchess of Malfi or a poem by Donne we

do not know surely what to feel. But we close *Samson* with a firm sense of resignation and settlement:

> Nothing is here for tears, nothing to wail,
> Or knock the breast, no weakness, no contempt,
> Dispraise, or blame, nothing but well and fair,
> And what may quiet us in a death so noble.

No matter how we rationalize or accommodate ourselves to the last scene, we cannot feel that *Hamlet* closes with any such decision. We know that, somehow, Hamlet has gained faith in the divinity that shapes our ends, and sees providence in the fall of a sparrow; he has made some discovery. And Horatio's farewell— "Goodnight, sweet prince, and flights of angels sing thee to thy rest"—has a tone of finality. Yet the meanings of the outcome are veiled, and "the rest is silence." What could Hamlet "have told us" if he had not died? And what, conceivably, can Horatio "tell" of these mischances at Elsinore, where purpose seems awry and where Hamlet—and Polonius—"with windlasses and with assays of bias/By indirections find directions out." By contrast, Samson's calamitous act is fulfillment, self-explanatory, ordained, bringing peace and consolation and "calm of mind, all passion spent." The baroque katharsis is achieved because the context of the drama is certain. We know "what to feel" because the values are assigned and not exploited only to gain an effect of crisis, because impulses at irrepressible pitch are firmly oriented toward a decisive act. In some such way Samson's gestures create about themselves an emotional theater, a tragic ethic without mannerist uncertainties. No accommodation is required; only denouement.

In the same way the baroque statue creates about itself its own emotional theater. Bernini's isolated figure of Longinus (Saint Peter's), with his hands extended in ardent devotion, leaves nothing unstated, and compellingly suggests, by a single gesture, the

whole drama of the Crucifixion and the awe of those
who beheld the stroke of the Lance. If the mannerist
figure "drives us about" its fluid contours, forcing us to
take a "revolving-view," the baroque statue demands
that we take a "one-view" approach. The baroque
sculptor so controls our access to his figure that it suddenly bursts into full view as a "flattened" or "broad"
spectacle which we see in a two-dimensional way as if
it were spread across a foreground plane. Although
baroque figures have great bulk, they are seen as if
they appeared on a proscenium stage. Thus they are
not really like renaissance profile-statues but highly
plastic volumes expanding freely into the "breadth" of
space about themselves. As Panofsky explains, our
"subjective experience" in looking at such figures "flattens" them because they are "fused with the surrounding space into a coherent visual picture." Bernini's
statue of the enraptured Saint Teresa generates about
itself, eloquently, its own spatial milieu and its own
passional meaning. The instant we come face to face
with this swooning figure we know what is happening
and surrender to its dominant emotional signature,
which is not ambiguous. The baroque image exists in a
powerfully but simply constructed context of obvious
values.

Almost like the baroque statue, Samson feels and
acts in the context of a simple but potent scale of moral
values; the figure has great "breadth" and is able to
organize about itself a coherent conflict of forces that
makes possible an unequivocal decision. An even more
simplified emotional theater is used in pietistic baroque painting, which is devoted to the prescribed
spectacular themes of Counter-Reformation legend:
the triumph of the Eucharist, the martyrdom of saints
with horrid tortures, scenes of the Passion, ecstasies
and levitations, astounding miracles. The high-baroque
theater discharges uncomplicated, powerful impulses

in "total" acts, releasing our emotions in ordained and polar directions. If mannerist theater utilizes the apparently unconditioned response, baroque art often depends upon the conditioned—or possibly stereotyped—reaction. With unguarded frankness the baroque theater stimulates us to feel rather than to think or discriminate; the energy of our response is so high that a few portentous gestures by heroic figures impel us headlong toward an overwhelming climax.

Any emotional release on this scale is necessarily public, and to an extent generalized and impersonal—not "depersonalized" in the mannerist sense of being aware of one's response, exploiting it curiously and with detachment studying it; but impersonal in the sense that it is magnified, primary, and having something of the classic or "universal" in it. The emotive discharge in Samson is as high as in Webster or Donne; but it is not private. Samson's self-examination is not so intricate as Hamlet's, so dissociated and disoriented. Furthermore, Donne and the mannerists do not trust their responses as do Samson and Othello, who are inclined to feel only one emotion at a time; therefore Samson does not appear to be so abnormally self-aware as the mannerist figure, and he does not venture to exploit or manipulate his sensibility; he is not quickly deflected. Unlike Hamlet, Samson never encourages us to examine the validity of his own responses; in its condition of doubt and instability mannerist art could not so openly commit itself to any act or release as Milton's play does. Of course *Samson Agonistes* is to an extent autobiographical, involving Milton's own political and sexual disillusions, and gains double meanings and intimacy through the poet's own unhappiness. Yet in spite of these personal overtones, the action has the public dimensions of high-baroque art, and is accessible to simple feeling as mannerist art was not; for in baroque the sensorium paralyzes the mind. This is not to say that *Samson* is merely "theater." It is much more. For one thing, the regularity of the action gives classic measure to events in Gaza; for another, there is the commanding Puritan gravity.

VII

RESOLUTION BY HEIGHT   Milton's drama is none the less a work of piety because it is Puritan, not Roman, piety. It has the devotional power of Counter-Reformation painting, statuary, and architecture. Usually it is said that the emotional key of baroque piety is "rapture," a *sursum corda,* an elevation of the spirit—or of the flesh. From time to time art historians have compared the "elevation" of baroque art with the vertical movement of gothic. Certainly baroque has abundant power to triumph over the horizontal by its pressure upward (its *Hochgedrang*) into mighty domes and pediments, into heavenly spectacles. The frail, constrained hovering of mannerist forms bursts into exultant baroque ascents. Baroque architecture accumulates massive materials and exalts them defiantly, easily, to inspiring heights. In painting, baroque accepts the flesh in its solidity, then lifts it up in space. An inherently baroque motif is the levitation of the body.

Congenial to this elevation, or levitation, of the flesh is the psychology of the Council of Trent, which set about inflaming otherworldliness and at the same time fostering the cult of splendid images. But there was also a geographic reason for the levitation of masses in baroque architecture, a style indigenous to Rome; and Rome is built upon hills. The very location of churches and palaces must have caused the Counter-Reformation architect to feel "the spatial rapture of the stair-

case." Michaelangelo felt it in planning his dramatic
flight to the Campidoglio, which, in turn, must have
inspired Bernini's Scala Regia and the ranging vistas
of baroque stagecraft. In such cases there is a steep
approach, a raised focus. This upward-looking (*di sotto
in su*) perspective had appeared in the "uncertain verticality" of mannerist composition, the wavering flamelike spaces in Tintoretto and El Greco, and the
thwarted upsurge of the anteroom of the Laurentian
Library. But Bernini's Scala Regia inspires us to make
ostentatious progress upward and *achieve* the heights.
Baroque solemnized and stabilized the aspiring mannerist vision; it fixed the point of view; it centralized
the axis; it enables us to mount on high with confidence and pomp. Bernini's stairway is a conquest of
upper space that resolves, daringly, the mannerist
longing to ascend. The baroque dome is an architectural *O Altitudo.* Unlike the renaissance Pantheon-
type dome or the half-concealed shrunken domes of
long-naved mannerist churches, the baroque dome is
treated as the obvious and imperious climax of the
broad façade and the wide interior, where the high
altar is ceremonially placed under a dynamic vast
space, from which light drenches the gaudy symbols of
piety. By means of paintings on the surface of the
dome and on the barrel vaults of baroque interiors, the
spatial rapture expands to an illusion of infinity, pillars
rising above pillars, clouds above clouds, until the spirits of the devout are swept upward into the operatic
heavens where great seraphic forms float in elastic
ease.

The high-baroque church is wider, more exposed,
more public than the long-naved mannerist church.
Baroque architects often reverted to a "centralized"
design more headstrong and *mouvementé* than the renaissance Greek-cross structure, or to a resplendent version of the Roman basilica. In such churches our sight

is drawn upward by the flood of light falling from
above; for often the baroque interior reveals everything. The walls of the first story are usually blind, the
nave opening into chapels or arms more disclosed than
those in the mannerist church. In each of these chapels
is displayed the altarpiece, that typical medium of baroque art. Amid such a setting these paintings are necessarily grandiose, and the artist naturally resorted to
a particular kind of "heightening": the large foreground figures must be dominant enough to make an
immediate impression, spread broadly upon the surface of the canvas just above the altar; above them, at
the top, as if the world were divided, glide huge saints
and angels in a celestial realm. Thus was created a
double world of space in baroque altarpieces, which
must take a theatrical, extravagant view of heaven. Already this double world had appeared during the high-
renaissance in Raphael's Disputà and Titian's Pesaro
Madonna, above an altar in the Frari in Venice. The
Titian Assumption, also, had suggested a formula for
the baroque pietistic scene—the dense foreground
group below gathered in rapture, looking up, across
an empty or cloudy space; and above, the panoply of
the heavenly host, superhuman figures in their substantial glory raising the hearts of the prayerful and
affirming the reality of the other world (for heretics
and Protestants had cast doubt upon these visions).
The figures in a baroque altarpiece are always gazing
upward, pointing our own attention toward the scene
above; the saints in ecstasy beholding the opened
heavens; the Madonna soaring, Murillo-like, above the
earth; the lush penitent Magdalen, tearful and half-
naked, glancing skyward over the scripture and skull
before her. We see the elevation of the flesh beginning
in Raphael's Sistine Madonna and even in the "realist"
Caravaggio, who painted Saint Matthew and the Angel for San Luigi dei Francesi. Domenichino's Last

Communion of Saint Jerome is a solemn pageant played under a tremendous Raphaelesque arch at the top of which float the cherubs waiting to embrace Jerome's soul.

During the evolution of the baroque façade, too, the law of gravity was increasingly denied. In the belated renaissance façade of Santa Caterina dei Funari, Rome (1564), pilasters are used to show how calmly the structure reposes upon solid earth. Signs of imbalance appear in the Gesù façade, about 1569–84, its features disturbed by awkwardness and unrest. With the greater warmth of Counter-Reformation piety, the façade of San Luigi dei Francesi (1589) hoists its most impressive volumes to the second story under a giant pediment. Then occur the high-baroque feats of sublimation, with levitated masses, ornate pediments surging to majestic heights, and richly treated superior orders and windows: Sant' Ignazio, that gaudy Jesuit spectacle (1626–85); Sant' Agnese in Agone (1653 ff.) with its triumphal towers and dome; Santa Maria in Campitelli (1665) and Sant' Andrea della Valle (c. 1665) with its operatic display; and, almost late-baroque, San Carlo alle Quattro Fontane (c. 1665–68) in voluptuous motion throughout its upper story. The history of the Roman baroque façade is coherent enough to justify the thesis that baroque architecture obeys a law of "upward-pressure" (*Hochgedrang*).

The center of gravity having been lifted, the particular art form suitable to express baroque piety was the divided world. In high-baroque churches the entablature between the first and second stories is broad and bold, horizontally dividing the façade and emphasizing the sumptuous handling of the upper orders. This treatment of the façade corresponds to the "Assumption-organization" of baroque painting, where the heavenly group is more gorgeous than the law of pictorial gravity allows. Mannerists like El Greco did not so clearly divide their world; it was left for the baroque painters to equate, courageously, the solidity of the realm above with the solidity of the realm below—another version of the dogma of transubstantiation, or secularizing the transcendental.

The elaborate devotional poetry of Crashaw has the triumphal, easily achieved "vertical" direction and daring materialism of baroque art. Technically, the baroque altarpiece or façade and Crashaw's poems alike resolve their energies by a feat of sublimation, levitating the material. Crashaw's "Stabat Mater" is like a Murillo Purissima, where both worlds take part in the sensuous drama of baroque art, and his "Prayer" is a gesture from Sassoferrato or Carlo Dolci:

> Effectual whispers, whose still voice
> The soul itself more feels than hears;
> Amorous languishments, luminous trances;
> Sights which are not seen with eyes;
> Spiritual and soul-piercing glances,
> Whose pure and subtle lightning flies
> Home to the heart, and sets the house on fire
> And melts it down in sweet desire. . . .
> Delicious deaths, soft exhalations
> Of soul; dear and divine annihilations. . . .

Crashaw's buoyant ardor reaches its fulfillment in the ecstasy of his Saint Teresa with her white breast, her beatific death of love, her delicious wounds, her transporting rapture in the flesh.

Crashaw does not have the mannerist imagination or feel the intense struggle of Teresa herself, or need the constant self-control and self-scrutiny of Saint Ignatius; for the tension between body and soul is loosened by his naive confidence in the fleshly image, which he lyrically exalts, then adores. Crashaw knows the triumph of piety, but not the anguish that caused Teresa to say that her "interior sufferings" cannot be described and "would make all physical sufferings seem very slight." He is not ravaged by Teresa's fear and doubt, her dread of "another very dangerous kind of temptation: a feeling of security caused by the belief that we shall never again return to our past faults and to the pleasures of the world." Crashaw's notoriously literal images—the tears that mount upwards, the walking baths in the Magdalen's eyes—are not, like Donne's understatements, ironic; they are the generous overstatements of a piety free to worship images without a bad conscience. Crashaw hopes to inflame devotion by his clever, if not outrageous, actualities that would seem almost metaphysical if the poet were able to "reserve" or "withhold" his meanings; but he is not metaphysical like Donne, for he is not critical of his own rapture, which he indulges without mannerist two-mindedness and dissonance. If Crashaw uses witty language, he completely trusts his own emotions. His mood is aspiration, approaching sentimentality. His literalism is not the sardonic literalism of Donne's metaphors. Indeed, if metaphor requires that an object be used as a symbol, Crashaw can hardly be said to use metaphor at all, for he simply describes fleshly experience—which he identifies with supernal experience, as Teresa did not. Crashaw's most material world is the heavenly world; his most sensuous exhibitions are on high, like the exhibitions in the divided baroque world.

If the two realms of baroque art—the world below and the world above—are separated, they are not, however, differentiated, since both are realized at the level of the senses. Again, baroque consolidates its experience in the material. Baroque piety simply performs a substitution, or a direct transference, using the world below to represent the world above; it affirms the glory of the eternal by overstating the temporal. This is one reason for the excessive magniloquence of baroque in its upper stories and celestial registers. The baroque artist is constantly tempted to overactualize his sublimities; and when he does so, he is in danger of being ridiculously literal rather than imaginative. Perhaps T. S. Eliot was justified in remarking that Milton has ascended "a perch from which he cannot afford to fall, and from which he is in danger of slipping." It demands a superhuman energy and vision to sustain the magnificence of this upper world: if it is not overpoweringly realized, it looks merely gaudy; if it is too extravagant, it is melodrama or travesty. Milton assumes the full risk of this divided world in *Paradise Lost*, where there is a double register of action, in Eden and in Heaven, and both must be realized in the same texture of material splendor. Thus Milton overactualizes his celestial spectacle; the war in Heaven with its uprooted hills, its oversized cannon and ethereal firepower betrays the sort of failure in baroque imagination we sometimes feel in Crashaw's visions, which are really not visions at all but only elevations of the flesh.

The double world of baroque art—its redundant heavenly extravaganza—is a tacit avowal that the Counter-Reformation paradise is not the invisible one, the inward Eden of man's spirit that Milton sought to enter. The baroque elevation, depending as it does on materializing or secularizing the other world, upon a false transfiguration, can become a coarse stagecraft. To triumph in the flesh may not be to reach the transcendent. Baroque art inherits from the renaissance, and impressively uses, an academic regularity, but it often reveals a specious psychology, a specious physics, lifting the center of attention and gravity to the dome, the canopy over the adoring group, enshrining the charms of common flesh until it looks celestial. In 1649 Francisco Pacheco wrote in his *Art of Painting* that the artist must be a Christian, and also that plastic form is more important than beauty, for plastic form can deceive the eye so that figures seem round and emerging from the frame. It is better, he says, to paint from nature than from any lay figure—even when painting the Virgin, who must be represented as follows:

. . . the Lady should be painted in the flower of Her youth, twelve or thirteen years old, as a most beautiful young girl, with fine and serious eyes, a most perfect nose and mouth and pink cheeks, wearing Her most beautiful golden hair loose, in short with as much perfection as human brush could achieve. Man possesses two beauties, namely body and soul, and the Virgin hath both beyond compare. Bodily she was a miracle. . . . She should be painted with a white tunic and a blue mantle. . . . She is clothed in the sun, an oval sun of whites and ochres which must surround the whole image, sweetly fusing it with the sky. She is crowned by stars, twelve stars in a light circle between rays parting from Her sacred forehead. . . . An imperial crown should adorn Her head, which should not hide the stars. Under Her feet is the moon.

The purpose of creating this image—this familiar image —is to inspire devotion, to assure the believer, says Pacheco, of gaining bliss and beatitude. Sometimes instead of elevating the flesh the baroque merely vulgarized heaven. Murillo's Immaculate Conceptions are early poster art.

VIII

FROM BAROQUE TO KITSCH   In fact, Murillo's beclouded, pleasant Virgins indicate the special peril in baroque art, which is liable to degenerate into a popular "art of delight" we have learned to call *Kitsch*. Since modern religious art is largely given to Kitsch, it seems worth remarking that the origins of this corruption of a style lie, by implication, in the policies of the Council of Trent; for again the Council is a watershed between the arts of the Catholic past and the arts of the Catholic present.

Turning against mannerism and its perplexities, its tendency to overexamine and distrust its own feelings, baroque art is an early "mass medium" devised to resolve doubts and give a sense of emotional satisfaction, triumph, or katharsis; it submerges scruples by dogma and resplendent images, releasing our feelings in a "unified" response. Baroque works many simplifications (Woelfflin's *Vereinfachung*). Often this reduction of dissonance within the self is gained at a sacrifice of intelligence and self-awareness, a yielding to the stereotyped reaction. A common opinion is that baroque confronts the world by "feeling" (*pathos*), not by "reason" (*logos*). The danger of sentimentality was, of course, inherent in the *pathos* of the baroque image. But as long as the Counter Reformation had to muster the energy needed to encounter evil and sin, baroque art expressed, along with its *pathos,* a kind of *logos* in the guise of a triumphant will.

Yet the triumph of the will occurs only when there is something for the will to triumph over, only when the conquest is achieved against a real existing evil. This is why the struggle in Milton's Samson is authentically baroque. In its eagerness for victory, however, the Council of Trent had insisted that error can be dispelled by reliance on the Church, that doubts can be subdued by authority, that belief can be easy, that the force and threat of evil can be annulled. As this sort of optimism grew, the Counter Reformation evidently did at last suppose it had cast out Satan; and after Satan has vanished, the exertion of the Christian will is an empty gesture. Then baroque art changes from a victorious exhibition of power to a gaudy display of self-assurance or self-satisfaction, which, in turn, can degenerate to sentimentality. When the will is enfeebled, devotion requires only a cheap efflux of feeling. As soon as the art of Michaelangelo and Milton in energetic strife (*agonistes*) is replaced by the art of Murillo and

Crashaw, the baroque image loses its full charge and becomes merely seductive or agreeable. It is agreeable enough in Crashaw, whose raptures are a very accessible kind of solace. Soon piety diffuses to pathos, and there are the girlish adenoidal madonnas and saints painted by Carlo Dolci and Sassoferrato.

When the baroque imagination fails in power, Counter-Reformation art decays to Kitsch—prettiness, and sentimentality. Milton himself has a few distressing passages of Kitsch in *Paradise Lost*, especially when Eve tries to be domestic and cultivate the middle-class virtues:

> . . . for nothing lovelier can be found
> In woman then to studie houshold good,
> And good workes in her husband to promote.

This is a sadly available range of virtue (Eve as efficient and self-effacing housewife who putters with the vegetables while Adam and the Angel, the menfolk, take up the serious business of life). In these episodes Milton writes the prologue to the bourgeois-baroque of the eighteenth century as practiced by Greuze and the "household" paintings with a usable, easy message for the ordinary man. There is a certain intellectual Kitsch, also, in Raphael's warning to Adam not to think too hard about thorny problems:

> Sollicit not thy thoughts with matters hid,
> Leave them to God above, him serve and fear.

This echoes the policy of the Council of Trent's Session XXV recommending that preachers avoid "the more difficult and subtler questions, which do not tend to edification" of ordinary folk. Adam is not advised to go, with John Donne, "about and about" to seek truth, or to gore his own thoughts. At first the Calvinist feared terribly the wrath of a mighty God; he feared with an intense concentration of piety. But Raphael makes Calvinism easy, lessening the terror by reassuring us that ignorance is the safest policy. When the Archangel says, in effect, "Don't try to know too much" he promotes a kind of Calvinism adapted to the man in the street, who is inclined to accept a sufficient stupidity as a warrant of normalcy and reliability. "Easy" Calvinism substitutes sufficient ignorance for sufficient grace; to know too much is high-brow. Donne wore his learning more insolently.

The Counter Reformation was fatally subject to intellectual Kitsch, and the more "devotional" rituals were the Kitsch of the Council of Trent, just as Murillo's glowing madonnas are the Kitsch of baroque painting and tinseled images are the Kitsch of baroque sculpture. Throughout the history of baroque styles the corruption is similar: first a baroque triumph in Bernini, Maderna, Borromini, and Milton; then easier access to feeling—to *pathos*—as a resolution; then a decline to gaudiness instead of splendor; lastly, Kitsch and popular devotion, images, literature, painting, and delights. Baroque begins with magniloquence and ends with "rhetoric" and "elegance." From this standpoint the Council of Trent inaugurates the larger reformation of the world, toward every form of Kitsch which destroys baroque vigor, the imaginative use of power.

Baroque found its popular "objective correlatives" in the sensuous images gathered in Caesar Ripa's *Iconologia* (1593, etc.) adapted by the new cults among Jesuits, Franciscans, Carmelites, and Augustinians; and the Counter-Reformation artist was obliged by the Church to use a lurid but trite iconology. The triumph of the Eucharist was among the set themes for painting, as were the horrors of martyrdom with their direct popular appeal: disemboweling of saints, flayings, beheadings, tearing out of tongues and eyes, cutting off of hands and breasts, innumerable flagellations. Practicing the *Spiritual Exercises* surely did not injure the talent of Bernini, who commanded the energetic baroque imagination; but under the soft and diffused influence of Correggio's painting, the Holy Night became a "show" with garish lighting and popular rejoicing in earth and heaven. The Annunciation became delectably Murillesque, with the Virgin's pneumatic rapture; and the Passion became a scene of torture involving such literal questions as whether three or four nails were used, whether the wound was on the right or left side, whether Mary was present at the Flagellation. Everything had to be obvious and orthodox. Thus the baroque imagination at its literal, popular level lost its transforming power.

This vulgar iconography concealed a new form of bad conscience about the fleshly image—prudery about the body. Uneasiness about the flesh is here and there concealed under Milton's own delight in the naked Eve, who wholly commands his poetic allegiance but who also causes him defensively to explain away some unidentified sense of shame. In its more hearty triumphs the baroque was able to treat the flesh, the erotic, without any sense of indecency—in Rubens, for example; but at the level of Kitsch, baroque soon reveals a middle-class pruriency. As early as 1582 Bartolommeo Ammannati wrote a Letter to the Academy cautioning fellow painters to "take care for the love of God and their own salvation not to fall into the errors and mistakes into which I have fallen in my work by making many of my statues nude and undraped. . . . I mean completely nude figures or anything else that might arouse evil thoughts in man or woman of any age." Here is the sexual problem as Donne never knew it; mannerism had a bad enough conscience, but it was not priggish. The more vulgar Counter-Reformation painting was prone to show the Magdalen in all her piety and only half-concealed charms. Mannerist images are *mondain*, ascetic, or neurasthenic, but not vulgar as the Magdalen was vulgar and enticing. There is nothing vulgar about Hamlet's overwrought conscience, foul as it may be. But a concern for modesty is a mark of the special bad conscience of a corrupt baroque style.

The enticing and popular iconography of sentimental baroque—perhaps like the images in Crashaw, the tears and milk of the Virgin, the cherubs and darts of love—accompanied a decay in rational theology and the rise of mere dogma in its place. The sensorium in its most literal activity became the instrument of faith. As the baroque imagination materialized itself at the familiar level, illusion became mere deception whenever the artist gave up the double world courageously erected by high-baroque art, and tried to obliterate entirely the distinction between the heavenly realm and the world of the worshiper. Baciccio's ceiling in the Gesù (1670–83) swirls with rosy clouds painted on areas of plaster or metal overflowing the architectural boundaries of the coffered vault until the ethereal mist seems to reach down into the space of the nave where we stand bewildered as to the division between the "other" world and "ours." This intimacy is clever and cheap, a vernacular approach to eternity. Heaven is entirely accessible in Fra Andrea Pozzo's ceiling (1685 ff.) in Sant' Ignazio, where the majestic soaring architecture, itself painted, is almost obliterated by the swarming angelic hosts flying about the very windows of the clerestory and obscuring the values of both illusion and reality by their facile descent. This art makes transubstantiation "easy" and credible.

In 1649 Father Jean Dubreuil in his *Perspective Pratique* (otherwise known as *The Jesuit Perspective*) suggested some of the advantages of having a new *theatra sacra* "for altars and oratories in churches, in gardens and summer houses, for alcoves, theaters, and ballets" —a final devaluation of baroque illusion, power, and expressiveness:

At Christmas Eve you could paint a stable on the first cutout; ruins, the Shepherds and the Angel on the second, with a view of Bethlehem at the back. For Holy Week you could make a Calvary by cutting mountains out of two or three boards placed one behind the other, with a Cross, Our Lady, St. John, the Magdalen, and some soldiers cut out at the back. For Easter Sunday the first cutout might show the mouth of a grotto, through which you would see the Sepulchre guarded by soldiers looking up startled at Our Lord above, while through an opening in the grotto, you could see Jerusalem and the Marys on their way to the Tomb.

These cutouts, the Father adds, are more effective if they are lighted by lamps to make the scene look deeper. The Counter-Reformation imagination has failed. This is no triumph of vision. It is not even the illusion of art. The potent baroque image created a baroque theater. The baroque theater at last became the religious peep show.

IX

RESOLUTION BY LIGHT   In the so-called Churrigueresque style (*c.* 1700) baroque, as if desperately, resorted to its most literal deceptions: the Virgin wearing real hair, the eyes of saints glassy, their wounds bleeding. High-baroque had guarded its illusions more successfully, its imaginative power transvaluing its densest materials, mass being resolved into movement, walls and domes into an idiom of dynamic space. But the ultimate baroque resolutions and transformations were attained by color and light. After the acid tints of mannerist art, its exploration of private obscurities, baroque casts a floodlight over the world. Under its bold effulgence vaults, piers, and domes become an atmosphere of radiance, the garments of Teresa seem to move while the warm glow is shed upon them, the columns of the Scala Regia vanish and emerge until they appear to be a pulse of light and shade. Baroque is indeed a "painterly" (*malerisch*) style, bathing volumes in light and dark (*Hell und Dunkel*) or pure tonality. Generously as baroque uses fat pigments and textures, its tonality does not necessarily depend upon color or hue (*Farbe*) but upon masses of brilliance and deep gloom, a released illumination (*Helligkeit*). Rubens conceives the structure of his world in exuberant molded color; but Rembrandt, having passed through the flickering shadows of mannerism, is able to dissolve the world in tonality, especially in his engravings, which press Tintoretto's analysis of substance to its extremity by his transforming light.

Roman baroque art was, chiefly, a resolution by mass, energy, and space; the northern baroque was a resolution by color and light. Milton's Eden, with its burnished groves, its flowers all hues, its purple grapes and umbrageous grottoes and streams, might have been created by Rubens' florid palette, and has something of the pastoral glory of high-renaissance landscape, its wealth of color, its *Farbenklang*. But in Milton's more severe passages there are deep "zones of shadow" (*Schattenstreifen*) reminding us of Rembrandt. Many have thought that Milton's sensitivity to light was due to his blindness; yet it must also have been due to the baroque and "painterly" quality of his seasoned imagination, which causes him to think of God as being Light, an eternal "bright effulgence of bright essence increate." His Inferno has the sultry splendor of Titian's Venetian baroque, the mysterious depths and luxuriant textures, together with a troublous, willful gloom that must be called not shadow but Rembrandtesque darkness:

> . . . a Cherube tall
> Who forthwith from the glittering staff unfurld

> Th'imperial ensign, which full high advanct
> Shon like a meteor streaming to the wind
> With gemms and golden lustre rich imblazd,
> Seraphic arms and trophies. . . .
> All in a moment through the gloom were seen
> Ten thousand banners rise into the air
> With orient colours waving: with them rose
> A forrest huge of spears; and thronging helms
> Appear'd, and serried shields in thick array
> Of depth immeasurable.

Milton's religious values can be symbolized by the fierceness of light, which is creative energy:

> Let ther be light, said God, and forthwith Light
> Etherial, first of things, quintessence pure
> Sprung from the deep.

The tragic ethic of *Samson Agonistes* is represented by light and dark: the darkness of the mind, of the day, of this action where the self is a dungeon and the blinded giant moves in obscurity. Samson speaks with the pain that led Rembrandt to immerse his self-portraits in the dusk:

> O dark, dark, dark, amid the blaze of noon,
> Irrecoverably dark, total eclipse,
> Without all hope of day! . . .
> The sun to me is dark
> And silent as the moon,
> When she deserts the night
> Hid in her vacant interlunar cave.
> Since light so necessary is to life,
> And almost life itself, if it be true
> That light is in the soul . . .

Milton's image for his terrible Puritan God is dark with excessive bright.

We enter deep shadow—darkness, at times—with Rembrandt, master of psychological and pictorial baroque art, who reduces the Roman problem of mass and energy to the final terms of a northern twilight resolution, like the resolution of baroque materialism in the philosophy of Spinoza, for whom matter is essential mystery, the breath of God Himself. After the mechanism and automatism of Hobbes there comes the pantheism of Spinoza—after the dichotomy of body and will, the resolving of flesh to spirit. For Spinoza "the power of nature is the power of God." This is the *Goetterdaemmerung* of baroque thought, the transvaluing of matter to force, the release from potency of the image to the motion of the soul. Thus the fleshly, willful, resplendent baroque completes (though we should least expect it in baroque art) the transformations that began during the renaissance. If, however, we think again, we recall that in high-baroque Rome the painted dome was resolved to music, and under the glare of noon the lavish altar, in its plastic majesty, was a blazing illumination.

Amid the waning glories of Italian baroque the French painter Claude Lorrain was irradiating his classic imaginary Roman world with a calm and vast transparency: beyond the pale and contrived architecture of his ports the sinking sun casts a light that never was on sea or land. It is an afterglow of baroque splendor—and also the clear, still atmosphere of a purified vision, the vision of Poussin and Racine.

NOTES

1. Much of the analysis of baroque style has been done by art historians who wrote in German, particularly Woelfflin (Renaissance und Barock), *Pevsner* (Barockmalerei in den Romanischen Laendern), *and Walter Friedlaender, whose various articles have examined the rise of an "anti-mannerist" style in the early seventeenth century. It again seems proper, therefore, to indicate some of the German expressions used by these pioneer scholars which may, or may not, have precise equivalents in English. At least it will suggest what I owe to them.*

2. J. B. Leishman holds this view about "unified sensibility" in The Monarch of Wit, *which marks the present re-*

action against earlier appraisals of "metaphysical" poetry by Eliot and others.

3. This discrepancy is mentioned by Basil Willey in The Seventeenth-Century Background; *actually it seems to be the discrepancy Eliot found in Milton in 1936 ("A Note on the Verse of John Milton"), an essay since qualified by Eliot himself, who had detected, he thought, an "interruption" between the surface and the "core" of Milton's poetry.*

4. The structure of baroque during its developing phases is defined, perhaps too schematically, by T. H. Fokker's Roman Baroque Art, *a book on which I have depended heavily in this chapter and the next. I have adopted Fokker's phrases to describe the baroque treatment of space and volume, and have referred to his illustrations of baroque principles, which in many ways agree with those in Denis Mahon's indispensable* Studies in Seicento Art and Theory.

5. This is Fokker's view, which, in essence, is supported by Walter Friedlaender and by Roger Hinks (Caravaggio), whose conclusions I epitomize.

6. My whole discussion of the relation of baroque to academic art depends on Denis Mahon's Studies in Seicento Art and Theory, *as well as on Fokker.*

LATE-BAROQUE

I

THE "NEOCLASSICAL" TRADITION   Before
the high-baroque displays had ended in Rome, the axis
of the arts was swinging northward to be stabilized,
during the latter seventeenth century, in the vicinity of
Paris, where newly founded academies of painting and
literature were conducting their stately "conversations."
After much grave consideration the French academicians succeeded in writing the last formulas for a cycle
of styles that originated in the renaissance and returned
upon itself in the many diplomatic rules of decorum,
propriety, unity, and *vraisemblance.*

If the French never produced an extravagant baroque
art, nevertheless the Parisian academies often found
their standards—their "judicious" standards—among the
baroque splendors of Rome. Relations with Italy were
maintained through solitary French artists left behind
in the sunset of Tridentine pomps. "The best of the
French School, Poussin, Le Sueur, and Le Brun," wrote
Sir Joshua Reynolds in 1771, "may be said, though
Frenchmen, to be a colony from the Roman School."
Since the earliest renaissance Paris had kept its contact with Italy, and just as in the mid-sixteenth century Primaticcio inspired the mannerist painters at
Fontainebleau, so Bernini's gusty visit to Paris in 1665
dramatized the prestige of Italian baroque among
French architects and sculptors of the age of Louis XIV.
And the more judicious British artists and writers of the
later seventeenth and the eighteenth centuries, like

Wren and Dryden and Reynolds, often served, though unwillingly, as a kind of Parisian colony in London. Dryden's dialogue on dramatic poetry, while asserting British independence from French dogma, also sanctioned a measure of regularity, "correctness," and "propriety"; and Pope lightly granted that "Critic-learning flourish'd most in France." We know, too, what Sir Joshua Reynolds owed to the French theory of painting, the doctrine of Du Fresnoy, and colloquies held in Paris academies upon paintings by Poussin and the Gallic colony in Rome.

One result of this swing in the axis from Rome toward Paris was a Franco-Roman-Augustan tradition heavily indebted to baroque, but usually called "neoclassicism" or "academism," a tradition that works itself out variously and lengthily in the fine arts from Domenichino, Borromini, and Bernini through Poussin, Le Brun, François Mansart, Jules Hardouin-Mansart, and Wren, and in literature through "heroic" plays by Corneille and Dryden, Johnson's "regular" tragedy *Irene*, and Reynolds' *Discourses*. The most influential academic critic of the whole seventeenth century was probably that well-born Roman Giovanni Pietro Bellori (1615 –96) whose words were echoed all over Europe, and Bellori's admiration for an "ideal beauty" surpassing nature proves that there is no inherent contradiction between the generous baroque style and the stately forms in painting and literature we have called "academic." The academic, or the Augustan, seems implicit in baroque itself. This tradition produces in Hardouin-Mansart's Church of the Invalides and in Dryden's heroic plays an art essentially different from the slighter decorative rococo art of Pineau, Alexander Pope, Watteau, Lancret, Guardi, Longhi, and Tiepolo. The academic-neoclassic tradition accepts a larger scale, keeping much of the baroque "augment," and relies on ideals of "elevation" and the "grand style"; but at the same time it has a strengthened sense of "decorum," regularity, unity, and whatever is tectonic.[1] Although British critics like Dryden and Johnson and Reynolds scorn the French "rules," they try to keep a "judicial" frame of mind. They admire the heroic, but they are devoted to an idea of "Nature" best defined by Reynolds when he says that "the whole beauty and grandeur of art consists in being able to get above all singular forms, local customs, particularities, and details of every kind." Dr. Johnson repeats that the poet's business is to examine not the individual but the species, to remark general properties and large appearances; he does not number the streaks of the tulip or describe the different shades of verdure in the forest. "The grand style" in Reynolds' sense does not tolerate any "inferior beauties." Corneille, Dryden, the French academicians, insist with Reynolds that poetry and painting must use "a language in the highest degree artificial, a construction of measured words such as never is, nor ever was, used by man."

This ill-defined Franco-Roman-Augustan tradition is international. In spite of their strong individuality Corneille, Boileau, Du Fresnoy, Dryden, Johnson, and Reynolds are kindred in their notions of style, "Nature," elevation, regularity, and judiciousness; so also Poussin, Le Sueur, and Le Brun belong to a tradition in style along with François Mansart at Val-de-Grâce, Perrault at the Louvre, Hardouin-Mansart at the Invalides or the Chapel at Versailles, and Wren at Saint Paul's or the Greenwich Hospital. There is diversity within this tradition: Dryden is more "heroic" than Johnson in *Irene;* François Mansart at Val-de-Grâce is less pompous than Wren at Saint Paul's or Hardouin-Mansart at the Invalides; Poussin is less frigid than Le Brun; Boileau is far drier than Reynolds, whose ill-disciplined affection for Michaelangelo is not quite orthodox. Indeed, Reynolds somewhat resembles the unruly

Dryden or Corneille, who confessed, "I love to follow the rules, but far from being their slave, I enlarge them or narrow them according to the demands of my subject." Above all there is a difference between Corneille and Racine, and between Dryden and the Milton of *Paradise Regained*. In these latter distinctions we find the difference between an heroic and a psychological form of academic art.

Sometimes art historians give their own name to this tradition, which is a residue from baroque but separate from high-baroque. For them, it is "late-baroque." The term is better than academic, neoclassic, or Augustan because it indicates both the origin and the course of this current, which runs through literature as well as the other arts, modifying the excesses of baroque by an effort to impose "regularity." Literary historians have long debated how far this academic or neoclassical practice, as found in Boileau for example, is indebted to "rationalism," or Cartesianism as it is often known, for this was the century that produced Descartes and his mathematical method. But this kind of art is not rationalist; rather, it has an instinct for "psychological symmetry," which is something else, and more subtle and humane, than rationalism. In fact, late-baroque is nothing less than a psychological reconstruction of baroque. Poussin and Racine, master artists in this tradition, purify baroque mass, flesh, volume, and gesture by a late-baroque psychology which amounts to a style—a style that returns to the tectonic principles of renaissance art.

II

THE SYSTEM OF REVERSAL AND BALANCE

Of Sir Isaac Newton's three laws of motion, the second, dealing with changes of momentum, acceleration, and mass, might be taken as the principle behind the dynamics of baroque art; but his third law is a basic premise of late-baroque style: namely, "To every action there is always opposed an equal reaction," or, in effect, the mutual actions of two bodies upon each other are equal and directly opposite. Late-baroque writes exact equations.

In the fine arts the mark of late-baroque style is the use of exaggerated contrast or counterpoise. As high-baroque gradually transforms itself into late-baroque, a rhythmical balance becomes metrical balance. We have seen that a high-baroque façade like that of Sant' Agnese in Agone in Rome balances its masses. The shift to late-baroque did not mean so much a change in form as a loss of "organic" or "total" movement and a stronger emphasis upon the units, the splitting up of masses into clearly arranged compartments. In a late-baroque façade like that of the Church of the Invalides the "regularity" is firmly imposed upon, and obviously controls, the powerful volumes of high-baroque; the walls are no longer internally "activated," and the movement does not seem so "free." Late-baroque masses are "closed" or contained within strongly defined limits and treated with a responsible, sober, or even methodical sense of order. The striking contrast between massive materials and their sedate arrangement gives to some late-baroque architecture an air of unconvincing splendor, as if there were an idiom to express energy without any compelling energy to express. The concern to regulate energy and statement is noticeable when we contrast one of Milton's enormous rhythmic verse-paragraphs in *Paradise Lost* with the contrived grandeur and rather brassy declamation of Dryden's "Song for Saint Cecilia's Day":

> From harmony, from heav'nly harmony,
>   This universal frame began;

> When Nature underneath a heap
> Of jarring atoms lay,
> And could not heave her head,
> The tuneful voice was heard from high,
> "Arise ye more than dead."
> Then cold and hot and moist and dry
> In order to their stations leap,
> And Music's pow'r obey.
> From harmony, from heav'nly harmony,
> This universal frame began:
> From harmony to harmony
> Through all the compass of the notes it ran,
> The diapason closing full in man.

The baroque pomps and overstatements of Dryden's "Grand Chorus" do not have the surging momentum of Milton's magniloquence.

The façade of San Carlo al Corso (*c*. 1682) illustrates the late-baroque treatment of masses, which now are set against each other with a rather clumsy insistence. The scale of the statement is gigantic, and at first glance the façade strikes us as one more overwhelming play of baroque power. The broken pediment has an outrageous violence, and the giant order running up the entire face in compound pilasters and columns has a truculent grandeur. If we move away a little, however, we see that in spite of all this abundance the façade places a coarse and uninspired stress on windows and portals, and is too crudely divided into three great "closed" areas by the colossal order, which looks fatter and more inert than it should. Despite, too, the louring pediment and the bulky columns, the masses do not "swing" freely but are measured into a pompous formula that soberly repeats its caesuras and accents. The lack of internal vitality would not be so evident if the scale were not so gross. Bernini's giant colonnades enclosing Saint Peter's Square, though they are exactly balanced, are not regularized in this heavy-handed way, but burst spontaneously into organic rhythm. The

façade of San Carlo has greater bravura than Bernini's
Scala Regia, which, however, reaches a melodramatic
climax without signs of rhetorical strain. By contrast,
the "combination of bulky and contrasting masses" [2] at
San Carlo al Corso seems to be a mere surplus in phrasing, as if baroque magniloquence had become bom-
bast, sound, and fury. The heightening and exuberance
of San Carlo alle Quattro Fontane bring no sense of
overexertion; yet there are abundant wealth and power
in spite of a scale that is tiny compared with the scale
at San Carlo al Corso, which swells its vocabulary by
rule instead of impulse.

The exaggerated contrasts and balances of late-
baroque appear in Bernini's latest sculptures like The
Angel with the Title (Sant' Andrea delle Fratte, Rome)
which simulates movement but is really fixed in a diagram of forces, the leg turned against the torso, the
torso turned against the head, the head turned against
the arm in a formula for *contrapposto*. For all its activity, this Angel lacks the organic rhythm of the earlier
Saint Teresa group in Santa Maria della Vittoria because the figure is divided into separate units or volumes. When the late-baroque statue falls into these
theatrical counterpositions its energy is expressed as an
"attitude," almost mechanically struck. The same exaggerated contrasts appear in late-baroque painting, like
Giacinto Brandi's Forty Martyrs (*c.* 1673) where the
masses are split up and congealed in separate units and
the bodies of the slain are thrown into contrasting postures. In the Spanish Steps at Rome (1723–25) the
late-baroque reversals occur with great precision and
a much simplified rhetoric; the formula of thrust and
counterthrust, swing and counterswing, is worked out
symmetrically within a diagram "closed" by the retain-
ing walls and the rather dry façade of Santissima Trin-
ità dei Monti, checking any full-baroque release. Whenever the encounter of opposite forces is thus metrical,

an effect of "number" replaces an effect of "mass," and
we think of the regularized framework of Dryden's late-
baroque verses:

> Who knows how far transcending goodness can
> Extend the merits of that Son to man?
> Who knows what reasons may His mercy lead,
> Or ignorance invincible may plead?
> Not only charity bids hope the best,
> But more the great Apostle has express'd:
> That if the Gentiles, whom no law inspir'd,
> By nature did what was by law requir'd,
> They who the written rule had never known
> Were to themselves both rule and law alone.
>   *Religio Laici*

This degree of formal control is unusual in high-
baroque, but common at Versailles and in the gardens
so hugely and methodically laid out by Le Nôtre.

These instances will suggest how late-baroque confines and redirects the energies of full-baroque by using a design of opposition, balance, and reversal. In
many of its phases the late-baroque does not lack
energy, but disciplines it anew in a dialectic of forces
that seem to obey Newton's third law of motion. Or
wherever there is a loss of willful imagination, as at
San Carlo al Corso and in "love-and-honor" drama,
there is a compensating noisiness of rhetoric, which
gives an appearance of overexertion, of amplitude in
material rather than in power.

While it was regulating and regularizing baroque
forces, late-baroque drama often treated the will under
a new aspect—as an obligation to behave according to
the demands of some idealized value like "honor" or
"love." Characters in Corneille, Dryden, and Otway do
not experience the will as a felt impulse but rather as
a need to comply with a formula of "love" and "honor"
which makes passion and duty a ritual performed by
an elite. The late-baroque will is often the directive of
a social code, a code operating at its full scope in the

heroic seventeenth-century plays in which everyone
obeys the "decencies" of a fictitious protocol. Dryden's
Almanzor in *The Conquest of Granada* obeys this sort
of code, which obviously owes a great deal to the
etiquette of a "grand century" attempting to maintain
the "heroic" baroque values in the face of an increasingly aggressive middle class:

> Vast is his courage, boundless is his mind,
> Rough as the storm, and humourous as the wind:
> Honour's the only idol of his eyes.

Dryden intended to elevate and control his gesticulating dramas, and to regulate the wills of his characters,
by some noble psychology that could give a formal,
even an academic, contour to heroic fables. He claims,
indeed, " 'Tis the moral that directs the whole action
of the play to one center." The late-baroque theater
often disguises its grandiose social conventions as moral
imperatives.

This sort of psychology, simplifying passion and will
to a conflict between the "duties" of a quasi-moral order,
appears in the English theater long before the Civil
War in Beaumont and Fletcher, whose characters have
been said to "walk among mirrors" because they are
controlled by absolutes that are only the ideals of a
coterie. Thus they move through symmetrical designs
of love and hate, loyalty and disloyalty, and produce
the "dialectical displays" of language which are the
rhetoric of the heroic play. In the coarse and violent
Maid's Tragedy (*c.* 1611) Beaumont and Fletcher used
a pattern of reversals required by a code of love and
duty, an hypothetic formula for morality. Amintor, who
is pledged to Aspatia, is betrothed to Evadne, who is
mistress of the King. When Amintor learns that his marriage is merely a mask for the King's lust, he confides
in Evadne's brother, Melantius, and both are caught in
the "moral" dilemma of having either to kill their king

or tolerate adultery. After many reversals of intention Aspatia, in disguise, is killed by Amintor, Evadne repents her crime and kills the King, and Amintor, Melantius, and Evadne die. Amintor wrongs Aspatia, Evadne wrongs Amintor, the King wrongs Evadne, and the system is almost closed in a scheme of countermovements. In their moral crisis Amintor and Melantius direct their wrath, in turn, against themselves, the King, and Evadne; then Evadne atones by murdering the King to prove herself worthy of Amintor's love; but Amintor will then not love her because she is a regicide. The contrary forces come to stability after each of the characters has taken, successively, the opposite "attitudes" available at the poles of this fictitious psychology. The hero of Fletcher's *Valentinian* (c. 1614) asks: "What is honour/We all so strangely are bewitched withal?"

The law of contradictory motives also operated in a baroque play like *Othello* or *Samson Agonistes;* however, the motives in Beaumont and Fletcher are not felt in the blood; they are not organic, passional forces but the need to maneuver within the terms of a convention. Othello knows his "honor" by a sickening black suspicion and a deep motion of his rage. Honor in Beaumont and Fletcher is a position or an attitude a character is expected to take. When moral values are only the manners of a coterie, the frontiers of drama shrink, as they sometimes do in Corneille and almost always in Dryden's heroic plays. This translation of moral impulses into protocol makes it possible for characters to conceive themselves, hypothetically, as taking different positions or "attitudes." Then the dramatic problem is reduced to one question: What is the correct attitude or posture, and what is the condition under which one assumes that attitude? In contrast to the blind struggle of passions in Othello's soul, drama in Beaumont and Fletcher seems like a debate about the rules of the code itself, so that the action tends to become dialectical. Amintor confesses that the very premise of his moral conduct is a formality:

> The thing that we call honour bears us all
> Headlong into sin, and yet itself is nothing.

This proposition would be too theoretic for the stricken Othello. When morality manifests itself as mere deportment, then there is a "*tragedy* of manners," and dramatic conflict occurs as an interchange of "postures assumed," each character raising, thematically, question after question in his effort to reach a solution within terms of the code. The counterplay of principles and positions must work itself out diagrammatically as do the forces in the Spanish Stairs. The forces in Restoration *comedy* of manners are equally artificial and schematic.

The late-baroque dialectic is clamorously used in Dryden's heroic plays with their "bulky and contrasting masses," their augmented vocabulary, and their extravagant gestures. We cannot call *Aureng-Zebe* a debate, although the characters obey an "elevated" formula of love and honor and reverse their positions, mechanically, by assuming a succession of contrasting attitudes within the limits of a pompous code. The Emperor loves Indamora; Aureng-Zebe loves Indamora; the Empress loves Aureng-Zebe. Aureng-Zebe defends the Emperor against Morat; but his love for Indamora drives the Emperor to betray Aureng-Zebe to Morat; meanwhile Morat has fallen in love with Indamora, and the Empress has confessed her love for Aureng-Zebe. Thus the characters take their contrary positions about Indamora; and their conduct is designed in a system of reversals between polar opposites: Morat is converted; the Emperor is converted; the Empress is converted. Aureng-Zebe in turn loves and hates Indamora. The passions are externalized and coarsened by passages of declamation at full cry:

> When I consider Life, 'tis all a cheat;
> Yet, fool'd with hope, men favour the deceit;
> Trust on, and think tomorrow will repay;
> Tomorrow's falser than the former day.

This magniloquence approaches platitude; the rhetoric often takes the form of generalizations vehemently stated. Othello's rhetoric ("Put out the light, and then, put out the light . . .") more fully inundates the meter and shows a more tragic involvement of the self with life. To have some notion of the mechanical reversals in Dryden, we may take two successive speeches of Aureng-Zebe to Indamora:

> Ah traitress! Ah ingrate! O faithless mind!
> Ah sex, invented first to damn mankind!

Then, when Indamora asserts her innocence:

> O, I could stifle you, with eager haste!
> Devour your kisses with my hungry taste!
> Rush on you! eat you! wander o'er each part,
> Raving with pleasure, snatch you to my heart!

Othello's moods ebb and flow with organic rhythm, not with these heavy lurches. However large the rhetorical scale, Dryden's tragic dimensions are not convincing; the pace of the action is too automatic.

Otway's *Venice Preserved* is another linguistic machine to magnify the clash of love with honor. Again the dramatic problem is to have the characters behave according to protocol when Jaffeir discovers that Renault has tried to seduce Belvidera, and Belvidera discovers that Jaffeir is conspiring to kill her father. The humanity of these people is sacrificed to the working out of a theme of duty, and declamation is substituted for tragic psychology. The signs of rhetorical overexertion are more obvious in Otway than in Dryden:

How I could pull thee down into my heart,
Gaze on thee till my eye-strings crack't with love,
Till all my sinews with its fire extended
Fixt me upon the rack of ardent longing;
Then swelling, sighing, raging to be blest,
Come like a panting turtle to thy breast,
On thy soft bosom, hovering, bill and play . . .

Milton's noble language was a reflex of his vision and
his will; Otway's is an effort to expand a given formula.

Some of the baroque strength of will activates Corneille, who does not operate his machines so noisily as
Otway and Dryden. *The Cid*, especially, has a kind of
sinewy power because its characters are impelled by
authentic emotions, not merely by a code of love and
honor. Although there is a clash of principles, Corneille
has a dramatic integrity that cannot be measured by
a formula of action and reaction. Roderick loves
Chimène; the Infanta loves Roderick; Don Sancho
loves Chimène. When Chimène's father insults Roderick's father, Roderick avenges the dishonor by killing
Chimène's father in a duel. Chimène, caught between
honor and love, offers herself to Don Sancho if he will
revenge her father on Roderick; yet when he has, she
presumes, done so, she hates Don Sancho. Roderick,
too, is caught between love and honor, and is eventually
reconciled with Chimène through the intercession of
the King. Quick and regular as the reversals may be,
Chimène is driven by a compulsion that has psychological as well as rhetorical force; she stands near the abyss
of an either/or choice that is felt rather than thought,
and is torn between the power of love and her duty to
her father:

Et quoi que mon amour ait sur moi de pouvoir,
Je ne consulte point pour suivre mon devoir:
Je cours sans balancer où mon honneur m'oblige.
Rodrigue m'est bien cher, son intérêt m'afflige;
Mon cœur prend son parti; mais malgré son effort,
Je sais ce que je suis, et que mon père est mort.

Roderick reduces his crisis to an equal severity when he urges Chimène to avenge her father with her own hand, not another's:

> Et pour venger un père emprunter d'autres bras,
> Ma Chimène, crois-moi, c'est n'y répondre pas:
> Ma main seule du mien a su venger l'offense,
> Ta main seule du tien doit prendre la vengeance.

The need for these gyrations is apparent in Chimène's unhappy confession when she sends Roderick from her sight: "Ne montre plus à ma douleur extrême/Ce qu'il faut que je perde, encore que je l'aime." But however impulsive these conflicts are, the equations balance with late-baroque exactitude.

It is significant that Roderick's bravery in battle is a public heroism, an epic gesture that reinstates him in honor and makes him eligible to accept Chimène's love. The potency of this gesture is a heritage from the baroque situation, where the hero openly performed his "one great act" to achieve a resolution. With great vigor Corneille claims his place beside Dryden and those who inherit the massive baroque images clashing against each other in thunderous, fully witnessed encounters. Racine does not need this sort of spectacular gesture: after all, he was a Jansenist and distrusted the potency of Corneille's images, their showy rituals. Racine locates his dramatic conflict in the soul; his expiations cannot be made in public. He does not have to resort to declamation, or to the overexertion of his characters.

III

PSYCHOLOGICAL SYMMETRY   There are, nevertheless, other values in Dryden than spectacular gesture; for he brings to English poetry an Augustan sense

of conformity, responsibility, and "closure," a certain
steady-eyed assurance:

> How can the less the greater comprehend?
> Or finite reason touch Infinity? . . .
> These truths are not the product of thy mind,
> But dropt from heav'n, and of a nobler kind.
> Reveal'd religion first inform'd thy sight,
> And reason saw not till faith sprung the light.
> Hence all thy natural worship takes the source;
> 'Tis revelation what thou think'st discourse.
>   *Religio Laici*

In these strong, if coarse, equations of Dryden's verse
appears "the rhetorical pattern of neo-classical wit,"[3]
which tends to be increasingly epigrammatic as the
seventeenth-century Cavalier poetry develops toward
the "propriety" of Restoration verse-essays. The neater
and neater oppositions of structure in the couplet were
well suited to convey a more exactly symmetrical pattern of thought, expressed as an antithesis of ideas. The
mannerist wit of Donne and the metaphysical poets
depended upon incongruities of image and ambiguities
of meaning and tone. But Dryden's wit is channeled
into parallel meanings and phrases, employing a pattern of contradiction, setting over against each other
mutually exclusive opinions or terms; and the meter
is confined by the design of the poet's forthright argument, which proceeds by firmly stated alternatives toward majestic solutions:

> Faith is not built on disquisitions vain;
> The things we must believe are few and plain.
>   *Religio Laici*

Dryden's attack brings into action a masculine authority without sacrificing control, direction, and judgment.
The movement in Dr. Johnson's verse is more deliberate
but quite as insistent; and the scale of statement is
even more general:

> Then say how hope and fear, desire and hate,
> O'erspread with snares the clouded maze of fate,

Where wav'ring man, betray'd by vent'rous pride,
To tread the dreary paths without a guide,
As treach'rous phantoms in the mist delude,
Shuns fancied ills, or chases airy good. . . .
Vanity of Human Wishes

Although Dryden's accent is more conversational
than Johnson's, nevertheless both poets break up the
"total" baroque rhythm of Milton's verse-paragraph
into more or less closed staves. Again, as in late-baroque
architecture, painting, and sculpture, an effect of
"number" dominates the effect of "mass." Dryden and
Johnson always propel their poems by compiling judicial phrases rather than by any swelling, tidal movement toward a climax. The articulation of their verse is
not Miltonic. There is a succession of well-considered
but forceful counterstatements, which progress to a
decision.

The language, too, differs from the magniloquence
of *Paradise Lost* with its richly sensuous texture. By
comparison Dryden's vocabulary seems prosaic; and if
Johnson's is hardly less sonorous than Milton's, it is far
more declarative or reflective. Both Dryden and Johnson speak of "general properties and large appearances," neglecting "minuter discriminations"; and Johnson, particularly, would accept Sir Joshua Reynolds'
view that "the mind should be elevated to the idea of
general beauty, and the contemplation of general
truth." Reynolds explained in his *Discourses*, "The
beauty of which we are in quest . . . is an idea that
subsists only in the mind; the sight never beheld it, nor
has the hand expressed it." Johnson and Dryden alike
give us summary opinions, and their "generalized" argument is sustained by that faculty called "judgment," so
much admired during the late-baroque era. To call a
writer judicious meant that he had reached certain decisions or conclusions—not necessarily intellectual,
rational, or theoretical conclusions, but observations

capable of being phrased in comprehensive, though not abstract, statements asserting the principles one accepts.

To be judicious does not mean to be doctrinaire; and though Dryden and Johnson appraise human experience in wide and formal terms, these poets do not exist in the luminously clear ideational atmosphere of Voltaire, or of Pope in his *Essay on Man.* Indeed, it would be hard to name a poem more heavily burdened with a sense of human distress than Dr. Johnson's *Vanity of Human Wishes,* where man is seen to roll darkling down the torrent of his fate. In this poem Johnson bears the full weight of his obscure doubts, prejudices, fears, and defeats; he attempts to make some reliable embracing judgment on life after considering the painful evidence of his own moral consciousness. He would never support any abstract concept like Pope's thesis that "Whatever is, is right." Johnson is judicious without being much concerned for logic; he cannot commit himself to the extreme clarity of an ideology, or to any syllogism held at an *a priori* distance from his own experience. If we ask who is the more intellectualizing poet, Pope or Johnson, we do not hesitate to name Pope, just as we should not hesitate to name Voltaire as being more rational than Racine. The climate of Dryden's verse essays, and Johnson's, is not theorizing, as was the climate in which the eighteenth-century encyclopedists and *philosophes* wrote. Johnson and Dryden base themselves upon felt convictions and are answerable to the prevailing moral situation of men; but they seek to deal with this situation by large affirmations.

In other words, although the judicious late-baroque art is addressed to the mind and speaks a reflective language, we must not think that this style is directly indebted to Cartesian "reasoning" or to Descartes' "mathematical" method of analysis, which reduces knowledge to rational abstractions like the clear brittle propositions of geometry. For Descartes' aim was to extend the form of "mathematical intellection" to all modes of thought. The late-baroque or Augustan tradition is, by contrast, primarily "psychological" rather than mathematical or rationalist in method and expression. A poet did not have "true wit" unless he used a certain tact or *esprit de finesse*, and even the rather heavy-minded Dr. Johnson defined good sense as "a prompt and intuitive perception of consonance and propriety." This sensitivity to "balance and harmony in form and effect" governs the Augustan architecture and decoration of Versailles—"symmetry conceived not in terms of mathematics but of human psychology."[4]

The instinct for psychological symmetry appears everywhere in the late-baroque aesthetics of Le Brun, Félibien, and Du Fresnoy, and those Frenchmen for whom Boileau speaks when he advises in his *Art poétique*:

> Il faut que chaque chose y soit mise en son lieu,
> Que le début, la fin, répondent au milieu.

These critics contribute largely to Sir Joshua Reynolds' *Discourses*, that most complete expression of the late-baroque frame of mind. In his Thirteenth Discourse Reynolds mentions "the sense of congruity, coherence, and consistency, which is a real existing principle in man; and it must be gratified." This felt need for order, unity, and proportion is one symptom of the late-baroque "settlement" after the excesses of baroque art. Furthermore, late-baroque art is, like high-baroque, compliant to authority and precedent. Or, more precisely, the high-baroque submission to authority takes, in late-baroque, a regulated and decorous form, a concern for tradition and "judgment" and a wish for responsibility in art and life. A sense of "propriety" and *bienséance* modifies the headstrong energies of baroque. The generality of late-baroque art—its acceptance of norms—is a mature and humane version of renaissance idealism and platonism.

Late-baroque architecture like Saint Paul's and The Invalides, or the Chapel at Versailles, retains some of the wealth of baroque volume and movement, but is simplified to a more plain and "general" statement, affirming with poise and authority a stable and convincing order. The façade of Santa Croce in Gerusalemme in Rome (1743) shows how a "neoclassical" structure and language finally reduced the plastic overflow of baroque masses to almost neutral elements. The convex wall is firmly bounded by giant pilasters with composite capitals; beside the richly arched portal the same plain pilasters are repeated, running up to a semicircular pediment, which is surmounted by a tall, cartouche-like cupola and a balustrade supporting statues. In spite of its two or three rococo flourishes this architecture is phrased in large, simple terms; the groundswell of baroque walls is here moderated, and the pilasters, especially, confirm the strong sense of decorum and propriety in the composition.

In his *Entretiens* upon Poussin's paintings, Félibien, quite in harmony with Boileau, adapts the baroque heroic style to the needs of a "psychological academism." According to Félibien, Poussin admired Domenichino as a painter who used a "strong expression" yet regulated his design. Poussin, he says, "felt obliged to remain within just bounds, and to work within a certain normalcy, moderation, and known order that established his work in its veritable being." For Poussin and the academicians who admired him, design is "the chief part of painting," and, reacting against the fat pigment of Rubens and the plastic excesses of baroque, they thought color to be less important than drawing. In his own *Observations on Painting* Poussin indicates exactly how late-baroque art chastened the high-baroque style by a psychological classicism:

The grand manner consists of four elements: subject or theme, concept, structure, and style. The first requirement, fundamental to all the others, is that the subject and the narrative be grandiose, such as battles, heroic actions, and religious themes. . . . As for concept, it is a pure product of the mind. . . . Order means the spacing of the parts. . . . The colors in painting are, as it were, blandishments to lure the eyes, as the beauty of the verses in poetry is a lure for the ears.

Du Fresnoy repeats Poussin: There is a mean in all things, with "certain limits or bounds wherein the Good and the Beautiful consist." The subject must be heroic, but judiciously composed:

The parts of it must be great and large, contrasted by contrary motions, the most noble parts foremost in sight, and each figure carefully poised on its own center. The parts must be drawn with flowing gliding outlines, large and smooth, rising gradually, not swelling suddenly. . . . In fine, let there be a perfect relation betwixt the parts and the whole, that they may be entirely of a piece. . . . Those things which are beautiful . . . ought to have somewhat of greatness in them; and their outlines to be noble; they must be disentangled, pure, and without alteration, clean and knit together; composed of great parts, yet those but few in number. (*The Art of Painting*)

Critics always speak of Poussin's paintings as "accepting the frame" and "closing" the composition. Among Poussin's major works The Funeral of Phocion shows this late-baroque psychological stability, and the reorganizing of baroque materials and forces: the masses are dense and balanced, the rhythms are firm and measured, the figures inhabit a clearly ordered world that is half-generalized with a kind of statement we find in Dr. Johnson's verses. This austere painting uses landscape with deep humanistic meanings, and, in the best classic tradition, employs architecture for dramatic purposes. Indeed the whole scene is architec-

turally constructed—built, that is, like a cubist painting to represent the authority of man's consciousness
over the appearances in nature.

In Poussin's classic landscapes the plastic values are
used chiefly to denote psychological relationships that
are controlled by what Reynolds called "the internal
fabric of our minds." This latter phrase occurs in the
Seventh Discourse, where Reynolds states, "My notion
of nature comprehends not only the forms which
nature produces, but also the nature and internal fabric and organization, as I may call it, of the human
mind." Reynolds names Poussin as "an artist strictly attentive to the most enlarged and extensive ideas of nature," precisely because his subject—always "some
eminent instance of heroic action, or heroic suffering"
—is "a general one." Poussin achieves the psychological
reconstruction of baroque mass, purifying it of its bulk,
reducing it to a degree of formal abstraction (which
is not the same as rational abstraction).

In his Seventh Discourse Reynolds defines the psychological premise of late-baroque art, and shows how
the full-baroque plenitude is brought into a community
of norms that passed for "nature":

The internal fabric of our minds, as well as the external
form of our bodies, being nearly uniform, it seems then to
follow, of course, that as the imagination is incapable of
producing anything originally of itself, and can only vary
and combine those ideas with which it is furnished by
means of the senses, there will be necessarily an agreement
in the imaginations, as in the senses of men. . . .

We may therefore conclude that the real substance, as it
may be called, of what goes under the name of taste, is
fixed and established in the nature of things; that there are
certain and regular causes by which the imagination and
passions of men are affected. . . .

The conforming of the material world to the internal
fabric of the mind: this is not Cartesian rationalism,

but a regulation of baroque materials according to a psychology of balance, equivalence, and symmetry, an inherent principle of congruence, coherence, and consistency. So also in contemporary drama, the academic "unities"—long since formulated by renaissance critics and used in high-baroque art—were being given a new psychological meaning, gaining for art a new concentration, and bringing the late-baroque hero under another dispensation than the massive baroque release. Boileau is among those who give the unities the force of a psychological law: "Qui ne sait se borner ne sut jamais écrire." In truly classic art the unities are a form of self-control, an instinct for order, intuited by the artist rather than prescribed by the critic; for as Reynolds says, "Unsubstantial as these rules may seem, and difficult as it may be to convey them in writing, they are still seen and felt in the mind of the artist." When the rules are mechanically used, late-baroque art fails, as Boileau warned it would: "Your cold discourse can never move the soul" ("Vos froids raisonnements ne feront qu'attiédir").

Dryden, with his blatant dramas, rebelled against the French unities; yet his heroic plays are actually only a transitional phase in the transforming of baroque into late-baroque art, during which the image in drama and painting retains, as its baroque heritage, its grandiose proportions and gestures, but is gradually removed into another world, amid more regular intervals, into a more formal and metrical space or "scene." The transformation is complete in Poussin's Shepherds in Arcadia (*c.* 1650) where the four great figures, their attitudes quoted, without overstatement, from Domenichino or Titian, rest in simple equation, two and two, one standing, one bending, on each side of the sarcophagus inscribed ET IN ARCADIA EGO. The trees on the right bracket the group, as do the mountains and the two trees, repeated in minor accents, on the left. The space falls away in adjacent planes to the rocky hills, which shut in the composition by their blue and jagged profiles, gently mounting towards two major accents. Over the head of the bending shepherd on the right, almost in the center, falls the caesura—a space between hills and trees. The four figures are in heroic but formal scale. The focus of their energy—a point of moral intersection within this pastoral drama—is determined by the two gracious hands, from left and right, pointing to the inscription on the pitiless stone.

IV

THE MECHANICS OF EXPRESSION   The gestures of these figures indicate their moods: resignation, surprise, curiosity, melancholy. Each of Poussin's compositions is a pantomime fixed at its most expressive moment. In his Massacre of the Innocents (1629) each figure is caught at an instant of psychological crisis, expressed in the attitudes of the actors: the executioner heedlessly raising his sword above the infant, the face of the mother a rigid mask, a second mother departing with a gesture of despair. The violence is baroque, but the action is arrested—this time mechanically—in each of these four, who serve as lay figures to portray a mode of feeling.

These baroque images have become "expressive" in a new way, by means of a late-baroque formula for behavior that literary critics have called "decorum" without denoting the complicated mechanism involved. I use the term mechanism, for here we meet one of the genuinely Cartesian contributions to late-baroque. Although the symmetry of this style and its regularity of form, its psychological reorganization of baroque forces, are not due to Cartesian rationalism, yet to explain the attitudes of the figures in Poussin's paintings the late-baroque critics utilized a theory of the mechanics of passion (we can hardly call it a psychology) that Descartes discussed in his *Passions of the Soul* (1649). In writing this treatise Descartes must have drawn upon earlier anatomies of passion such as Peter de la Primaudaye's *French Academy* or Coeffeteau's *Table of Human Passions*, or perhaps upon the many rhetorical treatises on the "expression" of the humours by bodily signs. During the renaissance the rhetoricians, following Aristotle and Quintilian, had assumed that the body is an instrument for *elocutio;* and the Elizabethan actor was trained in the practice of "decorum," that is, how changes in the soul are known by outward signs. In *The Passions of the Mind* (1604) Thomas Wright says that acting "is either a certain visible eloquence or an eloquence of the body, or a comely grace in delivering conceits, or an external image of an internal mind." While Poussin was painting his *Massacre,* the theater was already using a mechanistic ("Jacobean") psychology. Descartes' *Treatise* furnished the late-baroque academicians with a timely version of the various theories of "expression."

Without necessarily accepting the Cartesian rationalist spirit—the *intuitus intellectus* and the mathematical method—late-baroque critics believed that passion must be represented by a mechanism of gesture and feature. Boileau, who is no Cartesian, advises the poet to "clothe differing passions in a differing dress":

> La nature, féconde en bizarres portraits,
> Dans chaque ame est marquée à de différens traits;
> Un geste la découvre, un rien la fait paroître.

And in his *Art of Painting* (translated into English by Dryden) Du Fresnoy urges the painter: "You are to express the motions of the spirits, and the affections or passions whose center is the heart: in a word, *to make the soul visible.*" The French academicians, ceaselessly studying the attitudes of figures in Poussin and Domenichino, found in the Greco-Roman statue of Laocoön an accurate anatomy of "expression," illustrating how gesture and attitude convey emotions. Late-baroque or academic passion was not only a mode of behavior according to a certain protocol, as it was in heroic plays by Dryden and Corneille; it was also a manipulating of feature, gesture, and pose. In prescribing "attitudes" in painting, Le Brun, Testelin, and other academic critics accepted, almost verbatim, Descartes' account of the physiology of passion.

For Descartes, the seat of the soul is the pineal gland, which controls the machine of the body through the filaments of the nerves, which in turn are agitated when the spirits move this little gland. There are six chief passions—wonder, love, hatred, desire, joy, and sadness; the others are composite. Descartes' definitions of these passions are neat: hatred is an emotion caused by spirits inciting the soul to be separated from hurtful objects; love is the opposite. Each passion expresses itself physiologically by external signs, especially in the eyes and face:

There is no passion that is not evidenced by some particular action of the eyes. . . . We may say almost the same of the actions of the face which also accompany the passions, for although they are of greater extent than those of the eyes, it is at the same time hard to distinguish them; and they are so little different that there are men who present almost the same mien when they weep as when they laugh. It is true that there are some which are remarkable enough, as are the seams in the forehead which come in anger, and certain movements of nose and lips in indignation and scorn.

The features of passion may differ with the temperament of various persons; yet the signs of anger, jealousy, fear, admiration, or courage are usually unmistakable.

In discourse after discourse Le Brun and his fellow academicians sought to "read" Poussin according to this mechanism of expression. Le Brun illustrated a *Treatise on the Passions* (1698) with drawings of the features during fear, contemplation, laughter, astonishment, disdain, despair, inquietude, grief—since "expression marks the true character of each thing." The passions, he says, produce bodily action, and action is the motion of muscles caused by the ends of nerves; and the nerves are moved by spirits contained in the cavities of the brain; and the brain receives its spirits from the blood, which passes through the heart. Then Le Brun undertakes to describe the operation of the various passions, beginning with admiration, a "composite" movement of the soul. His discussion of the expression of anger is typical:

When anger takes possession of the soul, he who experiences this emotion has red and inflamed eyes, a wandering and sparkling pupil, both eyebrows now lowered, now raised, the forehead deeply creased, creases between the eyes, wide-open nostrils, lips pressed tightly together, and the lower lip pushed up over the upper, leaving the corners of the mouth a little open to form a cruel and disdainful laugh. He seems to grind his teeth, his mouth fills with saliva, his face is swollen, pale in spots and inflamed in others, the veins of his temples and forehead and neck are swollen and protruding, his hair bristling, and one who experiences this passion seems more to blow himself up rather than to breathe because the heart is oppressed by the abundance of blood which comes to its aid. Rage and despair sometimes follow anger.

It is often said that one of the neoclassical notions is *"ut pictura poesis"*—that is, poetry resembles painting because the poet "lays on" his verses the rhetorical phrases that correspond to the colors the painter "lays on" his design. This rhetorical manipulation of language has its corollary in the neoclassic notion of "expressing" passion by the proper features and gestures. " 'Tis the business of rhetoricians," Du Fresnoy asserts, "to treat the characters of the passions." Roger de Piles attempted to "catalogue" some of the best-known painters by arranging them on a scale, assigning to each a numerical value according to excellence in composition, drawing, color, and "expression." Domenichino, Raphael, and Rubens are nearly perfect in their "expression" of passion, with Le Brun and Le Sueur and Poussin not far below. In the records of the Conferences of the French Academy we find Le Brun's analysis of the psychological meaning of attitude and gesture in paintings like Poussin's Israelites Receiving Manna; and on June 6, 1675, Henri Testelin gave the most thorough and categorical discourse on Expression, summarizing and applying Descartes' treatise. "One can represent the passions of the soul by the actions of the whole body," Testelin explains: the elevation of the brows, the contour of the lips, the pose of the torso, the position of the feet. Aversion brings a recoil of the body, while the arms repulse the object; horror causes a similar gesture, but more forceful. In love the eyes are half closed, the lips red and humid; and the head is inclined toward the loved object. There are suitable "attitudes" for laughter, fear, desire, timidity, melancholy. Angels, he decides, cannot bear the marks of sensual passion, but only of contemplation; and the veins and arteries of the gods do not swell. The nose, adds De Piles, "has no passion which is particular to it." As usual, Testelin appends to his lecture a Table of Precepts for Expression, with a formula for each major passion. There are also tables prescribing proportions for the body, the tension of muscles, the aspects of youth, infancy, young men, young women, vulgar persons, more eminent personages, and degrees of light and shadow. In 1720 Antoine Coypel is still speaking the same language and cataloguing the various expressions of passion suitable to differing social ranks: the gestures of the wealthy man, a bigot, a hero, a philanderer, a prudent man—the natural, simple, grand air of a well-bred lord being quite unlike the brazen audacity of the *riche bourgeois*.

The plastic high-baroque image has thus become a late-baroque engine to express an attitude or imperative of the soul, and the "quantity of spirit" that stimulates it—another evidence that in late-baroque "number" tends to replace "mass." This mechanizing of passion occurs in Dryden's *Aureng-Zebe*, for when Arimant sees Nourmahal approaching in wrath, he says, like any French academician:

> The Empress has the antechambers passed,
> And this way moves with a disorder'd haste;
> Her brows the stormy marks of anger bear.

And Indamora warns Morat, as if she threatened him according to Testelin:

> Unsettl'd virtue stormy may appear;
> Honour like mine, serenely is severe;
> To scorn your person, and reject your crown,
> Disorder not my face into a frown.

These gestures in the theater and in painting show how the doctrine of the "expression" of passion is an academic bridge between the grand act of the high-baroque image and the automatic response of the "mechanical man" of Condillac and the associationist psychology of the eighteenth century. Reynolds and the eighteenth-century academicians inherit this dogma of the mechanics of expression, which is a theory parallel to the deterministic psychology developed by Locke, Hartley, Condillac, and the associationist school. The melodrama of the eighteenth-century stage, novel, and painting occurs in a tradition of late-baroque behavior. As late as 1806 Charles Bell's *Anatomy of Expression* appeared in London, an instance of the continuity of late-baroque doctrines of the mechanics of passion, which in turn arose from the earlier anatomies of hu-

mours. The famous Nightingale Tomb in Westminster
Abbey (1761), by Roubiliac, is, in style, a convulsive
late-baroque pantomime in which the frantic husband
seeks to interpose himself between his wife and the
brandished dart of Death, who starts from the gates of
the pit beneath. The group is obviously inspired by
Bernini's statuary (notably the monument to Alexander VII in Saint Peter's) but Bernini's figures have here
been mechanized by a theory of "expressive" attitudes.

However feeble the written drama of the eighteenth
century may have been, the period was histrionic; it
was an age of great acting, with Garrick, Mrs. Siddons,
and Foote. One need not dwell upon the stagy situations in Hogarth, or the arrested gesture of Reynolds'
Mrs. Siddons as The Tragic Muse; or the banal co-
quetry of Romney's Emma Hart or Greuze's nymphs,
or Boucher's; or the poses struck in Sterne's *Tristram
Shandy* and Rousseau's *Confessions*, which is literary
pantomime. Upon seeing West's painting of The Death
of General Wolfe, Garrick is said to have acted out
his criticism of the hero's appearance: as he was held
by two of his friends, he fell into the pose of the dying
Wolfe and "displayed in his features the exact coun-
tenance depicted by the artist"; then, to the applause
of bystanders, he expressed Wolfe's rapture as the British cried, "They run!" In his *Memoirs of the Life of
David Garrick,* Thomas Davies assures us that Garrick
"could without the least preparation, transform himself into any character, tragic or comic, and seize instantaneously upon any passion of the human mind.
He could make a sudden transition from violent rage,
and even madness, to the extremes of levity and hu-
mour, and go through the whole circle of theatric evolution with *the most surprising velocity.*" This theatric
velocity was possible by his commanding a mechanism
of expression. In 1765, Davies reports, Garrick performed, to the delight of a fashionable circle in Paris, a

little scene he once witnessed; and he performed it impromptu:

. . . A father, he said, was fondling his child at an open window, from whence they looked into the street; by one unlucky effort, the child sprang from his father's arms, fell upon the ground, and died upon the spot; what followed, he said, was a language which every body understood, for it was the language of nature; he immediately threw himself into the attitude in which the father appeared at the time the child leaped from his arms.

The influence which the representation of the father's agony produced on the company, and exhibited by this darling son of Nature, in the silent, but expressive language of unutterable sorrow, is easier to be imagined than expressed; let it suffice to say, that the greatest astonishment was succeeded by abundant tears.

The eighteenth-century "sensibility" was partly a mechanism of "expression," an idiom which Boswell, too, enjoyed using. It was not alone "feeling" but also an attitude, a pose. In late-baroque art the language of Nature was the theatrical gesture, which, as Garrick said, "every body understood," since the passions of the soul can be stated in "the actions of the whole body."

Poussin having used this idiom in paintings like The Massacre of the Innocents, the academies then developed the paradigms, with full inflections. If the passions of the late-baroque image are not rationalist or Cartesian, at least this image moves with Cartesian *gestures,* and its features are described in the *Treatise.* Félibien, writing of Poussin, says, "Among the essential and most considerable aspects of painting is expression . . . ; the painter intends to vary his scene by different movements of the soul as well as by gestures of the body and by the different attitudes of the persons he has portrayed."

V

THE LATE-BAROQUE PURIFICATION: RACINE

Racine records these movements of the soul. Late-baroque psychology provided him his diagram of dramatic forces, his reversals of will, his dialectic of passion, his conflict of imperatives; and Descartes had invented for him a machine of feature and attitude. It remained for Racine to free the structure and action of late-baroque art from its grossness, its automatism and externality, to reduce the late-baroque drama to its ultimate formal contour, to intensify it and press it to its final crisis of consciousness.

We appreciate Racine, as we appreciate Poussin, only when we abandon talk of classicism and academism and regard him as the voice of late-baroque sensibility. Then we feel Racine's force, his rarity, his transposing life into a naked conflict of impulses expressed by a logic of passion. Like Poussin, Racine liberates the baroque image from its plastic excess; he leaves us only its profile, its attitude, its idiom for defining the will of the self. Like Poussin, Racine refuses to solicit our interest by the external means of the scene. Racine's representation of the world is a "disposition" of human actions; and there also he resembles Poussin, who said that a painting is an "idea"—"if it portrays bodies, *it represents only the order and the mode* of the species of things." Racine operates, too, at a full and pure theatrical velocity, unencumbered.

Every Racinian action is organized into a late-baroque play of forces that a painter would call double *contrapposto* (counterposition) since the impulses of the characters "oscillate" between poles. This oscillation is a logic of dilemma. The essential structure of Racine's actions is suggested in the subtitle of his first play, *Les Frères ennemis*—the implacable strife at Thebes when Polynices opposes Eteocles his brother in a situation so tightly "closed" that only extreme alternatives are possible, without concessions. These perilous alternatives have their most direct and savage force in *Andromaque,* where the widow of Hector is wooed by Pyrrhus, slayer of Hector; and Hermione, daughter of Helen, is wooed by Orestes, but loves Pyrrhus. The key, the unseen figure, the invisible axis of the closed situation, where all the terms are known and there is only the logic of mutually exclusive responses, is the boy Astyanax, son of Hector, protected by Andromache, but held in charge of Pyrrhus; Orestes has come to seize him for the Greeks. At once Pylades realizes the double course open to Pyrrhus, scorning Hermione, himself scorned by Andromache: he might wed the one he hates and lose the one he loves—

> Il peut, seigneur, il peut, dans ce désordre extrême,
> Épouser ce qu'il hait, et perdre ce qu'il aime.

Orestes defines Hermione's position, scorning and scorned: "Elle me dédaignait; un autre l'abandonne":

> L'ingrate, qui mettait son cœur à si haut prix,
> Apprend donc, à son tour, à souffrir des mépris.

For her part Hermione feels a withering duplicity in her passion for Pyrrhus: "Ah! je l'ai trop aimé pour ne le point haïr!" From love to hate: here is the late-baroque psychological symmetry, like the clear symmetries in Poussin; the forces and characters are precisely confronted, the feelings swinging from pole to pole, each person occupying the position of the other as each in turn knows hope and despair. Orestes looks across his own torment to the torment he will inflict on Hermione:

> Je prétends qu'à mon tour l'inhumaine me craigne,
> Et que ses yeux cruels, à pleurer condamnés,
> Me rendent tous les noms que je leur ai donnés.

Then Pyrrhus, desperate in his rejected love, offers
Andromache a cruel choice: his kindness or his rage,
the queen's crown or the death of her son—

> Songez-y: je vous laisse; et je viendrai vous prendre
> Pour vous mener au temple où ce fils doit m'attendre;
> Et là vous me verrez, soumis ou furieux,
> Vous couronner, madame, ou le perdre à vos yeux.

The moral imperatives are strictly commensurate.
Hermione, Pyrrhus, Orestes, do not know whether they
love or hate; and after Andromache has wedded Pyrrhus, after Orestes has, for the love (and hate) of Hermione, killed Pyrrhus, Andromache assumes, as widow
of the slain Greek, the honorable duty of avenging her
husband, who in sacking Troy had killed her first husband. And once Orestes has killed Pyrrhus, he earns
not the love, but the hate, of Hermione.

The irony in these reversals is a major irony, the
irony of extremes that exclude each other, and it is
sharpened by the contradictions in situation and psychic forces. Hermione recognizes this ironic oscillation
of fate when she reproaches Pyrrhus, who has been
driven by his passion from Greece to Troy:

> Quoi! sans que ni serment ni devoir vous retienne,
> Rechercher une Grecque, amant d'une Troyenne;
> Me quitter, me reprendre, et retourner encor
> De la fille d'Hélène à la veuve d'Hector;
> Couronner tour à tour l'esclave et la princesse;
> Immoler Troie aux Grecs, au fils d'Hector la Grèce!

The tragic absurdity of man's position gives a bitter
edge to Hermione's taunt to a hero who is a traitor:

> Tout cela part d'un cœur toujours maître de soi,
> D'un héros qui n'est point esclave de sa foi.
> Pour plaire à votre épouse, il vous faudrait peut-être
> Prodiguer les deux noms de parjure et de traître.
> Vous veniez de mon front observer la pâleur,
> Pour aller dans ses bras rire de ma douleur.

It is the same in *Iphigénie*. It is the same with

Phèdre, torn between her duty to her husband and her illicit fatal love for her son. In this drama the full inconsistency, the impossible dilemma of the human situation, caught between contraries, is forced to a moral crisis in which the total consciousness and the total fate of man are "engaged," to use Racine's term. In his preface to this subtle play Racine says, "En effet, Phèdre n'est ni tout à fait coupable, ni tout à fait innocente: *elle est engagée,* par sa destinée et par la colère des dieux, dans une passion illégitime dont elle a horreur toute la première: elle fait tous ses efforts pour la surmonter." Thus late-baroque reduces the composition to a few powerful motives concentrated into an "interior" conflict with an effect of "chosen" fatality.

Racine spiritualizes the heroic code and, like Poussin, strips the baroque image of its brawn: he formalizes its behavior, its responses, its features, without abating its violence. After everything possible has been subtracted from drama, the tragedy remains as an almost theoretic design of forces without diminishing the psychic immediacy of these forces. A tragedy by Racine is stylized until it becomes almost a disembodied painting of an emotion.[5] Poussin must have meant something like this when he said that painting is "nothing but an idea of incorporeal things." For Poussin is as formal in his "disposition" as Racine—in his late-baroque equation of gesture with gesture, in his theatrical visage, his finesse and visibility.

After the high-baroque confidence in the flesh, its plastic redundance, Racine and Poussin discipline the late-baroque drama, translating baroque masses into moral energies. Racine designs *Bérénice* as a feat of "purity" very proper to the theater because of "the intensity of the passions it can excite." Concerning this play he explains that tragedy does not need the tumult of blood and death, but spiritual crisis:

It is not at all necessary that there be blood and death in tragedy: it is enough if the action be great, if the actors be heroic, if the passions be excited. . . . What is most advantageous is that I found it extremely simple. For a long while I had wished to attempt a tragedy with that simplicity of action which was so strongly to the taste of antiquity. . . . There are those who believe this simplicity to be a token of want of ingenuity. They do not consider that on the contrary all inventiveness consists in making something of nothing, and that all those numerous incidents have been merely an evasion on the part of those poets who did not feel in their talent either an adequate genius or an adequate force to hold their spectators for five scenes by a simple action, sustained by the fury of the passions, the beauty of the sentiments, or the eloquence of expression.

So he writes *Bérénice*, which for five acts is merely a repeated collision of the simplest and strongest imperatives: shall Titus sacrifice his love for his mistress in order to do his duty to Rome? This drama is played in the fabric of consciousness, not in the world outside. "Painting," said Reynolds, "is not only to be considered as an imitation operating by deception, but . . . it is, and ought to be, in many points of view, and strictly speaking, no imitation at all of external nature."

Racine himself in his more "heroic" actions like *Alexandre* and *Mithridate* makes "something" of what already was "a great deal" in the way of size and splendor. These plays are Drydenesque. But *Bérénice*, *Phèdre*, *Andromaque*, renounce each vulgar deception and evidence of actuality, and mount their late-baroque action in all its clarity as a stylized encounter of forces expressed by a theatrical mechanism of passion. For the *décor* in Racine is, no doubt, the human figure itself, its postures, its attitudes, its "presence." The features of the actor are an instrument of Racine's "elocution" of the soul; and the voice of the actor is the voice of the soul arriving at its decision, which is its fate.[6] Racine transposes humanity into language.

Indeed, Racine refuses the texture of the actual world and retains only the *expression* of imperatives within the self. Thus his plays are a mode of debate. The very motions of Phèdre's soul are audible in Phèdre's language, which is a style of action as well as a discourse, as when she tells Hippolytus she has been scorched by a love that concealed itself in hate:

C'est peu de t'avoir fui, cruel, je t'ai chassé;
J'ai voulu te paraître odieuse, inhumaine;
Pour mieux te résister, j'ai recherché ta haine.
De quoi m'ont profité mes inutiles soins?
Tu me haïssais plus, je ne t'aimais pas moins,
Tes malheurs te prêtaient encore de nouveaux charmes.
J'ai langui, j'ai séché dans les feux, dans les larmes.

Racine does not need, nor does Poussin, the high-baroque magniloquence—but only the dramatic diagram.

Dialogue in a play by Racine is the soul uttering its will in the word, the colorless word that is wholly *logos*, the discourse of the self. By this late-baroque transformation of drama Racine expresses the *pathos* (suffering or passion) of his characters as an activity of *logos* (intelligence or comprehension or insight). Even further: is it not possible to say that Racine's language (discourse or *logos*) is the vehicle of both *pathos* and *ethos*—that is, "action" in the sense Aristotle understood drama to represent "character in action"? The words that are spoken by Racine's people prove to *be* their conduct. If this is the case, Racine's art is almost unique in making the activity of the intelligence, or *logos*, equivalent to the moral life and to the dramatic imitation of "men in action." In a very profound sense indeed Racine's actions are the effort of the characters to gain a vivid comprehension of their situation, and drama is identical with the discourse of the self carried on in a state of "extreme attention." Racine's language —which is at the same moment *logos*, *pathos*, and *ethos*

—represents the existence of the self during its most acute and fatal periods of consciousness.

It has been much debated whether Racine's analysis of life is an aspect of Cartesian rationalism. It is not. His analysis is psychological rather than merely rational. Of course Racine shares with Descartes a certain seventeenth-century inwardness and immediacy; and just as the Cartesian mechanism of passion gave Racine his theatrical visage, the Cartesian spirit touches the Racinian spirit in its intensity of self-awareness. However, in Descartes self-awareness takes a philosophic, rational, geometrical mode of demonstration or thought; it speaks the clear language of mathematics and abstract ideas. Descartes thinks himself into being. This form of rational consciousness, the intellectual intuition, brings the self to a vivid self-awareness, but in one direction only. In effect Descartes says that Man is Consciousness; but he gives a limited meaning to consciousness. Racine also says that Man is Consciousness; but he does not restrict consciousness to mathematical analysis and logical perception. Cartesian analysis is merely the rational facet of consciousness; but consciousness can know other immediacies than those of geometry or science. Racine's consciousness embraces the whole "voluntary life" of the self, in all its modes. In art and philosophy the tendency of the seventeenth century was to occupy itself with the individual mind. Descartes turned his awareness inward upon his own rational premises and abilities. Racine turned his awareness inward upon the activity of the self through its whole range of consciousness. John Locke in the *Essay Concerning Human Understanding*, written to refute Descartes' notion that we have innate ideas, shares with Descartes and with Racine the seventeenth-century self-awareness. In one of his shining phrases Locke says that our abstract ideas are "precise naked appearances in the mind." Locke intended to be "empirical" and to seek the origins of these precise naked ideas in the experience of the senses. Descartes seeks them not in the senses but among the concepts of the mathematical reason, which are contours in the mind itself. Yet both Descartes and Locke turn inward upon the theater of the spirit, a theater where Racine achieved his extremities of consciousness.

Descartes, Locke, and Racine—each in a different way occupies the seventeenth-century interior theater of man's consciousness. But there is also the ultimate Protestant self-consciousness of John Milton, who at the end of his life finds that the most potent image of all is not the high-baroque image in the flesh, like Adam and Eve, but the inward, insubstantial self, inhabiting the invisible paradise nobler than the luxuriant Eden from which Man was banished. He found this Eden, this final Protestant theater of the completely self-aware self, in *Paradise Regained*, which (whenever it may have been written) belongs with Racine's *Bérénice* as a late-baroque encounter of opposing spiritual forces, Christ, the wise and virtuous, being tested by "temptation and all guile." *Paradise Regained* is a poem devoted to the "tormenter conscience," and with its debate between Satan and Christ resembles the morality play, as does Racine's *Britannicus* or *Bérénice:* the Son of God walks forth alone,

> . . . the spirit leading;
> And his deep thoughts, the better to converse
> With solitude, till far from track of men,
> Thought following thought, and step by step led on,
> He entred now the bordering desert wild,
> And with dark shades and rocks environ'd round,
> His holy meditations thus persu'd.

Christ refutes Satan in the wilderness by the power of the Word, a discourse carried on in the mind with a

sustained and extreme attention; and during this conflict *ethos* (action) expresses itself as *logos* (intelligence or self-awareness or decision). Here there is no
need for the baroque *décor* of *Paradise Lost;* or for the
magniloquence. This poetry is, like Racine's simplified
dramatic language, essentially anti-rhetorical, and the
action is reduced to a "pure" collision of imperatives,
as it is in *Bérénice:*

> I who e'er while the happy Garden sung,
> By one man's disobedience lost, now sing
> Recover'd paradise to all mankind,
> By one man's firm obedience fully tri'd
> Through all temptation, and the Tempter foil'd
> In all his wiles, defeated and repuls't,
> And Eden rais'd in the wast wilderness.

This tempting of the new Christ, the Protestant self,
occurs as a logic of dilemma, within terms of mutually
exclusive alternatives. Racine's heroes meet such temptations, and the resolutions come in both poets by the
same means: an intensely conscious choice which
closes the discourse of the self with the self after it has
reached a luminous perception:

> God hath now sent his living Oracle
> Into the world, to teach his final will,
> And sends his Spirit of Truth henceforth to dwell
> In pious hearts, an inward Oracle.

This oracle is the small voice of consciousness at its
most urgent pressure upon the will—for here the will
means, as it does in Racine, choice, not power. Christ
has the temperance that enables the self to discipline
the self and, with the consciousness fully involved and
enlightened, to choose with vivid comprehension. Such
a choice can be made only when the alternatives are
pitilessly clear—as clear as Hermione's love and hate
are to her own watchful self.

In *Paradise Regained* Milton the poet has come to
terms with his own Puritan ethic; he and Racine are

both image-breakers, and play the role of Eikono-klastes. They will not be seduced by any magnificent high-baroque spectacles; they will no longer invoke the power of the sensorium. Racine destroyed the heroic idols of the baroque theater. In *Paradise Regained* Milton has destroyed his baroque idols also, and the violence of his Protestant austerity speaks through the mouth of his Saviour, who is Milton's most conscious self, against the Counter-Reformation rites:

> . . . no, let them serve
> Thir enemies, who serve idols with God.

Paradoxically, the temptations of the flesh offered by Satan—the table spread for Christ, the visions of imperial pomp and Roman palaces—are here a kind of baroque anti-masque amid this barren perilous scene, which is the scene of Puritan consciousness. Ordinarily the masque is a scene of splendor, and the anti-masque is a scene of ugliness, deformity, or horror. In *Paradise Regained* the triumph occurs in the wilderness; the anti-masque, arranged by Satan, is the baroque feast and the Tridentine pageant of "great and glorious Rome." The Tempter soon finds that the "persuasive rhetoric" that "won so much on Eve" gains him nothing before Christ:

> . . . but Eve was Eve;
> This far his over-match.

So Milton and Racine, no longer needing the potent baroque image, the spectacle, the katharsis of the great act, reduce life to its essential inner debate, the *logos* which is the oracle within the will.

At about the same time, Mme de Lafayette in her *Princesse de Clèves* (1678) came to the same degree of self-awareness, the same discourse of the self with the self, which is the stranger because it is carried on amid the trivialities of the court, giving it a tone of preciosity. Mme de Clèves loves the Duke of Ne-

mours, but remains faithful to her husband in thought
and act because of the severity of her sense of honor.
Her life is a discourse, an encounter of conflicting imperatives. She watches her responses with extreme attention: "Shall I permit it?" she asks herself. "Shall I
make a return? Shall I engage in gallantry, be false to
Monsieur de Clèves, and be false to myself?" Behind
this fashionable novel is the dilemma of the tempted
soul. The tensions in Mme de Lafayette's fiction are
very inward; she cleanses the heroic and the "precious"
love-and-honor drama by taking an ascetic view of the
situation of one's self, and gives to the romance a new
psychological velocity.

At various moments Descartes carries on a sort of
formal discourse within his self, intensifying his
thought to a kind of dramatic activity; for we must
agree with Maulnier that any self-consciousness at a
certain pitch must be drama on account of its violence. "But what, then, am I?" asks Descartes. "A thing
which thinks. What is a thing which thinks? It is a
thing which doubts, understands, conceives, affirms, denies, wills, refuses, which also imagines and feels." This
self-regard swings over a wider arc than Descartes
needs to carry on his mere mathematical analysis. At
such moments Descartes' theater of consciousness does
not seem much more confined than the theater of consciousness within Pascal, who could not forgive Descartes his impiety but who also utilized the interior
stage of the self. For an instant Descartes in such a
passage seems to be carrying on his discourse in Racine's mode, as if he were someone like Bérénice con-
fronting himself with himself in the brightly lighted
arena of his sensibility. For both Racine and Descartes
consciousness is clarity, and the premise of Racine's
art, where imperatives collide, is Descartes' belief that
"there is nothing in us which we ought to attribute to
our soul except our thoughts, which are mainly of two

sorts, the one being the actions of the soul, and the other its passions." However he may explain its mechanism, the soul remains for Descartes the ultimate mystery and the focus of existence:

I knew that I was a substance the whole essence or nature of which is to think, and that for its existence there is no need of any place, nor does it depend on any material thing, so that this "me," that is to say, the soul by which I am what I am, is entirely distinct from the body, and is even more easy to know than is the latter; and even if this body were not, the soul would not cease to be what it is.

Pascal felt the radical identity of the self in the same way.

There is, then, a late-baroque mode of inwardness. Descartes, Racine, Mme de Lafayette, Pascal, the final Milton, all redeem the baroque image of man from its corpulence; they find the daemonic self; they discharge its forces, with all their urgency, as an unseen activity of consciousness, a conflict of a divided will, a discourse of the mind existing under the shadow of doubt.

This sort of debate is an examination of the self according to a logic of contradiction. And here we may resume an earlier question raised in connection with Beaumont and Fletcher's *Maid's Tragedy* as being a play that denotes the contrary positions a character can occupy. When self-awareness is sufficiently heightened, then there is always the possibility of conceiving one's self in another attitude, obeying another imperative. The debate—the conversation of the self with the self—may become hypothetical or problematic in tone; inquisitorial, in fact. In Racine's *Andromaque* Pyrrhus poses himself suddenly the question: What would his situation be if his cruelty remained after his fury had died:

> Mais que ma cruauté survive à ma colère,
> Que, malgré la pitié dont je me sens saisir,
> Dans le sang d'un enfant je me baigne à loisir?

This is a very hazardous state of self-consciousness because it means that regardless of the immediate motive, contrary motives are thinkable and, therefore,
possible. Inherent in this sort of inquisition of the self
by the self is a psychology not worked out fully until
the eighteenth-century skepticism of David Hume,
who remarked, with his ruthless bland logic, that every
proposition *implies* the existence of its opposite; consequently every affirmation involves a contradiction.
Boswell once wrote in his journals that Hume was tortured upon the metaphysical rack and had "walked the
wilds of speculation." When the opposite proposition
is always clearly conceivable, then the debate within
the self causes an existential anguish even while it
takes hypothetical form. After finishing a play by Racine, we have the sense that the characters have examined their possible attitudes to the point of exhaus-
tion because they have posed ultimate questions about
themselves from extreme and irreconcilable points of
view; they, too, along with Hume, have, to their pain,
walked daringly the far wilds of speculation and been
on the rack. Their drama is not a single action but ex-
plores double possibilities and perilous alternatives.
Thus their taking a certain position, after this self-examination, is decisive; they reach their "chosen" fate
by way of the internal dialogue, the insistent question-
ing of the self by the self in the presence of the self,
as if with duplicity.

Milton's *Paradise Regained* is this sort of examination. The Princess of Clèves, by taking a double view
of her own motives, belongs to a long tradition of Gallic
sensibility, the sensibility of self-regard originating
with the formal medieval examination of the duplicity
of the heart in the romances of Chrétien de Troyes.
The involutions, the reversals, the double modes of
thought, act, and conscience arising from this degree
of self-awareness, reappear in the novels and journals

of Gide, who so much desired to write a fiction as formally pure as Racine's theater, where polar attitudes are in the balance.

The examination of counterimperatives needs a Cartesian theater only in the sense that the self be left alone to obey the law of self-regard. With all their fierce clarity of consciousness Racine's characters recognize that conflicting passions, dispositions, and possibilities exist simultaneously within themselves, and like Pyrrhus, Orestes, and Phèdre they helplessly view their dilemma as a fatality of their divided wills. Such fierce crises of self-awareness release Racine's people from the dimension of time, for their situation is suddenly, as if by revelation, *there* before them, in its totality. A Racinian play has a "unity" or "immediacy" far more valid than any that can be gained by mere theatrical unities of time, place, and character, or *liaison des scènes;* it has the late-baroque unity that is entirely psychological—or shall we say intuitive. With a flash of insight Descartes also found that we intuit the essence of a truth, a situation, a state of being, instantaneously, in its entire contour, which is timeless: "Firstly," he says, "the proposition intuited must be clear and distinct; secondly, it must be grasped in its totality at the same time, and not successively." This is "enlightenment" as the eighteenth century seldom knew it; it is the illumination that comes with the final decisions reached by Racine's discourses within the self—like the decision of Bérénice to part from Titus:

> Je l'aime, je le fuis; Titus m'aime, il me quitte.

It is the illumination with which the Son, Milton's New Man with utter self-awareness, puts away the temptations of the Devil of knowledge and power, and triumphantly enters—creates, in truth—his eternal inward Eden. So also the Princess of Clèves after scrutinizing to the depth the impulses of her own heart renounces her lover and enters seclusion to die. Racine's drama is exempt from the casualties of time; the design of the action is "closed" with inevitable logic by the necessities of the self, a "geometry of fatality" to which those submit who suffer the oscillations of their double will. This logic brings its katharsis—not the baroque release in the flesh, in space, in the great furious act like Samson's destroying the temple, but an acceptance of the known imperatives of one's own being. Descartes accepts the finality of self-consciousness when he says, "Even bodies are not properly speaking known by the senses or the faculty of imagination, but by the understanding only, and since they are not known from the fact that they are seen or touched, but only because they are understood, I see clearly that there is nothing which is easier for me to know than my mind."

As Racine "closed" his theater by the limits of consciousness, so Poussin closed his pictorial world, which obeys the late-baroque psychological law of congruity, coherence, and consistency; this, says Reynolds, "is a real existing principle in man." And, he adds, it must be satisfied. The late-baroque satisfied this need for self-determination, for the values of a controlled psychology and vision, more completely than any art until cubism. Félibien said of Poussin, "The light which illumined his thoughts was uniform, pure, and without clouds." This is the achievement of late-baroque style: to shed over the world the light of the mind, to reduce life to the inward equation, to represent it as a fabric of consciousness—to set, finally, upon the arts of that whole great era we call the renaissance the measure of the human spirit.

NOTES

1. *Woelfflin has said: "Neo-classicism first leads back to the tectonic"* (Principles of Art History, 1951, p. 149).

2. *The phrase is from T. H. Fokker* (Roman Baroque Art, I, p. 294). *My account of late-baroque diagrammatic con-*

trasts, "attitudes," and masses is largely founded upon Fokker's theories and illustrations.

3. *George Williamson's article by that name* (Modern Philology, XXXIII, 1935–6) *neatly describes the essential structure of late-baroque verse and thought.*

4. *Joan Evans* (Pattern, II, p. 48) *so identifies the "vital inspiration" behind Louis XIV style. And Laurence Whistler writes as follows of the architecture of Vanbrugh and Hawksmoor, which was really an English version of late-baroque:*

The main obstacle that separates Vanbrugh from the Victorians is not his unromantic detail, nor his refusal to depart from candid brickwork and round-topped sash windows, but the law of symmetry. In his great works that law was absolute for him, as for any classical architect. There, symmetry could only be flouted where no angle of view would discover the lack of it, and in practice not often then. For symmetry on paper was desirable too. No doubt his orderly mind found pleasure . . . in contemplating the plan of Castle Howard, where the kitchen court is more or less the stable court in a mirror, although no eye could ever see both at once. . . . But one can imagine an uttermost Baroque where the idea of architecture as abstract sculpture is carried one step further; where symmetry still reigns, as it must, within the classical components of design (wing, portico, fenestration, cupola); but where the placing of those components is dictated by balance alone, in obedience to the needs of the plan. This, after all, is what begins to come about when a steeple is placed to one side of a portico, as at Hawksmoor's church in Bloomsbury. The Imagination of Vanbrugh and His Fellow Artists, 1954, p. 202.

5. *In an essay* (Racine) *printed in Paris in 1923, Malcolm Cowley states this in the course of one of the few discussions in English worthy of Racinian tragedy; another is Francis Fergusson's in* The Idea of a Theater.

6. *To my knowledge no one has dealt more brilliantly with this aspect of Racine than Thierry Maulnier* (Racine, 1947) *or, perhaps, Georges Le Bidois* (La Vie dans la tragédie de Racine, 1901), *who so well understands Racine's "mode of consciousness." Martin Turnell in* The Classical Moment *has made the point about the "inwardness" of the seventeenth-century mind.*

BIBLIOGRAPHICAL NOTE

The following lists indicate the chief works of art history mentioned in the text and will suggest the materials upon which each of the major chapters is based. As for works of literary criticism and literary history, my debts are so wide that I include only those items of which I have made very specific use, or which may not be generally known.

Gothic:

Adams, Henry: *Mont-Saint-Michel and Chartres*, 1905

Adhémar, Jean: *Influences antiques dans l'art du moyen age français*, 1939

Auerbach, Erich: *Mimesis*, 1953

Baltrušaitis, Jurgis: *La Stylistique ornementale dans la sculpture romane*, 1931

Bréhier, Louis: *L'Art chrétien*, 1918, 1928

Bunim, Miriam Schild: *Space in Mediaeval Painting*, 1940

Cohen, Gustave: *La grande clarté du moyen-age*, 1943

Coulton, G. G.: *Art and the Reformation*, 1928, 1953

Crombie, A. C.: *Robert Grosseteste and the Origins of Experimental Science*, 1953

Du Colombier, Pierre: *Les Chantiers des cathedrales*, 1953

Dvořák, Max: *Kunstgeschichte als Geistesgeschichte*, 1928

Evans, Joan: *Art in Mediaeval France*, 1948
   Cluniac Art of the Romanesque Period, 1950
   English Art, 1307–1461, 1949
   Nature in Design, 1933
   Pattern, 1931
   The Romanesque Architecture of the Order of Cluny, 1938

Focillon, Henri: *Art d'occident*, 1947
   L'art des sculpteurs romanes, 1931
   The Life of Forms in Art, second ed., 1948

Frey, Dagobert: *Gotik und Renaissance*, 1929

Gardner, Arthur: *Mediaeval Sculpture in France*, 1931

Harvey, John: *The Gothic World*, 1950

Hauser, Arnold: *Social History of Art*, 1951

Huizinga, Johan: *Waning of the Middle Ages*, 1924, etc.

Kernodle, George R.: *From Art to Theatre,* 1944

Mâle, Émile: *Religious Art in France, XIII Century,* 1913

Malraux, André: *The Voices of Silence,* 1953

Morey, Charles Rufus: *Mediaeval Art,* 1942

Panofsky, Erwin: *Early Netherlandish Painting,* 1953

    Gothic Architecture and Scholasticism, 1951

    "Die Perspektive als Symbolische Form," *Vortraege der Bibliothek Warburg,* 1924–5, 258 ff.

Porter, Arthur Kingsley: *Mediaeval Architecture,* 1909

Singleton, Charles: "The Perspective of Art," *Kenyon Review,* Spring, 1953

Worringer, Wilhelm: *Form-Problems in Gothic (Form in Gothic),* 1918, 1927

Renaissance:

Baker, Herschel C.: *The Dignity of Man,* 1947

Berenson, Bernard: *The Italian Painters of the Renaissance,* 1948, etc.

Blunt, Anthony: *Artistic Theory in Italy, 1450–1600,* 1940

Clark, Kenneth: *Landscape into Art (Landscape Painting),* 1949, 1950

Holt, Elizabeth G., ed.: *Literary Sources of Art History,* 1947

Ivins, William M., Jr.: "On the Rationalization of Sight," *Metropolitan Museum of Art* (N.Y.) Papers, No. 8, 1938

Laver, James: *Drama, Its Costume and Decor,* 1951

Meiss, Millard: *Painting in Florence and Siena After the Black Death,* 1951

Panofsky, Erwin: "Renaissance and Renascences," *Kenyon Review,* Spring, 1944

    "Renaissance Science and Art," *New England Conference on Renaissance Studies,* Harvard University, May 10, 1952

    Studies in Iconology, 1939

Pevsner, Nikolaus: *An Outline of European Architecture,* 1951

Stokes, Adrian D.: *The Quattro Cento,* 1932

    Stones of Rimini, 1934

White, John: "Developments in Renaissance Perspective," *Journal of the Warburg and Courtauld Institute,* XII, 1949, 58–79; XIV, 1951, 42–69

Wittkower, Rudolf: *Architectural Principles in the Age of Humanism,* 1949

Woelfflin, Heinrich: *Classic Art,* 1952

Mannerism:

Benesch, Otto: *The Art of the Renaissance in Northern Europe,* 1945

Blunt, Anthony: *François Mansart and the Origins of French Classical Architecture,* 1941

Bradbrook, Muriel C.: *Themes and Conventions of Elizabethan Tragedy,* 1935

Briganti, Giulio: *Il Manierismo e Pellegrino Tibaldi,* 1945

Crofts, J. E. V.: "John Donne," *Essays and Studies,* XXII, 1936, 128–43

Croll, Morris W.: "The Baroque Style in Prose," *Studies in English Philology in Honor of Frederick Klaeber,* 1929

Cruttwell, Patrick: *The Shakespearean Moment,* 1954

Curtius, Ernst Robert: *European Literature and the Latin Middle Ages,* 1953

Ellis-Fermor, Una M.: *The Jacobean Drama,* third ed., 1953

Focillon, Henri: *Benvenuto Cellini,* 1910

Freedberg, Sidney J.: *Parmigianino,* 1950

Friedlaender, Walter: "Die Entstehung des Antiklassischen Stiles," *Repertorium fuer Kunstwissenschaft,* XLVI, 1925, 49–86

Hinks, Roger: *Michaelangelo Merisi da Caravaggio,* 1953

Hoffmann, Hans: *Hochrenaissance, Manierismus, Fruehbarock,* 1938

Leech, Clifford: *John Webster,* 1951
    Shakespeare's Tragedies, 1950

Leishman, J. B.: *The Monarch of Wit,* 1951

Mather, Frank Jewett: *Western European Painting of the Renaissance,* 1939, 1948

Nicolson, Marjorie H.: *The Breaking of the Circle,* 1950

Pallucchini, Rodolfo: *La Giovinezza del Tintoretto,* 1950

Panofsky, Erwin: *Idea,* 1924

Pevsner, Nikolaus: *Academies of Art, Past and Present,* 1940
    "The Architecture of Mannerism," *The Mint,* ed. Geoffrey Grigson, 1946
    Barockmalerei in den Romanischen Laendern, 1928

Pinder, Wilhelm: "Zur Physiognomik des Manierismus," *Die Wissenschaft am Schiedewege von Leben und Geist,* 1932

Praz, Mario: *Secentismo e Marinismo in Inghilterra—John Donne—Richard Crashaw,* 1925
    Studies in Seventeenth-Century Imagery, 1939

Reed, Robert Rentoul: *Bedlam on the Jacobean Stage,* 1952

Riegl, Alois: *Die Entstehung der Barockkunst in Rom,* 1908

Schmarsow, August: *Barock und Rokoko,* 1897

Summerson, John: *Architecture in Britain, 1530 to 1830,* 1953

Tuve, Rosemund: *Elizabethan and Metaphysical Imagery,* 1947

Weisbach, Werner: "Der Manierismus," *Zeitschrift fuer Bildende Kunst,* XXX, 1919, 161–83

Spanish Baroque Art, 1941

Wittkower, Rudolf: "Michaelangelo's Biblioteca Laurenziana," *Art Bulletin,* XVI, 1934, 123–216

Woelfflin, Heinrich: *Principles of Art History,* 1932, 1951

Renaissance und Barock, 1908, 1926

Zupnik, I. L.: "The 'Aesthetics' of the Early Mannerists," *Art Bulletin,* XXXV, Dec., 1953, 302–6

Baroque:

De Tolnay, Charles: *Michaelangelo,* 1943, etc.

Fokker, T. H.: *Roman Baroque Art,* 1938

Frey, Dagobert: *Architecture of the Renaissance,* 1925

Friedlaender, Walter: "Der Antimanieristische Stil um 1590," *Vortraege der Bibliothek Warburg,* 1928–29, 214–43

Fry, Roger: *Transformations,* 1926

McComb, Arthur: *The Baroque Painters of Italy,* 1934

Mahon, Denis: *Studies in Seicento Art and Theory,* 1947

Mâle, Émile: *L'Art religieux après le concile de Trente,* 1932

Mayor, A. Hyatt: *The Bibiena Family,* 1945

Mora, José F.: "Suarez and Modern Philosophy," *Journal of the History of Ideas,* XIV, Oct., 1953, 528–47

Ors y Rovira, Eugenio d': *Lo Barroco,* [1944]

Pevsner, Nikolaus: "Gegenreformation und Manierismus," *Repertorium fuer Kunstwissenschaft,* XLVI, 1925, 243–62

Rosenberg, Jakob: *Rembrandt,* 1948

Scheffler, Karl: *Verwandlungen des Barocks in der Kunst des Neunzehnten Jahrhunderts,* 1947

Scholz, János, ed.: *Baroque and Romantic Stage Design,* 1950

Scott, Geoffrey: *The Architecture of Humanism,* 1914, 1954

Waterhouse, Ellis K.: *Baroque Painting in Rome*, 1937

Weisbach, Werner: *Der Barock als Kunst der Gegenreformation*, 1921

  "Gegenreformation - Manierismus - Barock," *Repertorium fuer Kunstwissenschaft*, XLIX, 1928, 16–28

Late-Baroque:

Beck, Leslie John: *The Method of Descartes*, 1952

Blunt, Anthony: *Art and Architecture in France, 1500 to 1700*, 1954

  "The Heroic and the Ideal Landscape in the Work of Nicolas Poussin," *Journal of the Warburg and Courtauld Institute*, VII, 1944, 154–68

Clark, A. F. B.: *Jean Racine*, 1939

Cowley, Malcolm: *Racine*, 1923

Danby, John F.: *Poets on Fortune's Hill*, 1952

Deane, Cecil Victor: *Dramatic Theory and the Rhymed Heroic Play*, 1931

Friedlaender, Walter: *David to Delacroix*, 1952

Hourticq, Louis: *De Poussin à Watteau*, 1921

Joseph, Bertram Leon: *Elizabethan Acting*, 1951

Jouin, Henri, ed.: *Conférences de l'academie royale de peinture et de sculpture*, 1883

Le Bidois, Georges: *La Vie dans la tragédie de Racine*, 1901

Lee, Rensselaer W.: "*Ut Pictura Poesis*: The Humanistic Theory of Painting," *Art Bulletin*, XXII, 1940, 197–263

Levitine, George: "The Influence of Lavater and Girodet's *Expression des Sentiments de l'Ame*," *Art Bulletin*, XXXVI, 1954, 33–45

Maulnier, Thierry: *Racine*, 1947

May, Georges C.: *Tragédie cornélienne, tragédie racinienne*, 1948

Mornet, Daniel: *Histoire de la clarté française*, 1929

Rogerson, Brewster: "The Art of Painting the Passions," *Journal of the History of Ideas*, XIV, Jan., 1953, 68–94

Rosenthal, Gertrude: "The Basic Theories of French Classic Sculpture," *Journal of Aesthetics and Art Criticism*, No. 6, 1942, 42–61

Segond, Joseph: *Psychologie de Jean Racine*, 1940

Turnell, Martin: *The Classical Moment*, 1946

Whistler, Laurence: *The Imagination of Vanbrugh and His Fellow Artists*, 1954

Williamson, George: "The Rhetorical Pattern of Neo-Classical Wit," *Modern Philology*, XXXIII, 1935–36, 55–81

INDEX